THE
STRUGGLE
TO REFORM
OUR
COLLEGES

THE
STRUGGLE
TO REFORM
OUR
COLLEGES

❧

DEREK BOK

PRINCETON UNIVERSITY PRESS

PRINCETON AND OXFORD

Published by Princeton University Press, 41 William Street, Princeton, New Jersey 08540

In the United Kingdom: Princeton University Press, 6 Oxford Street, Woodstock, Oxfordshire OX20 1TR

press.princeton.edu

Jacket images courtesy of Shutterstock

ISBN 978-0-691-17747-2

British Library Cataloging-in-Publication Data is available

This book has been composed in Minion Pro and Trajan Pro

Printed on acid-free paper. ∞

Printed in the United States of America

10 9 8 7 6 5 4 3 2 1

For

BILL BOWEN

Exemplary colleague,
excellent scholar,
exceptional leader

CONTENTS

∾

ACKNOWLEDGMENTS

ONE OF THE LASTING BENEFITS OF PRESIDING over a university for
twenty years is the chance to acquire a number of unusually accomplished friends. Several of these read versions of this book and kindly
offered valuable comments.

I would pay special tribute in this regard to my longtime colleague
and comrade in arms, the late Bill Bowen. For this book, as for others I
have written over the past twenty years, Bill gave me far more help than
I had any right to expect and supplied me with reams of good advice
that caused me to see the entire project in a clearer light and to improve
the final product immeasurably. Over four decades, we worked together
on a variety of other efforts to defend or improve universities. I count
these experiences among the happiest and most rewarding of my professional life. I was fortunate enough just before he passed away to tell him
that I wanted to dedicate this book to him in recognition of the friend-
ship and support he has given me over the many years we have known
one another.

Another good friend, Howard Gardner, also read a draft of this book
from beginning to end and made many helpful suggestions, which I
have tried to incorporate into the final version. Jonathan Fanton volun-
teered to read the entire manuscript and even gave me a splendid break-
fast at the American Academy of Arts and Sciences as a prelude to his
thoughtful comments. Other valued friends who read individual chapters include Richard Light, who critiqued an early draft of the chapter on
the quality of education, Barbara Brittingham, who gave me the benefit
of her vast experience in the practice of accreditation, and Eric von
Hippel, who read the final chapter and supplied me with many useful
insights concerning the process of innovation and the diffusion of new
ideas.

In addition to the help of these friends, the Princeton Press arranged
to have the book critiqued by two anonymous outside readers who

clearly knew a great deal about the subject matter and made many valuable suggestions.

As always, my wife, Sissela, dearest and most faithful of my critics, read the entire manuscript at least twice at different stages of its development and gave me all kinds of advice and encouragement to spur me onward.

Two other individuals deserve special thanks for their invaluable help. My research assistant, Meredith Krause, displayed an uncanny ability to locate all sorts of published and unpublished materials from which I learned an immense amount. Her work was truly outstanding, and much of the evidence for the statements in this book is the product of her labors.

Once again, my assistant for the past quarter of a century, Connie Higgins, lent her skills to the task of producing a readable manuscript for my publisher. Either because of the complexity of the subject or as a result of my advancing years, I made an exceptional number of revisions, reorganizations, and reorderings of sentences, paragraphs, and entire chapters. Through it all, Connie persevered with great patience and good humor until I was satisfied at last with the final version.

Finally, I owe a debt of gratitude to the Princeton University Press and to Peter Dougherty, its director and my editor for all the books I have written during the past twenty years. It has always been a pleasure to work with such a publisher, and I am forever grateful to have had the opportunity.

THE
STRUGGLE
TO REFORM
OUR
COLLEGES

Introduction

∾

AMERICAN HIGHER EDUCATION HAS REACHED one of the rare moments in its history when major reforms may be close at hand. Although the quality of research in our universities is still without equal, and our leading professional schools continue to enjoy an enviable reputation, concerns have been mounting over the condition of the forty-five hundred two- and four-year colleges that are currently responsible for educating some nineteen million students.

After boasting the world's most highly educated population for more than a century, America has fallen behind one country after another in the percentage of young adults earning college degrees. Economists talk of looming skill shortages that could hamper our ability to compete in the global economy. Far from promoting opportunities for all Americans to achieve a better life, higher education is now being accused of becoming a system that maintains existing differences in income and preserves racial inequality.

Evidence has also come to light casting doubt on how much our undergraduates are learning during college. International tests of basic skills find Americans with college degrees lagging behind their counterparts in many other advanced countries, while surveys suggest that undergraduates are spending much less time at their studies than they did half a century ago. Employers complain about the competence of many of the recent graduates they hire. Families throughout the United States have grown increasingly upset over constantly rising tuitions, and a majority of Americans now believe that colleges care more about the bottom line than they do about their students. A significant fraction of recent graduates wonder whether their college degree was worth the cost. These concerns seem all the more worrisome now that a college education is generally considered to be a necessary step toward finding good jobs, living fulfilling lives, and becoming active, enlightened citizens.

Even as doubts about undergraduate education have continued to grow, however, advances in psychology and educational research have created a wealth of useful insights to enhance teaching and learning. Technology is producing a variety of intriguing methods for improving college teaching and student services. Online education has brought courses taught by leading scientists and scholars within easy reach of audiences throughout America and around the world.

The combination of mounting dissatisfaction with the status quo and the emergence of innovative ideas for improving education has persuaded many observers that reform is not only needed but all but certain to occur. Commentators are predicting fundamental changes in the way students are taught rather than modest incremental improvements. Politicians are asking for massive increases in undergraduate enrollments and graduation rates. To sense the current mood, one has only to read the titles of recent books on higher education, such as *The End of College, Remaking College, College Disrupted*, or *The Online Education Revolution*.

Twice before, American higher education has experienced mounting pressure for change in the face of new opportunities and needs. On both occasions, major transformations took place. In the late nineteenth and early twentieth centuries, colleges became universities, and new institutions were established to meet the emerging demands of a rapidly industrializing society. Graduate programs were created to prepare scholars and scientists for careers of research and teaching. Professional schools were strengthened and new ones founded. College enrollments grew, and the traditional, heavily prescribed classical curriculum gave way to undergraduate programs with more practical courses and greater choice for students to pursue their own program of study.

Following World War II, higher education faced new challenges to enroll more students, strengthen basic research, and help America to play a more prominent role in world affairs. Once again, higher education responded. New colleges and community colleges opened their doors at a rate of one per week, as the number of undergraduates doubled, redoubled, and doubled yet again. American research expanded rapidly and increased in quality to become preeminent in the world. Graduate programs appeared in scores of universities to examine international problems and learn more about other regions of the world.

In 2009, shortly after taking office, the president of the United States called for another great effort by the nation's colleges and universities. In a speech to Congress, he set a goal of regaining America's historic lead in the education of its workforce by raising the share of twenty-five- to thirty-four-year-old Americans possessing "quality" college degrees by a whopping 40 percent in only eleven years. Corporate executives applauded this initiative. Several of our largest foundations made the effort a major priority. College officials expressed their support.

Now that almost a decade has elapsed, what can we make of the president's challenge and higher education's response? How reliable were his assertions that the current level of educational attainment is unsatisfactory, and how concerned should we be by such findings? Is attainment the only major problem, or are changes needed to ensure that college graduates will receive "quality degrees"? Finally, what have colleges and universities accomplished in the last few years to achieve these goals, and how can they be helped to do better?

These are the questions discussed in the chapters that follow.

PART ONE

The Challenge

CHAPTER ONE

Graduation Rates and Educational Attainment

UNTIL RECENTLY, GRADUATION RATES WERE NOT widely regarded as a national problem. Throughout the eighteenth and nineteenth centuries, fewer than 5 percent of young people entered college, and less than half of those enrolling graduated. Yet few people cared. Finishing college was rarely a matter of great consequence, since students did not need a degree to enter the vast majority of occupations and professions.

As the economy grew in size and complexity, college education became more important to the economy. Throughout most of the twentieth century, however, the percentages of young Americans who finished high school and graduated from college were above the levels of other countries and large enough in relation to the needs of the society that increasing the number who earned a degree did not seem a matter of much urgency. Until late in the century, dropout rates were seldom even considered a responsibility of the college. If students failed to stay the course, their departure was widely attributed to their lack of ability or perseverance, not to any failing on the part of the institution.

During the 1980s, however, Americans grew increasingly concerned about the nation's ability to compete successfully in global markets. By this time, rates of increase in the gross domestic product had become the principal measure of the nation's progress. Since economists identified the skills and knowledge of the labor force as important contributors to economic growth, policy-makers began to look more carefully at the performance of our educational institutions. Many state legislatures started to examine the benefits achieved by their appropriations to higher education and tried to make their colleges and universities more accountable by requiring them to submit detailed reports on their performance. Graduation rates were one of the outcomes included in almost all of these reporting requirements.

The problem of graduation rates attracted even more attention following the publication in 2008 of a book entitled *The Race between Education and Technology* by Claudia Goldin and Lawrence Katz.[1] The authors emphasized the importance of education not only for economic growth but also for equality of income and opportunity. In America, they claimed, the failings of our educational institutions over the past several decades, including a prolonged stagnation in college graduation rates, were a major reason for our sluggish economic growth and increasing inequality of income. These concerns were amplified by surging college enrollments in other industrialized countries that allowed many of them to overtake and even surpass the United States in the educational levels of their younger workers.

Research on college completion also revealed the large and growing income and racial gaps in the rates at which students were graduating from college. Among high school graduates academically qualified for college study, far more students from high-income families completed a bachelor's degree within eight years than did those from low-income families. This vast and growing difference was accompanied by rising income inequality, a problem that came to attract increasing attention in the twenty-first century.

Responding to these trends, President Obama declared to Congress in 2009 that the United States must regain its historic leadership in the educational attainment of its people.[2] To achieve this goal, he declared that America needed to raise the share of twenty-five- to thirty-four-year-olds earning a "quality" college credential to 60 percent by 2020. Since the existing percentage of college-educated Americans barely exceeded 40 percent, achieving the president's goal within little more than a decade would require a mammoth effort by all concerned, especially colleges and universities.[3] The percentage of Americans with college degrees had been increasing for several decades at a rate of roughly 0.5 percent per year, aided by growth in the college-age population.[4] Now, the percentage would have to rise at least *four times* as fast.

DO WE REALLY NEED SO MANY MORE
COLLEGE GRADUATES?

The call for a massive increase in college degrees echoed a widely shared view among business executives and policy-makers that America faces a shortage of highly educated workers, and that the problem will likely get worse if something is not done to increase the number of college graduates. The most authoritative estimates available, those of the Bureau of Labor Statistics, project that more than 60 percent of all new jobs created by 2018 will require at least some college education.[5] Anthony Carnevale, the widely cited director of the Center on Education and the Workforce at Georgetown University, has foreseen an even more serious problem, declaring that America will experience a skill deficit of roughly three million jobs by 2018 if the number of college graduates does not grow faster.[6] Already, the shortage of educated workers has helped to lift the earnings premium for college graduates to levels not seen for the last one hundred years.[7]

Reports of a serious shortage of highly skilled employees have continued to appear since the recession that followed the financial crisis of 2008. Most of these claims have been based on surveys of employers. For example, in 2014, the Business Roundtable projected shortages of college-educated workers even greater than those anticipated by Professor Carnevale. According to the Roundtable's "action plan,"

> By some estimates, the economy will create 54.8 million new and replacement jobs between 2010 and 2020 with 65 percent of all jobs requiring some level of postsecondary education and training. Unfortunately, we may fall short by as many as 5 million workers who do not have the postsecondary qualifications needed to meet this goal.[8]

Employers expressed particular concern over shortages of workers with degrees in science, technology, engineering, and mathematics, the so-called STEM subjects. In 2013, a poll, sponsored by the Bayer Corporation, of 150 talent recruiters from Fortune 1000 companies found that

89 percent of respondents reported "fierce competition" for STEM graduates and alleged that only half of the participating companies were able to fill job vacancies for STEM majors "in a timely manner."[9]

Is There Really a Skills Gap? Despite the concerns of employers and the projections of the Bureau of Labor Statistics, a number of analysts dispute the very existence of a "skills gap" in the economy and question the forecasts of a growing shortfall of college graduates over the next several years.[10] Some economists claim that such projections overlook the fact that large numbers of jobs currently occupied by BAs could be performed by employees with lesser credentials.[11] Other analysts point out that the demand for college-educated workers diminished during the first decade of this century, and that the average earnings of BAs (not counting those with advanced degrees) actually declined slightly, which they would hardly do if a genuine shortage existed.[12]

The most detailed attack on claims of a skills gap has been mounted by Peter Capelli, chair of the Wharton School's program in human resources at the University of Pennsylvania. In a paper published in 2014, Capelli pointed out that only 5 percent of employers indicated that they planned to raise their pay to cope with shortages of skilled employees.[13] With respect to STEM graduates, he cited figures showing that half of the engineering BAs take jobs in other fields, and that 30 percent of those who do mention the lack of employment opportunities in engineering as the reason. Although recent engineering graduates are less likely than most BAs to be underemployed, 22 percent held positions in 2010 that did not require an engineering degree, and an additional 7 percent were without a job.[14] Other analysts agree that the earnings of engineers have risen only modestly, not at all what one would expect if a serious shortage existed.[15]

After considering the evidence, Capelli concludes that employers are complaining about a nonexistent skills gap because they prefer having a surplus of qualified workers on which to draw rather than having to increase wages and provide more in-house training.[16] Since there has been no dearth of qualified candidates since the recession of 2008, Capelli claims that many companies wait to fill job openings in the expectation that ideal replacements will eventually appear possessing sufficient work experience to "hit the ground running" without a need for higher salaries or added training. Under these conditions, he concludes, "whether it makes sense for society as a whole to send a higher percentage of high school students to college expecting that they will all earn the same [earnings] premium, in the absence of any evidence of increased demand for college-level skills, is not obvious."[17]*

Well-known difficulties in estimating future economic fluctuations add to the confusion over the future educational needs of the economy. Estimating labor market trends, like predicting movements in the stock market, has always been an uncertain enterprise. Sharp differences of opinion over the likely effects of new technology make current projections of future job requirements even more problematic. Thus a recent study by two Oxford professors concludes that 47 percent of the jobs in America are now at high risk of displacement by machines, but that "computerization will mainly do away with low-skill and low-wage jobs in the near future."[18] On the other hand, author and Silicon Valley entrepreneur Martin Ford argues that advanced technology is already beginning to displace highly educated workers in fields such as law, radiology, and medical diagnostics, and that "we are running up against a limit both in terms of the people being herded into colleges and the number of high skilled jobs that will be available to them if they manage to graduate."[19]

---

* There are reasons why employers may have difficulty hiring qualified employees even though plenty of college graduates cannot find suitable jobs. Many BAs who have trouble landing a good job may not possess sufficient skills and other attributes that employers are seeking. Several reports (discussed in detail in chapter 2) suggest that the amount students learn in college has declined in recent decades, and that many current graduates are very weak in such fundamental competencies as writing and critical thinking. E.g., Barbara Kiviat, "The Big Jobs Myth: American Workers Aren't Ready for American Jobs," *Atlantic* (July 2012). The most recent decennial study of adult skills in America reports that large percentages of college graduates are deficient in reading comprehension, quantitative skills, and problem solving. *National Assessment of Adult Literacy: A First Look at the Literacy of America's Adults in the 21st Century*, National Center for Education Statistics (2006), p. 14. Other workers with college degrees may lack so-called soft skills, such as reliability, conscientiousness, and ability to work with others, that many employers understandably consider essential. If these conditions do exist, the argument over the existence of a skills gap may result not from a dispute over whether there are too few workers with college degrees but from differing perceptions about how many college-trained adults possess the competencies employers need.

The Immigration Solution. Even if a shortage does exist in subjects such as science and engineering, and even if the need for advanced skills grows more acute, it may not be necessary to solve the problem by massively increasing the number of people graduating from college. Instead, America could meet its needs by increasing the supply of well-educated immigrants. Large numbers of able young people regularly come to the United States to complete their education, and many of them want to remain here to work. Already, immigrants account for 15 percent of America's workforce, including one-third of all employees in STEM occupations and half of all employed engineering doctorates. The supply of highly educated workers could easily grow more rapidly if immigration restrictions were eased.

This situation may not last forever, once leading suppliers, such as India and China, develop their own economies sufficiently to offer more attractive career possibilities to their most talented graduates. Still, America could probably adjust immigration limits to meet the demand for highly educated talent for at least another generation or two, especially in STEM fields, a step enthusiastically supported by high-tech employers in Silicon Valley.[20] By responding in this way, policy-makers could avoid the risk of encouraging more young Americans to earn college degrees only to find no need for their skills.

At the same time, immigration would do nothing to increase the career prospects of employees who have seen their earnings stagnate or even decline over the past several decades. For generations, the American Dream has portrayed the United States as the premier land of opportunity where those who are willing to work hard enough can realize their ambitions, however humble their origins. This belief has been an important factor in maintaining social solidarity and securing acceptance of the existing economic system despite its high levels of income inequality. In recent years, however, a number of researchers have examined the evidence and concluded that the American Dream is actually just that—a dream. Far from being exceptional, our current rates of upward mobility appear to be lower than those of a number of advanced

European countries.[21] Relying on immigration to meet the demand for highly skilled employees will do little to change this situation.

In addition, the percentages of our young people who earn college degrees continue to be much higher for the offspring of white and well-to-do Americans than they are for blacks and Hispanics or for children from low-income families. From 1995 to 2015, the percentage of whites aged 25–29 with BA degrees or higher rose from 29 to 43, while the percentages for blacks rose only from 15 to 21 and those of Hispanics from 9 to 16.[22] The trends for young adults with an associate degree or higher followed the same pattern, rising from 38 to 54 percent for whites but only from 22 to 31 percent for blacks, and from 13 to 26 percent for Hispanics.[23] In short, the educational levels of blacks and Hispanics are not only much lower than those of whites; the gaps have widened rather than narrowed over the past 20 years. Immigration will do little to lessen these differences.

Much the same is true of the levels of educational attainment achieved by members of different income groups. Among Americans born between 1979 and 1982, 54 percent of those from high-income families earned a BA degree or higher compared with only 9 percent of those from low-income families.[24] Larger increases have occurred in the percentage of low-income students graduating from community colleges. Yet these gains, though beneficial, do not result in career opportunities or average earnings premiums as great as those achieved by graduates from a four-year college.

The gaps in educational attainment between children of rich and poor parents have also widened over the years. In part, this tendency reflects differences in academic aptitude between these groups of children. Yet substantial disparities remain even after such differences are taken into account. Thus analysts have found that among students who all scored in the top quartile in tests of mathematics proficiency, 74 percent of those from families in the top third of the socioeconomic scale graduated from a four-year college compared with only 41 percent of high-scoring students from the bottom third of the scale.[25]

The resulting differences in economic opportunity run counter to the ideal of an America in which all people have an equal chance to succeed according to their ability, ambition, and effort. Raising educational attainment levels will not automatically remove these gaps. Still, it is hard to imagine that current differences will ever narrow significantly *without* a substantial rise in the overall level of educational attainment. In this sense, raising attainment may not be *sufficient* to bring about greater equality of opportunity, but it is surely a *necessary* condition.

Beyond Economic Growth. There are also powerful reasons apart from economic considerations for increasing the percentage of Americans with college degrees.* Some of these benefits have to do with personal gains other than increased earnings. According to a large body of research, college graduates enjoy better health, not only for themselves but for their spouses and children.[26] They tend to live longer than those with only a high school diploma. They suffer less from depression, get divorced less often, and enjoy greater happiness. Fewer among them commit suicide or indulge in substance abuse. They are also more likely to enjoy their work and find it meaningful.[27]

Increased education likewise contributes far more to the society than increased productivity. College-educated adults tend to pay more in taxes, go to prison less often, receive fewer unemployment benefits and food stamps, and spend less time on welfare than those with less education. They also volunteer more often in their community, exhibit greater racial tolerance, and give larger amounts to charity.[28] They are less likely to have children before the age of twenty, and their offspring are more likely to do well in school and go to college themselves, extending the consequent personal and social benefits to another generation.

Finally, according to yet another large body of research, valuable civic benefits are associated with higher levels of education—less corruption, more efficient government services, more respect for property rights,

---

*Unfortunately, most studies of the noneconomic benefits of higher education merely record the later-life benefits associated with earning a BA degree. Much less is known about exactly what experiences in college produce these benefits. There is likewise little research about the noneconomic effects of a community college education.

and greater belief in political freedoms.[29] As citizens, college graduates not only vote more; they are also more informed about political matters, more open to other points of view, and less susceptible to political propaganda than those who did not go to college.

Social scientists who have tried to quantify all of the nonmarket benefits conclude that their total value is, if anything, even greater than the purely economic gains emphasized by politicians and economists.[30] Other studies in at least two states have found that spending more money on higher education produces tangible public benefits such as additional tax receipts and lower welfare expenditures and prison costs, which yield handsome returns on the investment. A report in Texas concluded that every additional dollar spent on higher education returned four dollars to the state.[31] A similar study in California found that each dollar spent for higher education would eventually yield $3.65 for the state.[32] If these calculations are correct, the money governments spend on increasing college enrollments and graduation rates may be a wise investment even if it temporarily increases the national debt. Far from benefiting current taxpayers at the cost of burdening generations to come, such expenditures could increase the future welfare of both today's children and their children as well.

At this point, skeptical readers may ask whether the nonmarket gains attributed to increased levels of education simply reflect the fact that those who go to college tend to be smarter and more self-disciplined than those who do not. If so, increasing the number of college graduates will not achieve the hoped-for private and civic benefits, since these gains will derive from attributes students possess whether or not they go to college.

Many investigators have examined this possibility by trying to isolate the effects truly attributable to college. This is not an easy task. Natural abilities and the effects of college are highly interdependent, so that separating them requires considerable ingenuity.

Some researchers have sought to overcome this problem by comparing the lives of identical twins who acquired differing amounts of education.[33] Others have compared the results of large populations of young people who spent differing amounts of time in school, not by their own choice but because of a legislative change in the age for compulsory education.[34] Such studies recognize that the differing abilities and other attributes of students independent of schooling do have some effect on achievements in later life. Nevertheless, many observers have concluded that these effects are largely canceled out by other factors, such as the tendency of survey respondents to exaggerate the amount of education they have received. Thus, although disagreement persists, most observers conclude that the nonmarket benefits described in earlier paragraphs can be largely attributed to additional education, and not to the superior intelligence or intangible values and dispositions that college students possess relative to those with only a high school education.*

It is odd that current debates about raising educational attainment levels focus so often on economic outcomes and ignore the array of other potential benefits. Yet this omission has appeared regularly in the recent pronouncements of political leaders on the significance of education. A particularly egregious example is the statement made by President Clinton on the passage of a new education law. "We measure every school by one high standard: are our children learning what they need to know to compete and win in the global economy."[35] Statements of this kind are eminently bipartisan. As Republican Governor Rick Scott of Florida observed in 2011: "Is it a vital interest of the state to have more anthropologists? I don't think so. If I'm going to take money from a citizen to put into education, then I'm going to take that money to create jobs."[36] In 2015, Governor Scott Walker of Wisconsin even proposed deleting from the state university's mission statement such purposes as "to educate people and improve the human condition" and "to serve and stimulate society" while substituting language that would narrow the university's goals to meeting "the state's workforce needs."[37]

---

*For a dissenting view, see Jason Schnittker and Jere R. Behrman, "Learning to Do Well or Learning to Do Good: Estimating the Effects of Schooling on Civic Engagement, Social Cohesion, and Labor Market Outcomes, in the Presence of Endowments," 41 *Social Science Research* (2012), p. 306.

These assertions differ sharply from those of earlier political leaders. From Thomas Jefferson to Lyndon Johnson, presidents have justified expanding education on very different grounds, such as the value of an enlightened citizenry for a self-governing democracy and the need to extend opportunities for advancement to all segments of the population.[38]

Perhaps the recent pronouncements reflect a judgment that economic results are the only ones that matter today to students and to the public. National surveys of entering freshmen regularly find that being able "to get a better job" is the most frequently cited reason for coming to college. In 2015, 82.24 percent reported that they went to college for that reason. "Being very well off financially" was the next most important reason, cited by 81 percent.[39]

A closer look, however, reveals that students have many other reasons for attending college. More than 82 percent of freshmen in 2015 also claimed to be hoping "to learn more about things that interest me," while 70.6 percent said they sought a college degree "to gain a general education and appreciation of ideas."[40] In addition, "influencing social values," "helping others who are in difficulty," "developing a meaningful philosophy of life," "keeping up to date with political affairs," "helping to promote racial understanding," "becoming a community leader," "increasing understanding of other countries and cultures," and "protecting the environment" were each cited as important by one-third to one-half or more of the entering freshmen.[41]

The shrunken rationale for education expressed by many current political leaders is not without practical consequences. If public officials look only at the impact on the economy, they will greatly underestimate the value of increased learning and invest too little in our schools and universities. By doing so, they threaten to weaken the quality of education and diminish its many contributions to the nation's welfare, contributions that extend beyond the marketplace and would be well worth having quite apart from any effects they have on economic growth and global competitiveness.

REASONS AND RESPONSIBILITIES

The discussion thus far has revealed several reasons for seeking a major increase in the number of college graduates. The most commonly cited argument rests on official estimates of the economy's need for many more skilled and knowledgeable employees. Such forecasts are not very reliable, and not every economist accepts them. Nevertheless, most analysts seem to agree that the demand for skilled labor will rise sufficiently over the next decade to require large increases in the number of college graduates.

In addition to satisfying our future employment needs, there are a variety of other important nonpecuniary benefits resulting from increasing the number of college graduates, both for the graduates themselves and for society as a whole. Most of these benefits, such as higher voting rates, better health, and less substance abuse, will exist whether or not the estimates of future labor market trends turn out to be accurate. These advantages provide an independent reason for raising the level of educational attainment substantially.

Finally, college degrees create opportunities for graduates to compete for jobs and careers that offer better incomes, greater intrinsic interest, and higher status. Quite apart from the economy's needs, increasing the number of college graduates gives more individuals a chance to compete for a satisfying career and achieve the success they deserve in light of their interests, abilities, and effort.

Together, the justifications just described make a powerful case for increasing our current level of educational attainment. They also give rise to somewhat different responsibilities for the various segments of our higher education system.

The task of educating the many additional students needed to increase attainment levels will mainly fall to the public colleges and for-profit institutions that accept nearly all of the applicants seeking admission. Most of these students will not possess sufficient academic aptitude and preparation for college study to qualify for admission to the "flagship" state universities or to selective private colleges.

However, by the policies they adopt in choosing which students to recruit, selective colleges can help revitalize the American Dream by opening their doors to deserving students who would not otherwise enroll. Large segments of the population, notably blacks, Hispanics, and members of low-income families, have traditionally had a relatively small presence in the professions and other desirable occupations, as well as in positions of leadership throughout the society. Many students of this kind do not enjoy the social, economic, and educational advantages that benefit other applicants seeking admission to selective colleges. As a result, these colleges have accepted a responsibility to make special efforts to seek out and enroll applicants from underrepresented groups who have the potential to meet the academic standards of the institution and earn a degree.

In recognition of this responsibility, most selective colleges have encouraged academically qualified black and Hispanic students to apply and have given them special consideration in the admissions process. Campus officials overwhelmingly support this practice, not only to provide students from minority groups with a greater opportunity for later-life success but also because racial diversity can enrich the educational experience of all undergraduates.

For similar reasons, selective colleges have long sought to assist qualified students from lower-income families by offering them financial aid so that they can enroll and graduate. Such policies have helped to expand the educational opportunities of many students of limited means, but progress has been limited for several reasons. In competing with other colleges for highly talented applicants, many selective colleges have increasingly used substantial portions of their financial aid budget for merit scholarships even though many of the recipients come from families that could afford to pay all or a large part of the costs of attending. As a result, less money is available for deserving low-income applicants.

In addition, it has recently come to light that many thousands of low-income students with very strong academic records never even apply to selective colleges because they do not know of their existence, do not believe that they could afford to attend, or do not realize that their chances of graduating will normally be much higher than they would be at an open admission school. Many selective colleges are now making greater efforts to seek out and enroll more of these promising students. A number of well-endowed institutions have revised their financial aid policies to make it much easier for such individuals to attend. Nevertheless, since these potential applicants are widely scattered in high schools across the country, the challenge of locating them and persuading them to apply has proved to be more difficult than anticipated, and progress has been slow.

In short, despite the advances already made, the challenge for selective colleges to provide adequate opportunities for all students qualified to enroll, regardless of their race and income, remains ongoing. This challenge is unquestionably important, and selective colleges need to continue their efforts to recruit and graduate more students from disadvantaged groups that have traditionally been underrepresented. However, since I have already written at length on this subject, I will not pursue it further in these pages.* Instead, the chapters that follow will focus on the formidable task of greatly increasing the total number of Americans who earn college degrees while making sure that all those who enroll receive a "quality" education.

---

* See William G. Bowen and Derek Bok, *The Shape of the River: Long-Term Consequences of Considering Race in College and University Admissions* (1998); Derek Bok, *Higher Education in America* (2013), pp. 129–40.

CHAPTER TWO

ॐ

The Quality of Education

EVERYONE IS IN FAVOR OF A "QUALITY EDUCATION." But commentators have had differing meanings in mind when they discuss what this term implies for America's colleges. For years, much of the writing on the subject had to do with specific concerns, such as complaints that faculties were not devoting enough attention to studying the "Great Books," or American history, or foreign languages, or some other subject. Today, however, two other questions are more likely to arise in discussions about the quality of teaching and learning in college. First of all, how responsive is the curriculum to the evolving demands of students and society, and how suitable is its design for achieving the important aims of undergraduate education? In addition, how well are courses being taught, and how effective are the methods instructors use to help their students learn? As the following pages will reveal, there are reasons for concern about both of these questions.

THE CURRICULUM

Meeting the Changing Needs of Students and Society. Most colleges do well in adjusting their curriculum to meet new needs. Surveys suggest that students consider the programs and majors that colleges provide to be the most important factor in deciding where to enroll.[1] As a result, in order to compete successfully for students, every college must create courses and programs that reflect their interests and concerns.

It is also important that curricular requirements be designed to achieve the most important aims of undergraduate education. A broad consensus exists among faculty members and academic leaders about what these purposes are. The Higher Education Research Institute (HERI) at the University of California, Los Angeles periodically asks professors to indicate which goals they consider "essential" or "very important."[2] More than 99 percent regularly point to "critical thinking." More than three-quarters mention skill in writing, preparation for a career, and the development of greater tolerance for other ideas and beliefs. More than two-thirds include increasing racial understanding and a respect for differences in culture and beliefs, acquiring a breadth of knowledge, and developing ethical awareness and a capacity for moral reasoning. While the HERI surveys do not always mention preparing students to be active, knowledgeable citizens, most academic leaders seem to consider this aim to be fundamental, judging by their college brochures. Other frequent additions to the list include developing a basic competence in mathematics (or numeracy) and fostering global awareness (i.e., some knowledge of other cultures and international affairs). Each of these aims is important. Together, they help define a quality undergraduate education.

Colleges and universities have also achieved a high degree of consensus on the basic structure of the undergraduate curriculum. For generations, almost all four-year institutions have divided their course requirements into three parts: the major, which typically occupies 40–50 percent of the course credits needed for graduation; the general education program, which takes up roughly one-quarter to one-third of the required number of courses; and electives, which fill the remaining space in the curriculum. Community college curricula are necessarily more constrained, since their program of study is only half as long as that of four-year institutions. Nevertheless, most community colleges provide vocational or liberal arts programs and electives, and are required by accrediting agencies to reserve one-third or one-quarter of their total number of credit hours for general education in order to award the associate of arts degree.

Despite its widespread use, the tripartite structure just described seems poorly designed to embrace all of the goals that faculties and their leaders claim to value. The major, which occupies the largest portion of the curriculum, does make room for vocational programs of study that prepare students for careers. Most majors may also contribute to other basic aims, but they rarely do so systematically to ensure that all students receive instruction relating to all the important goals. Thus majoring in government may help prepare students to be citizens, but one can scarcely make the same claim for studying fine arts or physics. Majoring in English literature may lead a student to write with clarity and style, but the same is not necessarily true for students majoring in a vocational program or in the sciences and social sciences. Almost all majors claim to help their students acquire a competence in critical thinking, but critical thinking may not mean the same thing in classics as it does in cultural anthropology or computer sciences. In fact, many scholars who have studied critical thinking assert that the skills implied by this term in a given discipline are not readily transferable for use in other fields of knowledge.[3]

The portion of the curriculum allocated to electives is an even more uncertain path toward the basic aims of undergraduate education, since students in four-year colleges are typically free to select the courses they want from a long list of offerings covering all sorts of subjects. The very purpose of electives is to allow students to pursue any interest they choose rather than acquire a prescribed set of essential intellectual skills and bodies of knowledge.

Almost by default, the remaining portion of the curriculum, commonly referred to as general education, is the place for most of the requirements to ensure that all students pursue the basic goals. Even here, however, the pursuit of common aims is heavily constrained, since many of the course credits allocated to general education are reserved for a very different purpose—to prevent students from choosing an excessively narrow course of study. Most colleges achieve the desired breadth of knowledge by simply requiring students to choose two or three courses from each of several vast fields of knowledge, such as humanities, social sciences, and sciences. As with electives, such an open-ended requirement cannot ensure that every student will pursue each of the important aims of undergraduate education.

Any further effort needed to attend to the remaining goals of undergraduate education must be fitted somehow into the few credits left over after majors, electives, and distribution requirements have all received their allotted slice of the pie. It is in this residuum that one is likely to find required courses in writing, or moral reasoning, or quantitative skills, or diversity, or foreign languages, or global understanding.

The difficulty is that there is seldom enough space remaining to achieve all of these purposes. The situation is even more constraining in community colleges, since accreditors require students seeking the associate degree to take many fewer courses in the liberal arts. Faculties resort to various expedients in an effort to solve the problem. Some purposes are simply ignored. For example, very few colleges prescribe even a single course to prepare students to be active, knowledgeable citizens. Of course, some undergraduates will acquire civic preparation by taking one or more classes in government or economics, but large proportions of the student body do not choose to take even an introductory course in these subjects. The latter may gain useful civic skills such as critical thinking or leadership in other courses and extracurricular activities, but suitable preparation is not guaranteed and is probably minimal for large numbers of students.

Many colleges do not require students to take even a single course in mathematics; while many others prescribe no study of ethics or moral reasoning. Curriculum committees occasionally acknowledge these omissions but content themselves with the hope that students will gain some exposure to these subjects in other courses. Most students probably never do.

Colleges deal with other important aims by simply prescribing a single course or two. For example, almost all colleges require students to take a basic course in writing unless they can demonstrate sufficient proficiency by passing some sort of test. Few teachers of writing, however, would agree that a single course is sufficient for the purpose, and some colleges do take active steps to provide a number of courses on other subjects in which instructors agree to pay special attention to student writing. In most colleges, however, curriculum committees are content to assume that students will improve their writing by preparing papers for other courses, despite the lack of concrete steps to ensure that these papers will be critiqued for the quality of their prose. Thus it is not surprising that many employers complain about the writing ability of the college graduates they hire. Some corporations even contract with individuals or firms to give mandatory classes in writing for their newly hired college-educated employees.

In short, the curriculum in most colleges is not well aligned with the basic aims that most faculty members, academic leaders, and employers consider essential. Every student may receive an adequate amount of instruction in furtherance of *some* basic objectives, but few will have sufficient opportunities to achieve *all*, or even nearly all, of the acknowledged goals. The reason is simple: so many courses have been assigned to the major and to electives that too little room remains to make certain that every student will pursue each of the important objectives.

The explanation for this state of affairs is quite clear. The basic structure of the curriculum was never created to accommodate all the aims of undergraduate study. It was the outgrowth of two separate decisions arrived at during the early decades of the twentieth century. The first of these choices was to replace the heavily prescribed classical curriculum by giving students great freedom to select whatever courses they wished. The elimination of almost all prescribed courses meant that professors trained as specialized scholars would not be forced to offer courses outside their field but could teach the subjects in which they did their research. In the words of a leading champion of the elective curriculum, Harvard's president Charles W. Eliot, "the largest effect of the elective system is that it makes scholarship possible, not only among undergraduates, but among graduate students and college teachers."[4] Or, as Frederick Rudolph put it in his history of American higher education, "the elective principle was the instrument by which departments of knowledge were built, by which areas of scholarly interest were enlarged, and therefore it was the instrument that enabled colleges to become universities."[5]

Before long, however, faculties and their leaders discovered that many students did not take advantage of the elective system to dig deeply into academic subjects that interested them. Instead, they took easy subjects, many of them introductory courses, in different fields of knowledge. As a result, many undergraduates were completing their degrees with only a superficial understanding of a wide variety of subjects. To counteract this tendency, faculties arrived at the second key decision: to require every student to study one subject, or major, in depth while also acquiring breadth by having to learn a little about each of several fundamentally different fields of knowledge.[6]

This basic structure has remained intact for a century, not because it provides an ideal way to pursue the basic goals of undergraduate education but because it succeeds so well in serving the interests of the principal parties involved. Faculty members are given ample opportunity to teach the subjects in which they specialized as graduate students, while students are given great freedom to choose a major, choose electives, and choose which courses to take to satisfy the distribution requirement. The price paid to achieve these results is the creation of a basic structure virtually guaranteeing that many students will fail to achieve at least some of the purposes that faculty members themselves consider "essential" or "very important" aims of a college education. This is a steep price to pay. By now, however, the basic structure has endured for so long that it is taken for granted without discussion in most faculty reviews of the curriculum.

HOW MUCH DO STUDENTS LEARN IN COLLEGE?

A persistent feature of the recent debate over workforce needs is the tendency to classify individuals under headings such as "high school only," "some college," "BA degree," or "advanced degree" as if every individual in each of the several categories were equally equipped to meet the economy's requirements. In fact, however, seniors vary greatly in how much they have learned in college. These differences matter far more than the mere fact of having earned a degree. As Eric Hanushek and Ludger Woessmann observe after a careful study of the subject, "There is strong evidence that the cognitive skills of the population—rather than merely school attainment—are powerfully related to individual earnings and to economic growth." In fact, they add, "the effect of the quality of education dwarfs the variation between quantity of education and growth."[7]

The same is probably true of other benefits of a college education apart from preparing students for jobs. How successful a role college graduates play in civic life and how discerning they are in choosing the most suitable health-care plan, completing their tax return, or perceiving a moral problem and considering how to respond are all likely to be affected far more by how much they learned as students than by whether they earned a degree. In fact, the recent international survey of skills by the Organization for Economic Cooperation and Development (OECD) found that college graduates who achieved higher levels of literary proficiency not only earned more money but exhibited greater trust, better health, higher participation in civic activities, and increased political efficacy.[8]

Although these findings seem obvious, few commentators paid attention to how much students were learning until recently. Critics of undergraduate education were not hard to find, but most of them were chiefly concerned with college curricula, not with the progress students were making in acquiring knowledge and mastering basic intellectual skills. Although many observers faulted university professors for neglecting their teaching in favor of research, far fewer suggested that the prevailing *methods* of instruction might leave something to be desired.[*]

Without attracting much attention, however, a growing body of empirical research began to appear in the 1970s and 1980s seeking to measure the effectiveness of different teaching methods and the intellectual growth of students during their undergraduate years.[9] This work has gradually increased our understanding of how college affects students. Yet even now, little is known about whether today's undergraduates in four-year colleges are making more or less progress than their predecessors

[*] An exception in this regard is Clark Kerr, *The Uses of the University* (3rd ed., 1982), pp. 118–19.

did in earlier times, and even less has been discovered about student learning in community colleges. Such knowledge as exists consists of separate scraps of evidence, like bits of a jigsaw puzzle, that leave readers to decide for themselves which pieces belong and what those that do can tell us about the finished picture.

Do Larger Course Catalogs Mean Greater Learning? Any comparison of college catalogs today with those from several decades ago will reveal that the number and variety of courses have greatly increased. The constant addition of new subjects constitutes progress of a sort and makes it easier for almost all students to find courses that interest them. Yet most undergraduates must still take about the same number of credit hours to graduate as their forebears did in generations past. As a result, one cannot assume that students are gaining more knowledge or acquiring greater intellectual skill merely because they have more courses from which to choose.

In many subjects, however, notably the sciences, the body of knowledge has clearly increased in quality as well as quantity. Erroneous beliefs have given way to more reliable conclusions, and more important discoveries have replaced less significant findings. In this sense, students today may not be learning more from the wealth of courses available, but what they do learn may be more valuable.

Developing Greater Intellectual Competence. An essential question to ask is how much progress students are making in acquiring the basic skills, such as critical thinking or writing well, that professors regard as the most important aims of a college education. Developing these competencies is more valuable than merely acquiring information, because students who master them tend to retain them longer and use them more than the facts and figures presented in lectures. Moreover, many of the skills are also valuable in a wide variety of occupations, a matter of no small importance for young people whose ambitions are not yet fully formed and whose future is subject to unforeseeable changes.

The most comprehensive summary of how much intellectual growth occurs in four-year colleges is the mammoth review of hundreds of prior studies authored by Ernest Pascarella and Patrick Terenzini.[10] Their study

Freshman to Senior Gains in the 1990s

Critical thinking	.50
Reflective judgment (use of reason to address ill-structured problems)	.90
English (reading and writing)	.77
Math (quantitative skills)	.55
Science	.62
History, social science	.73
Moral reasoning	.77

Ernest T. Pascarella and Patrick T. Terenzini, *How College Affects Students*, vol. 2, *A Third Decade of Research* (2005), p. 179.

concludes that students do make progress in college, including progress toward acquiring basic competencies, but that most of the improvement is rather modest. The accompanying table summarizes the results measured in percentages of one full standard deviation. (A gain of one full standard deviation implies that students testing at the median of their entering class would be able, as seniors, to rise from the 50th percentile of the class to the 84th percentile if they were to take the test again with a comparable group of entering freshmen.)

Among these several competencies, the most important in the eyes of the faculty is critical thinking, which over 99 percent of professors regard as either an "essential" or a "very important" goal.[11] In recent years, a new test, the Collegiate Learning Assessment (CLA), has been developed to evaluate this skill. The CLA differs from most earlier measures in that it is not a multiple-choice exam but an essay test in which students are asked to prepare a well-argued solution to a practical problem drawing upon an accompanying collection of documents filled with relevant information.[12]

Richard Arum and Josipa Roksa recently published the results of a study in which they administered the CLA to students in several hundred four-year colleges both as freshmen and later on as seniors.[13] They discovered that, on average, seniors gained a bit less than half a standard deviation during college over what they achieved as entering freshmen.

Concretely, this meant that seniors of average ability who entered college with scores at the median of their class in critical thinking—that is, at the 50th percentile of their classmates—would be able, on average, to reach approximately the 65th percentile if they could take the test again as seniors with a similar group of freshmen.

This conclusion was not surprising since it was very close to the results derived by Pascarella and Terenzini from a host of studies in the 1990s using different tests and different samples of students. Of greater significance was the finding that the most successful one-third of the students improved their critical thinking by 1.5 standard deviations, or more than three *times* the average amount of progress for the group as a whole. What provoked the most reaction from the Arum-Roksa study, however, was the authors' conclusion that roughly one-third of the students did not make *any* statistically significant progress at all during their four years of college.

Since Arum and Roksa published their study, many commentators have cited their conclusions as a reliable account of how much progress undergraduates make in learning how to think. Yet there are at least three reasons for questioning these findings. The first involves the estimate that one-third of students did not make *any* significant progress. The authors derived this result by simply assuming that all students who were not shown to make significant progress must have failed to improve. This conclusion suffers from a basic statistical flaw. In order to be more certain of reaching a reliable estimate of student progress, the authors provided a generous margin for error, which led them to disregard a substantial number of modestly positive results that could turn out to be erroneous—in other words, "false positives." The trouble was that having refused to count these seemingly positive results in the interest of ensuring greater reliability, the authors lumped them together with the results of undergraduates who made no progress at all, which almost certainly exaggerated the percentage of students who failed to improve.[14]

The second difficulty with the CLA exam involves the concept of critical thinking itself. Educators are deeply split on whether one can treat critical thinking as a single skill that is transferable to other fields of knowledge or whether its meaning differs widely depending on whether one is talking to a professor of physics, forestry, or fine arts.[15] If the latter is true, it is hard to imagine that a single test of critical thinking can accurately measure the improvement of all undergraduates in college.

The third and final problem with the authors' findings is even more fundamental. The CLA is typically administered as a "low stakes" exam—that is, nothing much turns on the results for those taking the test. Under these conditions, it is likely that many of the students will not be especially motivated to do their very best. Several investigators have found, unsurprisingly, that lack of motivation can make a substantial difference in test results.[16] Thus it is possible that entering freshmen, who are typically eager to please and willing to do what they are told, try harder to excel than seniors, who tend to be more blasé and must frequently be paid in order to take the test at all. If such a motivational difference exists, of course, the results could significantly understate the amount of progress that seniors have actually made.

It is still possible that Arum and Roksa's findings are accurate, the more so since they are very similar to the results from other studies using different tests and students.[17] Yet it is also conceivable that a similar lack of student motivation may have affected all or most of the earlier test results as well. In the end, therefore, the Arum and Roksa findings may be the best estimates available, but they cannot be called definitive.

Are Undergraduates Learning More or Less Than They Once Did? Whatever weight one chooses to put on Arum and Roksa's study, the results they reached are too recent to give any hint of whether students today are learning more or less than they did in previous generations. On this point, the National Assessment of Adult Literacy casts a ray of light, since scores on prose literacy, document literacy, and numeracy are available for college graduates who took the same test in both 1992 and 2003.[18] Although BAs and community college graduates performed significantly better in both years than those with only a high school education, their scores for document and for prose literacy in 2003 were well below those from ten years before. (Their numeracy scores remained about the same.)*

Here, too, one cannot be sure how hard the students tried when they took the tests, but there is no apparent reason why they would have been less motivated in 2003 than in 1992. It is also possible that college graduates in 2003 were not as academically talented as a group as they were in 1992. Over the eleven intervening years, the proportion of four-year college graduates grew from 10 percent of the test-takers in the earlier cohort to 12 percent in the second, and much of the growth could have resulted from a larger number of students possessing below-average academic ability.

Further evidence of a genuine decline, however, is available from Ernest Pascarella and Patrick Terenzini in their aforementioned review of the multitude of studies on student learning conducted both before and during the 1990s. In their words, "the evidence from the 1990s ... suggests that [on average] students are making gains in critical thinking

*

	1992	*2003*
Prose Literacy		
High school only	268	262
Community college graduates	306	298
College graduates	325	314
Document Literacy		
High school only	261	258
Community college graduates	301	291
College Graduates	317	303
Quantitative Literacy		
High school only	267	269
Community college graduates	305	305
College graduates	324	323

National Assessment of Adult Literacy: A First Look at the Literacy of America's Adults in the 21st Century (2006).

In addition, while 40 percent of college graduates were "proficient" in prose literacy in 1992, only 31 percent could be so designated in 2003. The percentage of graduates proficient in document literacy dropped from 37 percent to 25 percent over the same period.

skills that are appreciably smaller in magnitude than the gains we observed in the [1970s and 1980s]."[19] As a result, the authors lowered the average student gains in critical thinking from a full standard deviation in the earlier period to half that amount for students in the 1990s.

How Do American College Graduates Compare with Their Counterparts Abroad? A first-ever survey of working-age citizens from economically advanced nations published in 2013 throws some light on the *comparative* academic progress of American college graduates. The survey tested people in 22 nations aged 16–65 for literacy, numeracy (quantitative skill), and problem solving with computers. The results hardly reveal exceptional competence on the part of American college graduates.* Our BAs ranked only 14th in problem solving, 16th in literacy, and 20th in numeracy.[20] They fared somewhat better in the percentage scoring at the highest levels (levels 4 and 5) but still finished only 8th in literacy and 9th in numeracy.[21]

A serious difficulty in interpreting these results is that they do not show how much the performance of college graduates reflects the quality of undergraduate education and how much stems from deficiencies in the public schools. There are reasons to suspect that the latter was an important factor. A recent analysis of test results from multiple countries has concluded that American high school students are a full year behind students of the same age from six other countries and a half year behind students from another six countries.[22] Moreover, the OECD report notes in passing that college graduates from the United States, along with those of Japan, showed an unusually *large* improvement over adults with only a high school education or less.[23]

All in all, existing studies that seek to measure how much students learn in college seem to suggest that American undergraduates, as a whole, are making modest though significant progress in acquiring important competencies taught in college, but that they may actually be learning less today than their counterparts did a generation or two earlier. Still,

---

*Once again, however, those who participated in this survey may not have tried their hardest, although there is no apparent reason why Americans should have been any less motivated than their counterparts in other countries.

much of the evidence tends to be sketchy, methodologically shaky, and limited with respect to trends over time. It is necessary, therefore, to look further for helpful clues.

Time Spent Studying and Going to Class. One of the most troubling pieces of evidence on student learning is a study by Philip Babcock and Mindy Marks revealing a startling decline in the hours per week that undergraduates in four-year colleges devote to studying and going to class.[24] According to self-reports from students in a long series of surveys, the total amount of time spent on these activities, after remaining quite stable between 1920 and 1960, dropped sharply from 40 hours per week in 1961 to 27 hours in 2003. The average number of hours devoted to studying fell especially steeply, from 24.38 hours per week to 14.42 hours. While 67 percent of college students reported studying more than 20 hours per week in 1961, only 13 percent did so in 2004. More than one-third of undergraduates now spend less than 5 hours per week preparing for class.[*]

Several studies have found that the amount of time spent studying and going to class has a greater effect than any other behavior under the control of students on how much they learn and what grades they receive.[25] If so, it is hard to imagine how such a steep decline could occur without affecting the amounts students learn during college. The downward trends involved seem to have occurred in all kinds of four-year institutions including some highly selective colleges. They cannot be explained by students working more hours or commuting longer distances, or by the proliferation of part-time students.

In ethnographic studies of student life, undergraduates in residential colleges sometimes say that though they may spend little time studying, much of what they learn that matters most to them comes from their very busy lives outside the classroom. Careful inquiries into how undergraduates use their time, however, cast doubt on such rationalizations.

---

[*] The methods used to derive these results were subsequently reviewed with care by Alexander McCormick, Director of the National Survey of Student Engagement, who found them reliable. "It's about Time: What to Make of Reported Declines in How Much College Students Study," 97 *Liberal Education* (Winter 2011), p. 30.

One survey of undergraduates on nine campuses of the University of California found that students spent an average of 5.79 hours per week watching television, 11.43 hours using the computer for fun, 5.47 hours on hobbies, and 11.43 hours socializing with friends.[26] While students may certainly have learned something valuable from these activities, it is hard to believe that they could not find time amid these leisurely pursuits to devote more effort to their homework.

The Quality of Student Effort. Some researchers claim that the total amount of time spent on homework is not as important as *how* students study—alone or with others, giving undivided attention or not, and so forth.[27] In America, surveys uniformly show not only that the time college students spend studying has declined, but that it is used less effectively today than it was several decades ago. The results indicate that large and growing percentages of undergraduates now "multitask" while studying by checking for e-mail, using Facebook, texting, and engaging in other forms of social networking.* The annual reports from the National Survey of Student Engagement reveal that two-thirds of students sometimes use social media even while sitting in class, and that 39 percent of freshmen and 31 percent of seniors do so "frequently."[28] Studies analyzing the effects of such multitasking on student performance regularly find that learning declines significantly.[29]

Grade inflation may be another trend that contributes to reduced effort on many campuses. Although the extent and severity of this problem is a matter of dispute, the prevailing consensus is that after remaining quite stable from 1920 to1964, grade averages surged during the Vietnam War period when a poor academic record could result in a student being drafted. Once the draft ended in the early 1970s, grade averages declined slightly for a decade, after which an upward trend (fewer Cs, more As) began on many campuses that seems to have continued to the present day. Although the gravity of the problem is a matter of some

---

* An *Educause* study has found that over 73 percent of students text message daily, 99 percent own a computer, 92 percent use Facebook, and 90 percent use social networking websites. Those on Facebook use it more than one hour and forty minutes per day, while students who use messaging spend over one hour and twenty minutes daily.

dispute, almost everyone agrees that grade averages today are higher in most colleges than they have been during the past fifty years, and that As are often given more frequently than any other letter grade.*[30]

Grade inflation is not unrelated to the effort students devote to their academic work. According to a recent empirical study by Philip Babcock, as good grades become easier to get, students feel less challenged, and the time they spend studying for their classes tends to decline.[31] This effect is especially pronounced when students expect a higher average grade not only for themselves but for the class as a whole. Taken together with the rise of multitasking, therefore, grade inflation provides another indication that both the quality and the quantity of student effort in the courses they take may have deteriorated significantly in recent decades.†

IS ALL THE EVIDENCE GLOOMY?

Thus far, the evidence about the quality of undergraduate education and its trends over time seems heavily weighted on the negative side. There is other information, however, suggesting that the quality of undergraduate education may be starting to improve. During the last few decades, a mounting number of empirical studies have shown that methods of instruction that engage students actively, such as problem solving, collaborative projects, or instructional computer games, along with asking

* A few commentators dispute the very existence of any significant upward movement in grades, arguing that the rate of dismissal for academic reasons has not fallen, and that the decline of low grades may simply reflect the more liberal use of extensions and pass/fail grading. See the chapter by Clifford Adelman in Lester H. Hunt (ed.), *Grade Inflation: Academic Standards in Higher Education* (2008), p. 13.

† Not everyone will agree with this conclusion. For example, John Etchemendy, former provost at Stanford, has argued that the quality of undergraduate education must be improving because the premium in earnings for college graduates over those with only a high school education or less has climbed to historic heights. "Are Our Colleges and Universities Failing Us?" in *The Big Picture: Assessing the Future of Higher Education*, Carnegie Corporation of New York (2014), p. 44. Most analysts, however, believe that the earnings premium for college graduates reflects a variety of factors apart from the quality of college education, such as changes in the supply and demand for college-educated workers resulting from trends in the number of BAs and changes in the skill needs of the economy. See, e.g., David Autor, "Skills, Education, and the Rise of Earnings Inequality among the Other 99 Percent," 344 *Science* (2014), p. 843.

Teaching Method	1991–93	2013–14
Extensive lecturing	54.2	50.6
Class discussions	69.4	80.7
Cooperative learning	31.7	60.7
Experiential learning	19.8	23.4
Group projects	31.6	45.5
Multiple drafts of written work	14.4	21.7
Students' evaluations of each other's work	10.0	28.0

Kevin Eagan et al., *The Undergraduate Teaching Faculty: The 2013-2014 HERI Faculty Survey*, Higher Education Research Institute (2014), p. 6.

students to think about the methods they are using to solve problems, produce deeper and more lasting learning than the more passive experience of listening to lectures and taking notes.[32] While faculties have been slow to adopt the newer techniques, the figures in the accompanying table suggest that their use has increased substantially while the prevalence of lecturing has gradually receded.

In addition to the growth of active teaching, colleges have begun to do more to try to measure how much their students are learning in order to identify problems and areas of improvement when they occur. This tendency too is at an early stage, and the methods used are not always rigorous. Moreover, although college administrators are collecting more data about student learning, they are often reluctant to discuss the results with the faculty to demonstrate the need for improvement. Still, such discussions are beginning to take place and seem likely to become more frequent in the future. By now, the signs of progress are too obvious and widespread to be ignored.

Another hopeful sign is that more than 80 percent of American colleges, at the behest of accrediting organizations, have now defined their learning outcomes and hence are equipped to start thinking about how well their curriculum and its course requirements relate to these goals.[33] Like the growing effort to utilize more promising methods of instruction, this process should eventually lead to progress toward a closer alignment.

HOW MUCH DOES LEARNING IN COLLEGE MATTER?

Some investigators have tried to discover how much the intellectual gains made in college matter in later life. The answer seems to be "a lot." In the previously cited work of Eric Hanushek and Ludger Woessmann, the authors conclude, "There is strong evidence that the cognitive skills of the population—rather than mere school attainment—are powerfully related to individual earnings, to the distribution of income, and to economic growth."[34] In fact, they estimate that raising the level of math achievement by 0.25 of a standard deviation—not enough to catch up with leading countries such as Japan but sufficient to bring America up to countries such as New Zealand and the Netherlands—would add forty-four trillion dollars to our GDP over a period of eighty years.

Another analysis estimating the long-term *noneconomic* benefits of learning was carried out by the Organization for Economic Cooperation and Development in their survey of the competency of adults from twenty-three industrialized nations.[35] According to this study, "Proficiency in literacy, numeracy, and problem solving.... is also positively associated with other important aspects of well-being, notably health, beliefs about one's impact on the political process, trust in others, and participation in volunteer or associative activities."[36] These findings are correlational only and do not prove that greater intellectual proficiency *caused* the later-life results. Together with the evidence just noted, however, the OECD findings are consistent with what common sense would suggest: namely, that acquiring greater knowledge and intellectual competence is likely to have a variety of beneficial consequences for students and society long after graduation.

SUMMING UP

The discussion in chapter 1 found persuasive reasons for increasing the percentage of Americans earning college degrees in order to meet the needs of the economy, expand opportunities for young people, and realize an impressive variety of noneconomic benefits both for the individuals involved and for society. It may not be feasible to set a precise goal for such an increase, given the problems of educating so many additional students and the difficulty of trying to predict how many more college graduates the economy will require. What one can safely say is that there are persuasive reasons for trying to increase the number of college graduates as much as we can over the next several years.

At the same time, helping more Americans to earn college degrees will accomplish little either for students or for society unless the graduates learn a lot along the way. The challenge is not merely to maintain standards of quality in the face of increased numbers of entering students, many of whom will come to campus poorly prepared for college study. As chapter 2 has endeavored to show, there are disturbing signs that current undergraduates are not learning as much as they should or as much as their counterparts did several decades ago.

Improving the quality of education will not be easy. Professors will have to relinquish their heavy use of lectures and adopt more active methods of instruction. They will have to reexamine the traditional structure of the curriculum and seek a better framework to achieve all of the important goals of a well-rounded undergraduate education. They will need to convince their students that acquiring the capabilities their homework assignments seek to foster and pondering the questions raised by their readings will matter enough in their future lives to warrant serious effort.

In short, the quality of education is just as important as its quantity. Each should be increased, and each deserves equal attention. It is the need to make progress toward *both* objectives simultaneously that presents the greatest challenge for America's colleges in the coming generation.

PART TWO

Sources of Influence

CHAPTER THREE

᠒

Can Colleges Meet the Challenges by Themselves?

IN THEORY, AT LEAST, THERE IS SOMETHING to be said for letting colleges deal with educational problems on their own without external interference. Academic leaders and their faculties have far more experience than anyone else in educating students and helping them earn a degree. In order to improve endeavors of this kind, which call for expert knowledge and judgment, it is usually best to set a goal and let those who do the work decide how best to do it. Otherwise, it will be difficult to generate the enthusiasm and expertise to get the job done well.

Could it be, then, that efforts from outside to influence how universities go about raising graduation rates and providing a quality education are unnecessary, even unwise? After all, most professors want their students to learn and achieve success in later life. They spend much of their working lives trying to help students reach this goal. Why not leave them alone and let them figure out how to meet the challenge of improving teaching and raising graduation rates?

FINANCING A MASSIVE INCREASE IN THE LEVEL OF EDUCATIONAL ATTAINMENT

One familiar reason why colleges might require outside help in raising levels of educational attainment is the need for money.* Graduating millions more Americans with a college degree promises to be an extremely costly undertaking. The community colleges and comprehensive

---

*By levels of educational attainment, I mean the percentage of Americans who have achieved a particular level of education, such as earning a high school, college, or professional degree.

universities that will enroll the bulk of the additional undergraduates have been given less and less funding per student over the past thirty years by their state and local governments. They can hardly be expected to raise all the money they will need from private sources, which have rarely shown much interest in supporting these institutions. As a result, leaving colleges to their own devices to achieve larger enrollments and higher graduation rates threatens to fail for lack of adequate funding.

A recent study by McKinsey consultants, however, suggests a possible way out of this dilemma.[1] According to the authors, if all comprehensive universities and community colleges adopted the methods of education and administration already used by their most successful peer institutions, they could "produce more graduates [and achieve President Obama's goal] for the same total expenditures without compromising the quality of degrees awarded or reducing access."

In arriving at this conclusion, the authors examined institutions with the same kinds of students as the community colleges and comprehensive universities that will educate most of the millions of additional young people needed to reach the president's goal. They quickly discovered that some of these colleges graduated students at much higher rates and lower cost than others. They then looked especially carefully at six of the most successful institutions to discover how they managed to perform so much better than their peers.

The successful colleges used a combination of measures to increase graduation rates and cut costs. They improved graduation rates by offering students a limited number of well-structured programs leading to good jobs after graduation instead of having them choose from a bewildering array of courses and majors. Better advising kept students from delaying their completion by taking courses they did not need. Stronger job counseling helped motivate them to persevere and earn a degree. Among the steps the exemplary colleges took to reduce their costs were shifting to year-round instruction to make more efficient use of facilities, centralizing the purchasing and creation of course materials, making greater use of online instruction and adjunct faculty, and eliminating activities, such as intercollegiate athletics, that were not essential to the institution's core mission.

The results accomplished by the six exemplary colleges are impressive. Is it realistic, however, to expect the vast majority of institutions to equal their achievements? Even with the limited information provided in the report, a number of difficulties spring to mind.

To begin with, some of the six colleges studied intensively by the McKinsey team had the benefit of exceptionally able and resourceful leadership. For example, one of them, Brigham Young University–Idaho, has undergone a remarkable transformation under its president, Kim Clark.[2] As it happens, Clark turns out to have been a highly successful dean of the Harvard Business School who was chosen by the Mormon Church hierarchy to take the helm at BYU-Idaho. How likely is it that hundreds of community colleges and comprehensive universities could attract presidents of this caliber?

Another of the six exemplary institutions is Western Governor's University (WGU), founded in 1997 to offer exclusively online instruction for careers in a small number of vocations, chiefly school teaching, health care, and business.[3] WGU is notable for its use of online teaching and its embrace of competency-based, self-paced learning that gives course credit to students who pass an appropriate examination without requiring them to take a course or sit through a prescribed number of classes. Study materials for its courses are purchased from a large publisher by the WGU administration, and there are no professors, only mentors who are available to advise and encourage students. Charges for each six-month term were only $2,890 in 2014.

These methods are imaginative and deserve to be tried, although WGU's graduation rates by the government's estimates are still too low to improve educational attainment levels.[4] Moreover, the WGU model may be feasible for a new institution but hard to follow for most existing colleges that have their faculties already in place and often represented by unions. In these institutions, efforts to have instructors use teaching materials bought from a commercial publisher may be stoutly resisted. Even more problematic are attempts to replace existing members of the teaching faculty with less expensive "mentors." Why would colleges even attempt to introduce such contentious changes without substantial pressure or inducement from some external source?

For community colleges and comprehensive universities with significant numbers of tenure-track professors, several of the other money-saving suggestions in the report also seem problematic. Replacing tenured faculty with part-time adjunct instructors, as the authors recommend, might be difficult to bring about. Even if it could be managed, researchers have found that extensive use of adjunct faculty tends to increase dropout rates and possibly impair the quality of education, the very opposite of what colleges need to accomplish.[5] According to some studies, degree programs taught entirely online can also reduce learning, especially for low-income and minority students.[6] Efforts to award credit for skills acquired at work or elsewhere or for courses completed online may do away with aspects of a traditional college education that are responsible for noneconomic benefits that are valuable in later life both for graduates and for society. Giving up athletics (for being a costly activity unrelated to the colleges' "core mission") has also proved difficult to accomplish for institutions that have tried to do so. Even year-round education, as was instituted by BYU-Idaho, may be opposed by faculty members who wish to have their summer free to vacation with their families in July and August when their children are out of school.

Although few colleges may duplicate the performance of the exemplary institutions, they must clearly do whatever they can to eliminate unnecessary expenses and lower the cost of educating students.[*] But costs are not the only problem that colleges must address in order to achieve substantially higher levels of educational attainment. Two-thirds of the students seeking to enter community colleges today, and 40 percent of those coming to four-year colleges, require remedial classes to

[*] The subject of college costs is not a primary focus of this volume except as it bears upon the effort to increase levels of educational attainment and improve the quality of undergraduate education. It is worth pointing out, however, that the community colleges and comprehensive universities that will enroll the great majority of additional students needed to achieve higher levels of educational attainment charge the lowest tuitions and spend the least amount of money per student of all the types of nonprofit colleges. They have also had to adjust to more than three decades of gradual decline in funding per student from their state and local governments. As a result, it is not clear how much room remains for further cost cutting by these institutions without damaging the quality of education they provide. For more on the subject of tuitions and college costs by two experienced analysts, see William G. Bowen and Michael S. McPherson, *Lesson Plan: An Agenda for Change in American Higher Education* (2016), especially pp. 46–61.

ready them for college-level study. Half of them do not manage to complete these courses and drop out as a result. Others never even try. Most of the additional students needed to raise attainment levels are likely to be even less prepared for college-level work. Faculties may simply not know how to help these students succeed.

Once enrolled in regular courses, many students drop out before completing their studies. Approximately one-third of those who enter a four-year college do not earn a degree within the next eight years. The numbers for community colleges are considerably worse. More than 60 percent neither earn a degree within six years nor transfer successfully to a four-year college. Most of the additional students who will have to enroll in order to raise attainment rates will be even less likely to graduate unless someone discovers more effective ways to help them succeed.

In short, while colleges and their faculties must be deeply involved in any successful effort to increase the level of educational attainment, there are plenty of reasons why they cannot succeed by themselves. A few institutions may manage to raise their graduation rates substantially without any loss of educational quality, but their success does not prove that the entire higher education system can follow suit. Most colleges will need a lot of help and encouragement from outside sources in order to achieve the desired goal.

ENHANCING THE QUALITY OF EDUCATION

If past experience is any guide, colleges will also need outside prodding and assistance to improve the quality of the education they provide. Throughout the history of American higher education, colleges have been slow to institute reforms of this kind. During the first 250 years of American higher education, academic leaders clung stubbornly to the traditional classical curriculum despite mounting dissatisfaction over its heavy use of ancient languages and texts taught by means of recitations and disputations.

Throughout the century or more since that curriculum gave way to a new model, colleges have added many courses and programs and have engaged in much tinkering around the edges, but the basic structure and the prevailing methods of instruction have remained pretty much the same. In a large majority of four-year colleges, faculties still embrace the familiar tripartite division into majors, general education, and electives. Moreover, while some progress has occurred of late in introducing newer, more active methods of instruction, lecturing to passive student audiences continues to be one of the most prevalent forms of teaching.[7] According to Myles Boylan, director of the National Science Foundation program on undergraduate education, "In almost every discipline, I could point to a variety of really effective, wonderful sets of instructional materials and instructional practices that if we could magically click our fingers and get everybody using them, there would be a major improvement in undergraduate education. But we are nowhere near that."[8]

Why Such Inertia? Responsibility for the sluggish rate of change must surely rest with the tenured faculty, since they are by far the most important force in determining the nature and quality of undergraduate education. For over fifty years, they have had virtually complete control over the undergraduate curriculum, the content of its courses, the methods of instruction used, and the training of the graduate students who eventually become college teachers.

The usual explanation by critics for the reluctance of faculties to reform is that professors are much more interested in research than in teaching undergraduates. Yet resistance to change in undergraduate education was evident long before research became prominent in universities, and it remains so not only in major universities but in the community colleges and many of the comprehensive universities where research is not a high priority. Within higher education as a whole, more than 75 percent of professors report that they consider teaching the most important activity in their professional lives.[9] At least when classes are in session, faculty members, even in research-oriented institutions, act according to these priorities, spending an average of 60 percent of their working hours on their courses and only 15 percent on research.[10]

At the same time, most of the effort that tenure-track professors devote to preparing their classes takes the form of keeping up with their field, incorporating recent material into their lectures and readings, and trying to convey their ideas with greater clarity. They have been much less interested in working collectively to make major changes in the curricula or in striving individually to experiment with innovative methods of instruction.*

As explained in the preceding chapter, faculties continue to support the existing curriculum, in part because it is now so well established that it is taken for granted by almost everyone and in part because the basic structure adopted by most colleges does such a good job of accommodating their professional interests. In a majority of four-year institutions, tenure-track professors have been trained as specialists in a particular discipline or field of knowledge. The curriculum is designed to fit their fields of expertise. It is therefore not surprising that these faculties rarely question the established structure, let alone agree to change it substantially.

Professors are likewise disinclined to alter their methods of instruction significantly unless they become convinced that their familiar ways are not working. Such epiphanies do not come often. Surveys suggest that 90 percent of faculty members believe that they are above-average teachers.[11] Since there is no accepted method of measuring just how much students are learning, most professors see no convincing reason to change.

---

*In a most informative study, three authors from the University of Washington recount the efforts of fifty-five faculty members in evolving and improving as teachers. Caroline H. Beyer, Edward Taylor, and Gerald M. Gilmore, *Inside the Undergraduate Teaching Experience: The University of Washington's Growth in Faculty Teaching Study* (2013). The study highlights the many ways in which instructors can learn through experience and improve their teaching by a continuing process of experimentation and adjustment. The authors succeed in dispelling the common misperception that all professors in research universities are concerned only with their scholarly pursuits and do not care about how much their students are learning. At the same time, the participants in this study were all professors "known to be thoughtful about their teaching." As such, they do not seem representative of an entire university teaching corps, which includes junior faculty preoccupied with establishing a record of publications that will warrant a tenure appointment, and adjunct instructors who now make up some 70 percent of college teachers and are often overworked and shabbily treated. Even tenured professors are frequently too preoccupied with their research or too set in their ways to experiment with new methods of instruction.

To be sure, instructors can and often do detect difficulties encountered by students in grasping new material or understanding lectures and problems assigned in class. In smaller classes, the expressions on students' faces, the questions they ask, the tests and term papers they write can reveal when teachers are not accomplishing what they intended. Such signs often cause instructors to revise their lectures or reorganize their reading assignments. But most of them are too preoccupied with their existing duties to contemplate fundamental changes in their methods of instruction. Many teach large classes in which they cannot easily observe the reactions of their students or even read their essays and tests, relying on their teaching assistants to perform those functions. Others who do read term papers and exams often assume that any shortcomings are the result of insufficient effort on the part of the students rather than deficiencies in their own teaching. Student course evaluations give professors a sense of how their teaching is received, but they seldom provide reliable evidence of how much students are learning.

Most college professors also work close to fifty hours per week or more and find it hard to spare the time to master new methods of instruction. If they are receiving positive student evaluations, as many do, they see little reason to change. Even if their evaluations are less than glowing, the reward structure in most four-year colleges gives little incentive to make substantial changes. In many comprehensive institutions and independent liberal arts colleges, as well as leading universities, investigators have shown that published research brings higher salaries, while extra time and effort in the classroom does not.[12] Publications also lead to promotions, lucrative consulting opportunities, and invitations to speak and attend conferences in exotic places, not to mention attractive job offers from other universities. Teaching seldom offers such rewards. Under these conditions and lacking knowledge of how much their students are learning, many professors see no compelling reason to abandon their familiar methods of instruction. Even those who do perceive a need to change may fail to act because they do not know exactly how to proceed and often get little assistance or encouragement from the administration to help them do so.

In almost all colleges, moreover, especially in comprehensive universities and community colleges, large majorities of the teaching faculty are not tenure-track professors but instructors serving on short-term contracts. Many of them are part-time, sometimes working at more than one institution. While they are seldom expected to do research, the colleges most likely to employ them tend to have little money to spend on helping them improve their teaching. At current rates of pay, most of these instructors either have other jobs or heavy classroom duties that leave them few opportunities to experiment with new methods of instruction. Even if they found the time, they would often be deterred by worry that their efforts might not succeed, causing student dissatisfaction that would compromise their chance to have their contract renewed.

For all these reasons, in most kinds of colleges, a faculty left to itself will usually be slow to make basic changes in its methods of teaching and even slower to rethink its curriculum. The incentives to spend the time and energy to make a collective effort are weak, while the disadvantages are considerable. Just as in the effort to raise graduation rates, some other entity will have to help both to demonstrate the need for change and to provide the money, encouragement, and assistance to ease the task of learning to teach in new ways.

The Role of College Leaders. Presidents and provosts are the obvious candidates to lead the charge to improve undergraduate education. In the past, they may have lacked convincing evidence of the need for major reform. Today, however, most of them are presumably aware of the growing number of studies and reports criticizing the quality of teaching and learning and arguing for alternative methods of instruction.

In fact, many academic leaders today *are* doing more than they once did to gather evidence and encourage experimentation and reform. As most of them acknowledge, however, much of the impetus for these efforts originated externally through the prodding of accrediting organizations.[13] Moreover, although colleges have now taken steps to clarify their learning objectives and gather evidence of student progress, most academic leaders have been reluctant to discuss the findings with their faculties, let alone provide sufficient funds and technical support to facilitate the use of new teaching methods.[14]

Why haven't academic leaders taken more initiative to try to bring about reform? Part of the explanation may be that presidents today are preoccupied with other matters—raising money, balancing budgets, and dealing with trustees, alumni, government officials, community groups, and other interested constituencies. A recent survey by the Council of Independent Colleges sought to determine how college presidents spent their days by asking leaders of public doctoral universities, private doctoral universities, comprehensive universities, community colleges, and independent colleges to rank twenty familiar presidential tasks in order of the amount of time they devoted to each during a typical work week.[15] Presidents of private doctoral universities rated academic issues fifth in the amount of time they spent, while heads of independent colleges placed them eighth. Among presidents in the three categories of public institutions that together educate the vast majority of undergraduates, academic affairs stood no higher than eleventh.

Feeling burdened with so many other responsibilities, most presidents have long since delegated responsibility for educational matters to provosts, deans, and vice presidents for academic affairs. But these deputies are also preoccupied with a host of day-to-day matters. Lacking the ultimate authority held by the president, they are usually inclined to concentrate on keeping things running smoothly rather than start a major effort at academic reform. Most of them serve for too short a period to contemplate such an undertaking, which often takes many years to complete.

The press of other duties is not the only reason why many leaders are reluctant to make a determined effort to reform undergraduate education. Some have an instinctive reluctance to risk antagonizing the faculty by seeming to suggest that their teaching is not as effective as it should be. Presidents and provosts want to be appreciated by their faculty. Disapproval is always unpleasant. Besides, professors cannot be ordered about; they must cooperate if anything is to be accomplished, and cooperation does not come easily from a faculty that feels criticized and unappreciated.

Other academic leaders may be reluctant to evaluate student learning or discuss the results of such assessments with the faculty out of fear of adverse publicity. Such inhibitions are especially acute in the most selective institutions. These colleges charge high tuitions yet still attract several times the number of applicants as there are places in the entering class. They compete vigorously for the very best students, many of whom assume that such highly regarded institutions must be doing a better than average job of helping students learn. Yet no one really knows whether this is so, and some analysts claim that it is not.[16] Under these conditions, leaders in the most prestigious colleges can easily conclude that they have little to gain and a lot to lose if they conduct assessments and discuss them with their faculty, only to find the results made public in the local newspaper.

Finally, the very nature of the duties performed by academic leaders today can lead them to underestimate the need for reform. Presidents spend the bulk of their working days trying to assure one audience after another that their institution is in excellent shape and getting better all the time. They repeat this message constantly to alumni, donors, students, government officials, and media representatives. Over time, they may come to believe what they are saying, and to overlook indications to the contrary.

According to a 2013 survey reported in the *Chronicle of Higher Education*, 82 percent of college presidents felt that they were doing a good or excellent job of providing academic programs that met the needs of the economy, and 73 percent believed that their graduates were well prepared for jobs, even though only 20 percent of employers agreed.[17] A mere 12 percent of the presidents acknowledged that their college was "not too effective" or "not at all effective" in teaching writing skills, although most tests administered externally have found that a majority of graduates are not proficient.[18]

Chief academic officers seem to share these tendencies. According to one recent survey, only 16.5 percent of such officials feel that "academic rigor has fallen at my campus in recent years," whereas 72 percent believe that "while my campus is doing well on rigor and quality issues, the issues pose real problems elsewhere in American higher education."[19] Academic leaders who are this confident about the quality of education in their own college can scarcely feel much urgency to reform, especially if they think that their faculty might resist such an effort.

The Role of Trustees. In an ideal world, boards of trustees would play an important role in maintaining high standards both by choosing presidents who are interested in academic reform and by making clear that the improvement of teaching and learning is a high priority on the campus. After all, trustees are ultimately responsible not only for supporting their university but for discussing its priorities and making sure that it pays appropriate heed to the legitimate needs of society.

Lay boards of trustees, at least in state colleges and universities, are specifically charged with representing the public in helping choose the goals of their institution. As a result, one would assume that they would give special attention to having their college address the two principal challenges facing higher education today. However, few observers feel that boards are fulfilling this responsibility well. According to one report from a committee composed of trustees, former college presidents, and former governors: "A lack of clarity of institutional purpose—or a failure of governing boards to ensure that institutions adhere to their stated purpose—is a major contributor to the rapidly rising cost of higher education over the past several decades. Competition among colleges and universities has caused many [institutions]—regardless of the mission or community they are intended to serve—to adopt a 'bigger and better' model of growth, as opposed to a focus on quality and prioritization."[20]

In many colleges, when trustees choose a president for their institution, they do not appear to put much emphasis on candidates' willingness and ability to carry out reform. That was clearly the conclusion of a recent study by the Aspen Institute of the selection process used by community college trustees.[21] Authors of the study interviewed members of search firms frequently employed by community colleges to assist them in finding a president. According to these sources, "trustees pay inadequate attention to the ability of presidential candidates to lead and manage change."[22] "Nearly every search consultant we interviewed strongly suggested that boards sometimes neglect or take for granted candidates' commitment to student access and success."[23] "The hiring process commonly favors candidates who are risk averse" and do not take "the kinds of risks that may spark controversy or result in irresolvable conflict with faculty or others."[24] Instead, trustees look for other qualities, such as fund-raising ability, external relations, and communication skills. Once new presidents are selected, added the report, programs to prepare them for their leadership positions "infrequently teach skills in ways that clearly aim to prepare [them] to lead institutions to higher levels of student success."[25]

Most trustees claim to be aware of the need for colleges and universities to work harder at helping students to graduate and improving the quality of their education.[26] In practice, however, according to a recent Public Agenda report, in-depth interviews with trustees from a range of public and private higher education institutions found that most were "focused on the short-term challenges facing their institutions" and had "not yet fully engaged with broader issues of higher education reform."[27] In another report by the Association of Governing Boards, more than 60 percent of trustees admitted that they spent too little time on academic affairs.[28] Asked for reasons for not getting more involved, 63 percent felt that other issues required more attention; 45 percent claimed that there was not enough time; 30 percent believed that the measures of student learning were not reliable enough to sustain a useful discussion; and 21 percent concluded that student learning was not an appropriate subject for board involvement.[29]

Former trustees agree that the boards they served on had no influence in such matters.[30] More recently, chief academic officers have indicated that boards (and presidents) are beginning to have a part in encouraging assessments of student learning but still rate trustee influence as only "moderate."[31]

There are reasons why trustees are often hesitant to play a more active role. Few members of a typical board start off knowing much about teaching and learning, and few are chosen for possessing such expertise. Once they begin to serve, they seldom receive much training on these subjects. Most new trustees are given no more than a half day of orientation; only 20 percent have as much as a full day.[32]

Once they join the board, trustees often complain that they do not receive adequate information to permit them to understand the issues and engage in meaningful discussion. According to a 2015 Public Agenda report, "trustees told us they often feel overwhelmed by complex information and uncomfortable asking for help."[33] Another board member described his experience more colorfully: "The staff likes to treat you like mushrooms: keep you in the dark and shovel you with manure."[34] Trustees from state institutions add that having to conduct all meetings in public because of sunshine laws tends to inhibit frank discussion about sensitive subjects such as dropout rates and the quality of teaching.[35]

It is theoretically possible, of course, to appoint more trustees who know enough about education to contribute to discussions of academic issues. Every university has alumni with extensive academic experience who could play a useful role in encouraging leaders to undertake needed reforms. As a practical matter, however, such an outcome is unlikely. State governors who appoint trustees for public colleges and universities often prefer to use their power to reward campaign donors and political allies or to please important constituency groups. Private colleges can choose their own trustees but invariably try to appoint a goodly number of wealthy donors. For the remaining vacancies, college authorities tend to prefer successful alumni who are loyal to the institution and unlikely to cause trouble by insisting on discussing the quality of teaching and learning in the college.

Most academic leaders are probably content to maintain the status quo and less than eager to have their boards become an active force in matters of teaching and learning. The line between asking for information about teaching and learning and pressing for specific reforms is not always easy to maintain. Few presidents wish to risk trustees' interference with their management or relish the prospect of having to cope with impractical proposals introduced by an inexperienced board member who means well but knows little about the subject. In their eyes, it is hard enough to persuade members of the faculty to embrace reform without getting trustees into the act and risking conflicts between board and faculty on what needs to be done.

THE TASK AHEAD

This chapter has outlined reasons why the challenges facing higher education today are unlikely to be overcome by colleges and universities acting alone. Universities tend to be conservative when it comes to changing their educational practices. Tenure-track faculty, who have almost complete control over teaching methods and curriculum, are reluctant to consider basic changes in a system that serves their interests well. Adjunct instructors lack the time or the security to experiment with major changes in their methods of teaching. Few college presidents are inclined to undertake a process of major reform that could prove to be time-consuming, contentious, and ultimately unsuccessful. Trustees feel ill suited for intervening in matters outside their competence and rarely seem eager to search for presidents who are intent on reforms that might create controversy.

To be sure, forceful leaders do emerge and manage to bring about transformative change. Michael Crow at Arizona State University, Paul LeBlanc at Southern New Hampshire University, and, in an earlier time, Bob McCabe at Miami-Dade Community College and Sister Joel Read at Alverno College are all prominent examples. Still, such leaders are few and their efforts often prove to be controversial. Moreover, even they will usually require additional funding from outside sources in order to carry out their ambitious reforms.

Finally, there is much we still don't know about how to improve remedial education and increase graduation rates. Major advances in the quality of teaching and learning will also require the discovery of better ways to measure student learning, together with innovations that technology conjures up to aid in the task. Such progress may not occur without the aid of government funding and help from other sources outside the academy. In short, meeting the challenges facing undergraduate education will almost certainly depend not only on what colleges do but on support from the various external forces that affect the performance of our higher education system. The influence these forces exert and how their role might be improved are the subject of the chapters that follow.

CHAPTER FOUR

ॐ

The Influence of Students

LIKE ALL ORGANIZATIONS BUILT TO PERFORM services for others, colleges pay close attention to the needs and desires of their students. In contrast to commercial firms, however, responsiveness to student "customers" is not always a good thing. While consumers may be the best judges of what they wish to eat in a restaurant or buy from a clothing store, students do not always know what is best for themselves, let alone what they most need to learn to become a successful employee and a responsible member of society. As a result, while college leaders and their faculties ought to pay close attention to the desires of their students, it is important that they exercise their own judgment in deciding how to respond.

As pointed out in chapter 2, colleges have been especially responsive in adding new programs and expanding others to meet the evolving needs and aspirations of undergraduates. They reacted promptly to the massive shift in student preferences during the 1970s, from the liberal arts to vocational programs, and moved quickly to create new programs in fields such as computer science and health-care services that offered growing career opportunities for their graduates.[1] It is no accident that colleges react so quickly to changing student interests about what to study. According to one survey, "the majors and programs that are offered are considered by prospective students the most important factor in deciding where to go to college."[2]

At times, when colleges have been slow to meet their needs, students have brought pressure to bear on the faculty and administration to make the desired change. In the late 1960s and early 1970s, applicants to college voted with their feet for coeducation, with the result that one all-male institution after another (along with several women's colleges as well) felt compelled to begin admitting members of the opposite sex.[3] On many campuses, black, Hispanic, and female undergraduates resorted to sit-ins and other demonstrations to obtain the appointment of more minorities and women to the faculty and the creation of programs in African American, Hispanic, and women's studies. While student activism declined after the early 1970s, it has grown stronger in recent years, both to enlist the support of the college administration for various social causes and to make the campus environment more welcoming and supportive for diverse groups of undergraduates.

The influence of students on graduation rates and the quality of instruction is more complicated. Undergraduates necessarily have a great deal to do with completion rates, since most who leave without a degree do so of their own volition and not at the insistence of campus authorities. Yet students do not make this choice in isolation. Parents often play an important part in the decision. Financial pressures, including the need to work long hours in order to earn enough to stay in school, can also cause students to withdraw. A capable, caring adviser, an interested faculty member, or supportive friends and teammates can all help to sustain the resolve to keep going. According to one close observer of undergraduate behavior in residential colleges, "by far the most compelling reason given for staying in college [is] the college experience"— friendships, extracurricular activities, student organizations, and the sheer enjoyment of being on one's own, free to make one's decisions and live more or less as one chooses without having to bear the responsibilities or endure the hazards of living as an adult in the "real world."[4]

Most colleges make considerable efforts to keep their students from dropping out, not only for budgetary reasons or concern for the institution's reputation but, most of all, because they care about their students and want them to persevere and earn a degree. However, with the possible exception of some recent demands to increase mental health staff, students seldom appear to exert much deliberate pressure on their colleges to take steps to lower dropout rates. Instead, most undergraduates seem to regard the decision to leave college as a matter of personal choice rather than the result of some institutional policy or neglect that calls for collective protest.

The impact of students on the quality of their education is quite different and not always beneficial for undergraduates themselves. Because applicants to college have no way of comparing the effectiveness of teaching at the various institutions they are considering, they do not exert the kind of pressure that their predecessors did during the 1960s and 1970s in forcing all-male colleges to begin admitting women. Once enrolled, however, students have significant effects on the quality of the education they receive, although the nature of their influence is not always what one might have anticipated.

The vast majority of freshmen claim that their principal reasons for coming to college are to prepare for a successful career and to earn a lot of money. Surprisingly, however, most undergraduates do not behave in the ways best calculated to achieve these ends. To be sure, some students in every college take a serious interest in their studies and work hard at doing well academically. In highly selective colleges, substantial numbers may behave this way. In the vast majority of institutions, however—according to surveys of how undergraduates spend their time, observations by professors who have spent a semester or two living in a campus dorm, and accounts of instructors teaching in community colleges—most students do not seem to care a great deal about many of their courses or how much they learn from their professors.[5]

As pointed out in chapter 2, undergraduates in four-year colleges study far less today than they did in the early 1960s when their vocational ambitions were less pronounced. Surveys suggest that they are completing fewer of their reading assignments than they did in earlier decades and reading for enjoyment much less frequently.[6] When they do study and go to class, they are often distracted by surfing the Web and communicating with friends via social media, despite much evidence that such behavior will hurt their academic performance and limit their chances for employment.

If students care so much about getting a good job and making a lot of money, why don't they work harder at their studies to help them succeed?

Many students of low or moderate income may lack the time or the energy to study more because of the hours they have to work in order to earn enough money to stay in school.[7] Others simply yield to temptation. At residential colleges in particular, the campus is filled with all manner of social and extracurricular diversions that compete for undergraduates' time and attention. On every campus, companies led by very clever people do their best to capture more of students' waking hours for television programs, social media such as Facebook, or absorbing new computer games.

The limited effort of most undergraduates does not appear to originate in college. Surveys have revealed that a majority of high school seniors spend less than five hours per week on homework.[8] Other surveys show a marked decline in the hours per week that seventeen-year-olds spend reading.[9] A 2007 survey of entering college freshmen found that more than half disagreed with the statement "I get a great deal of satisfaction from reading," while more than 40 percent agreed that "I don't enjoy reading serious books, and I only do it when I have to."[10]

Although professors may believe that the principal value of college lies in courses and preparing for class, that is not necessarily how students view the matter. For many eighteen- to twenty-one-year-old undergraduates in four-year colleges, the most important learning occurs outside of class in their relationships with other students.[11] It is these encounters that give them ideas about how to live their lives, and equip them with the social skills to interact easily with a variety of other people. In contrast, they often find their courses boring and feel that many lectures convey a lot of facts and information that have no practical use and will probably be forgotten within a few weeks after the final exam.

While students often spend little time on their courses, they do care about getting good grades (preferably without having to work very hard to achieve them). Researchers who observe students closely, especially those attending selective colleges, report that undergraduates define success more by the grades they receive than by any other factor.[12] Grades are the clearest evidence of what they have accomplished. Many of their parents take a keen interest in the marks their children receive and remind them periodically of how important their academic record will be in gaining admission to a good graduate school or landing a desirable job.

Curiously, however, the preoccupation with grades does not necessarily lead students to work harder at their courses. What it does do is cause them to argue over the grades they receive. According to the National Survey of Student Engagement, 95 percent of college seniors reported that they had discussed their grades with a faculty member, many more than the number who recalled having talked to a professor about ideas.[13]

Some commentators ascribe this behavior to a "consumer mentality" among undergraduates resulting from the growth of student loans, the lower voting age, and the spread of commercial and material values.[14] Because many students must now pay a substantial share of their college costs, they are more inclined than they once were to think of themselves as customers who are buying educational services and expect full value for their purchase. In their opinion, professors should give good grades to any student who makes a reasonable effort in exchange (with students themselves defining what is reasonable).

Some commentators also point to the fact that today's students grew up in an era when parents, teachers, and various youth-oriented organizations put much effort into building children's self-esteem.[15] As a result, surveys reveal an unusual increase in the number of young people who believe that they are "special," "important," and destined for success. Graduation speakers have repeatedly told them that they can be "anything they want to be," and that they should "follow their dreams" and never stop believing in themselves. Students with this mind-set can ultimately come to feel that they are almost "entitled" to succeed, and that any setbacks along the way are probably the fault of someone other than themselves. With this frame of mind, it is easy for many of them to believe that they "deserve" high marks, at least if they have done what they believe to be a reasonable amount of work.

Whatever the explanation, undergraduates have been quite successful in reducing the effort required of them in their courses while still obtaining good grades. Although the average amount of time they spend studying and going to class seems to have sharply declined since the 1960s, the grades they receive have apparently *increased* on many campuses, especially in selective colleges where an average of 43 percent of all grades today are As.[16] Meanwhile, the academic demands on students in most colleges appear to be modest. According to the National Survey of Student Engagement in 2007, only half of seniors in four-year colleges reported being called upon to complete a paper in excess of twenty pages, while one-third did not take a single course in which they were required to read more than forty pages per week.[17]

Why have many faculties failed to hold the line? If grades matter so much to students, one might have thought that instructors would have the power to insist on high academic standards in their courses. But matters are not that simple. Professors are understandably concerned not to put their students at an unfair disadvantage vis-à-vis undergraduates from other colleges in the intense competition for admission to good graduate schools and a successful career. Such concerns are especially prevalent at a time like the present when grading practices are unstable, and instructors are not sure exactly what the appropriate standards are or how to treat their students fairly in relation to those enrolled in other courses and other colleges. When no one is exerting countervailing pressure to maintain rigorous standards, and the standards themselves have become quite fuzzy and subjective, it is hardly surprising that many instructors respond by giving students the benefit of the doubt.

Another cause of grade inflation and easier course requirements is the widespread use of published student evaluations. Faculty members do not relish the prospect of being identified as poor teachers and having students shun their courses. As a result, consciously or unconsciously, they may be hesitant to award bad grades or require heavy readings for fear of damaging their evaluations and their reputation among students. This tendency is especially likely among the large majorities of faculty who are not tenured but serve under short-term contracts. For such instructors, student evaluations are often the most important evidence available to those who will decide whether to renew their appointment. Under these conditions, gaining a reputation as a tough grader with demanding intellectual standards may not seem a prudent thing to do. Students can sense the vulnerability of their teachers and sometimes even threaten them with poor evaluations or complaints to higher authorities if assignments are not shortened or grading standards relaxed.[18]

As pointed out in chapter 2, when students learn that they can get a high grade without trying very hard, the effort they spend on homework diminishes. This tendency seems intuitively obvious. As one student put it, "If I get the same grade for my very best work that I get for work that is not my best, I'm less motivated to try to stretch as far as I can."[19] Philip Babcock undertook to test this reaction empirically by examining the grades and reported student effort in almost eight thousand classes at the University of California, San Diego.[20] He found that student effort did indeed decline as the expected grade increased. The effect was especially great when the average anticipated grade *for the entire class* was higher. Thus when students expected that the average grade in a given class would be an A rather than a B, the time spent by individual students preparing for the class declined by more than fifty minutes per week, while the average study time dropped by one-half if the average expected grade was an A rather than a C.[21]

Grade inflation has also made most students more optimistic than they should be about how much they are learning in college. According to the National Survey of Student Engagement in 2010, more than 85 percent of college seniors claimed that their undergraduate experience had contributed "very much" or "quite a bit" to their ability to think critically, even though the Educational Testing Service found that 72 percent of such students were in fact "not proficient" at critical thinking, while another 20 percent were only "marginal."[22] As they near graduation, seniors are much more likely than employers to consider themselves fully competent in the qualities and competencies they need to succeed in the workplace.[23] Only after they have taken their first job do many of them recognize their inadequacy and regret not having studied harder in college.[24]

Why haven't deans and other academic leaders done more to resist grade inflation and insist on appropriate academic standards? Part of the explanation may be a concern that gaining a reputation for tough grading and rigorous requirements will deter potential applicants from applying. Another reason could be that college officials are reluctant to publicly acknowledge the existence of grade inflation or reveal any evidence of limited student learning for fear of irritating the faculty and stirring up concern among alumni and trustees.

In many cases, however, there may be an even simpler explanation. Most academic leaders appear to be unaware that grade inflation exists on their campus. In a recent survey of chief academic officers, only 30 percent of the respondents felt that grade inflation was a significant problem in their own college, although 65 percent considered it "a serious problem across higher education."[25]

Such misperceptions are seldom entirely inadvertent. They usually serve some purpose, and ignoring easy grading is no exception. Not only does it avoid controversy; as Roger Geiger has observed, "Grade inflation, after all, has a positive effect on student retention, faculty teaching ratings, and the satisfaction of student consumers."[26] Unfortunately, another of its effects is to keep many students from recognizing the limited progress they are making in college, thus diminishing their incentive to work harder at their courses.

THE BOTTOM LINE

As the preceding discussion makes clear, students have a pervasive influence on the behavior of colleges and their faculties. They are second only to the faculty in their impact on campus policies and practices. They determine graduation rates by the decisions they make to stay the course or leave college prematurely. They have a powerful influence on the undergraduate curriculum by virtue of their power to choose which college to attend and what courses to take. They have important effects on the amount they learn and the way their instructors teach through their power to decide how much effort to expend on their classes.

The motives that shape the way undergraduates use their influence are more complex than many commentators assume. In particular, the desire to earn a lot of money after graduation appears to have a more mixed effect on student behavior than one might think. Although it clearly influences the decisions of many students in choosing a major, it does not cause most undergraduates to work especially hard at their courses.

Whatever makes students behave as they do, one thing is certain. Few undergraduates today are clamoring for longer readings, harder questions, innovative methods of instruction, or tougher grading standards. All too often, they use their influence to bring about shorter, less demanding homework assignments, more lenient grading, fewer requirements, and greater freedom to choose. As a result, student behavior on many campuses probably helps to undermine the effectiveness of undergraduate education rather than to strengthen it. Regrettably, the response of academic leaders and their faculties has often been to accommodate rather than resist such pressures.

There is no sign that these tendencies will diminish any time soon. Nor can colleges reverse the trend merely by toughening grading standards and lengthening homework assignments. Colleges are most likely to improve their academic program by doing more to persuade students of the value of their coursework to their future lives, by teaching in ways that engage them more actively in learning, and by informing them more clearly and candidly about how well (or how badly) they are doing in acquiring the habits and competencies that will serve them well after they graduate.

CHAPTER FIVE

ॐ

Employers

AMID THE MANY DIFFERENCES OF OPINION over the state of undergraduate education, one point commands wide agreement. Almost everyone acknowledges that preparing students for a career is an important aim of undergraduate education. More than three-quarters of the faculty agree. Incoming freshmen are even more convinced; year after year, they list getting a good job as their most important reason for attending college. Business executives are naturally fully in accord. Politicians also share this opinion. As we learned at the end of chapter 1, some governors even talk as though preparing students for the workforce is the *only* purpose of a college education that really matters.

Observing this consensus and the emphasis placed by so many students and corporate leaders on preparing for a career, some educators have expressed concern that the values of liberal learning are at risk of giving way to the narrow vocational demands of the marketplace. In fact, however, most corporate CEOs and human resources executives claim to value many of the same qualities that large majorities of college presidents and professors consider essential to a proper undergraduate education. The table on the next page illustrates the point.

Chief executives also express a strong preference for broad knowledge and skills rather than practical know-how for specific jobs. Ninety-one percent agree that acquiring basic, general competencies, such as proficiency in critical thinking and written and oral communication, is more important than the choice of a major.[1] The human resources executives who actually do the hiring are more likely to value the practical skills and knowledge that will enable new employees to "hit the ground running," but even 55 percent of these managers claim that broad knowledge and competencies are more important.[2]

Most Important Qualities for Recent Graduates

CEOs[1]		Human Resources Executives[2]		College Presidents[3]	
Communicate orally	85%	Critical thinking, problem solving	72%	Communication, written and oral	94%
Work effectively in teams	82%	Teamwork, collaboration	61%	Make decisions, solve problems	79%
Communicate in writing	82%	Communication skills	54%	Analytic, research skills	66%
Ethical judgment	81%	Technical skills	54%	Collaborate with others	55%
Critical thinking and analytic reasoning	81%	Adaptability	48%	Work with diverse groups	48%
Applying knowledge to the real world	80%			Job-related knowledge	45%
Solving complex problems	70%				
Locating, organizing, evaluating information	68%				
Innovating, being creative	65%				

[1] Hart Research Associates, *Falling Short? College Learning and Career Success*, survey carried out for Association of American Colleges & Universities (January 20, 2015).
[2] Economist Intelligence Unit, *Closing the Skills Gap: Companies and College Collaborating for Change* (2014).
[3] Pearson, *Breakthrough to Greater Student Achievement* (2013), p. 29.

With this much consensus among business representatives and academic leaders on the basic goals of a proper undergraduate education, the stars seem perfectly aligned for satisfying both groups. As it happens, however, campus officials and corporate leaders have widely different views about how well colleges are succeeding in giving employers what they seek.

HOW WELL DO COLLEGES PREPARE STUDENTS
FOR EMPLOYMENT?

The View from the Bridge. Academic leaders claim to be well aware of the importance of the college's vocational mission. Fully half of them acknowledge feeling either "great" or "very great" pressure from employers to equip their students with the necessary knowledge and skills to succeed in their jobs.[3] Fifty-eight percent report hearing similar concerns from the parents of current students. Even more (59 percent) declare that they are made aware of such sentiments by prospective students and their parents.

In recognition of the widespread desire to prepare students for a career, presidents and deans report that their institutions use a variety of ways to keep in touch with the job market and employer needs.[4] The means they employ vary according to the nature of the college and the kinds of jobs their graduates fill. The large for-profit colleges often work closely with industry councils or employer advisory committees composed of representatives from the industries they serve who give them up-to-date advice about the kinds of courses and specific skills they need. Community colleges with strong vocational programs also form employer advisory committees to keep them informed of changing skill needs, although these committees are usually created to advise on a variety of vocations rather than one specific occupation. Representatives of four-year colleges report using several methods to stay attuned to vocational needs. They may meet regularly with company representatives, or survey employers for feedback on the skills and preparation of recent graduates, or even poll young alumni to learn their thoughts about the adequacy of their preparation for the jobs they hold.

Overall, college leaders seem quite satisfied with their efforts to equip students for careers. In one recent survey, 82 percent of college presidents claimed that they were doing an "excellent" job of providing academic programs that meet the needs of the economy.[5] In another survey, 23 percent of presidents considered their graduating seniors to be "very well prepared" for their first jobs, 50 percent considered them to be "well prepared," 25 percent regarded them as simply "prepared," and only 2 percent felt that they were "unprepared."[6]

Other surveys asking more specific questions evoke a slightly more nuanced appraisal. In a 2014 poll sponsored by Gallup and *Inside Higher Ed*, college presidents evaluated the effectiveness of their institutions in different aspects of preparation for the workplace.

Activity	Somewhat Effective	Very Effective
1. Developing critical thinking	54%	40%
2. Emphasizing writing skills	62%	28%
3. Real-world problem solving infused into classroom	60%	31%
4. Providing internships with employers	48%	38%
5. Working with employers	48%	19%

Gallup and *Inside Higher Ed*, Poll of College Presidents (2014).

In another survey, provosts gave a fairly positive though slightly less upbeat assessment of their college's effectiveness in preparing students for jobs. Oddly, the two types of colleges receiving the highest rating from their chief academic officers were the very institutions employers consider *least* effective in meeting their needs. Since many community colleges and most large for-profits try especially hard to consult with employers to learn their needs, the most likely explanation for this result is that these colleges enroll the least academically qualified students.

Percent of Provosts Giving Their Institution a 6 or 7 on a 7-Point Scale

All Institutions	Public Doctoral	Public Masters	Community Colleges	Private Doctoral	Private BA	For Profit
50	43	29	54.9	51	49.6	74.2

Inside Higher Ed (January 25, 2012), p. 11.

Students. College seniors are almost as confident as college presidents in evaluating their qualifications for good jobs after they graduate. They seem well informed about the preparation they need for the jobs they seek. In fact, their impressions of the qualities that matter most for success in the workplace are strikingly similar to the views of employers.[7] As the following table makes clear, a solid majority of seniors feel that college has prepared them well in each of these skills and competencies. Curiously, however, while most academic leaders stress the value of undergraduate education over the lifetime of their students, seniors tend to think that colleges do best at preparing them for their first job.[8]

Competency	Percentage of Students Feeling Well Prepared
Critical thinking	65
Written communication	65
Oral communication	62
Analyzing and solving complex problems	59
Working in teams	64
Locating, organizing, analyzing information	64
Ethical judgment	62
Applying skills to real world	59

Hart Research Associates, *Falling Short? College Learning and Career Success*, survey carried out for Association of American Colleges & Universities (January 20, 2015), p. 8.

Recent Graduates. Once students finish college and find a job, their opinions change dramatically. In 2014, Bentley University sponsored a survey of recent graduates from a representative sample of colleges to obtain their views about their preparation for the workforce.[9] Sixty-six percent replied that unpreparedness was a "real problem" for graduates like themselves. Sixty percent blamed themselves for not working harder to master basic skills, such as communicating in writing, critical thinking, and analyzing and solving problems. Forty-two percent blamed their college. Thirty-one percent held their professors responsible.

A McKinsey survey of recent graduates in 2012 reached slightly less discouraging results. Only 30 percent of those who had attended four-year colleges thought that they had not been well prepared. A higher proportion (40 percent) of those who graduated from community colleges felt the same way.[10]

Employers. Business executives strongly support President Obama's goal of increasing the number of Americans with college degrees. In a Hart Research Associates survey of 450 corporate leaders in 2011, 79 percent of the participants replied that increasing the supply of post-secondary graduates would have either an "extremely positive" or a "very positive" impact on the economy, while 70 percent replied that it would have an "extremely" or "very positive" effect on workforce produc-tivity.[11] An even greater majority (87 percent) felt that a larger number of college graduates would have a "very positive" or "extremely positive" effect on America's ability to compete in the global marketplace.

While strongly supporting the campaign to raise existing levels of ed-ucational attainment, employers are much less impressed than college seniors and academic leaders with the qualifications of the graduates they hire.

Are Graduating Students Well Prepared?

Competency	Percentage of Employers (answering yes)	Percentage of College Seniors (answering yes)
Working with others	37	64
Staying current with technology	37	46
Ethical judgment	30	62
Locating, organizing, evaluating information	29	64
Oral communication	28	62
Quantitative literacy	28	55
Written communication	27	65
Critical thinking, analysis	26	66
Innovation, creativity	25	57
Analyzing complex problems	24	59
Applying knowledge to real world	23	59

Hart Research Associates, *Falling Short? College Learning and Career Success,* survey carried out for Association of American Colleges & Universities (January 20, 2015), p. 12.

Employer views about the capabilities of recent college graduates are also much less positive than the estimates of college leaders. A Pearson survey from 2013 provides a quick summary.

How Well Prepared Are Recent College Graduates?

	Employers	College Presidents
Very well prepared	2%	23%
Well prepared	18%	50%
Prepared	49%	25%
Unprepared	28%	2%
Very unprepared	3%	0%

Pearson, *Breakthrough to Greater Student Achievement* (2013), p. 15.

Echoing these results, Dana Linn, who oversees the Workforce Committee of the Business Roundtable, recently declared: "Colleges and universities think they're adequately preparing students for the workforce. You couldn't have a more stark difference of opinion. They're [i.e., colleges and universities] not getting anywhere close to what [we] want."[12]

While the figures listed above indicate much dissatisfaction among employers with the college graduates they hire, other polls of business leaders seem to point in the opposite direction. In a 2012 survey of employers appearing in the *Chronicle of Higher Education*, almost 70 percent of the respondents rated colleges as "good" or "excellent" in preparing successful employees.[13] In another survey, this one by Public Agenda in 2014, more than 90 percent of human resources professionals at medium and large corporations rated the quality of the public and private four-year colleges they knew as either "good" or "excellent." Eighty percent gave a similar rating to community colleges, while 69–70 percent said the same about for-profit colleges.[14] Moreover, if so many employers feel that the recent graduates they hire are inadequately prepared, why did 79 percent of the business leaders in the Hart Associates survey in 2011 declare that increasing the supply of postsecondary graduates would have an "extremely positive" or "very positive" effect on workforce productivity?[15] And why did 87 percent maintain that such an increase would have a "very positive" or "extremely positive" impact on America's ability to compete globally?[16] The surveys give no explanation for these seeming inconsistencies.

MAKING SENSE OF THE EVIDENCE

Part of the dissatisfaction employers feel about the qualifications of the recent graduates they hire may reflect a difference of opinion over how much of the preparation should be done by colleges and how much by employers. Many American companies are wary of investing much money in workforce training for fear that recipients may leave the company after a brief time and take their skills elsewhere, perhaps even to a competing enterprise. As a result, the total amount of training the average worker receives per year in the United States is just shy of eleven hours, and much of this total is directed at workplace safety, not on how to do the job effectively.

According to Peter Capelli, director of the University of Pennsylvania's Center for Human Resources, "a huge part of the so-called skills gap actually springs from the weak employer efforts to promote internal training for either current employees or future hires."[17] While most companies assert that they cannot afford to provide more training, Capelli points out that "teaching work-based skills outside the workplace is both inefficient and impractical in the long run," because it forces employers to spend excessive amounts of time and money searching for applicants who already possess the necessary practical skills.[18]

At least one management consultant firm, Accenture, agrees that many employers demand too much of the college graduates they employ. Based on its own surveys of students and employers, Accenture discovered that 77 percent of graduating seniors in 2013 expected their first employer to provide formal training to develop their company-specific skills. In fact, only 48 percent of college graduates in 2011 and 2012 received such assistance. According to the consultants:

> Based on [our] findings, as well as on our work with hundreds of companies around the world, it is hard to avoid the conclusion that many employers have overblown expectations for the skills of new hires—believing falsely that recent college graduates should be able to hit the ground

running. Because of that misplaced expectation, companies are not making adequate commitments to, and investments in, the long-term training that would attract, develop and retain the talent needed for their companies to achieve high performance.[19]

Recent graduates have another explanation for the dissatisfaction of employers with the applicants they hire. Many of them seem to agree with employers that they were not well prepared for their first jobs. Yet many fewer hold their alma mater responsible.[20] Instead, according to one survey, 60 percent blame themselves for not having worked harder in college.[21] An earlier survey of alumni from twenty-nine highly selective colleges found that almost half faulted themselves for studying too little as undergraduates, especially those who finished below the top third of their class.[22] Such regrets are not surprising. As pointed out in chapter 2, college students today appear to be spending much less time than they did fifty years ago studying and going to class.[23] More than one-third claim to have spent less than five hours per week on their homework.

While many recent graduates feel personally responsible for their inadequate preparation, and some commentators fault employers for offering insufficient training, colleges must surely share some of the blame. Most of the employer complaints do not involve disagreements over teaching specific job-related skills. They reflect dissatisfaction with basic competencies, such as writing and critical thinking, that presidents and their faculties have long included among the most important aims of undergraduate education.

Colleges must also accept some responsibility for failing to provide their students with a more accurate view of how much (or little) progress they are making in acquiring the competencies required for success in the workplace. The striking differences between the views of college seniors and those of employed recent graduates in evaluating their readiness for work clearly suggest a failure of communication on the part of many colleges. As pointed out in chapter 4, although undergraduates today appear to be studying much less than they did several decades ago, they receive better grades today than their predecessors did then.[24] By awarding higher marks for less effort, colleges may be doing their students a disservice, giving them an unrealistic impression of their readiness to perform when they begin their careers. In addition, most faculties have become much more lenient in allowing students to hand in papers late and excusing them from other rules and deadlines, thus failing to prepare them well for the world of work where most employers will be less forgiving.[25]

On the basis of the available evidence, then, each of the parties involved—colleges, students, and employers—appear to deserve some blame for the gap that apparently exists between the capabilities of college graduates and the needs of the workplace. Of the three parties, however, only recent graduates seem willing to acknowledge any responsibility for the problem. Many employers complain about a skills gap while failing to do much of anything either to raise compensation to attract better applicants or to provide more on-the-job training that could give employees the skills they need. Many students claim to be primarily interested in going to college to obtain a good job yet devote surprisingly little time to learning what they need to know to succeed in their careers. Many academic leaders simply appear to be in denial. While almost half of college presidents in one survey awarded a grade of C or lower to the job done by colleges as a group, over 80 percent think their own college is performing well in meeting workforce needs.[26]

REFLECTIONS ON THE INFLUENCE OF EMPLOYERS

The evidence presented in this chapter yields one other intriguing insight. Despite the concerns about excessive vocationalism frequently heard in academic circles, employers do not appear to have *too much* influence over undergraduate education. One can even make an argument that they have *too little*.

The most apparent indication of employer influence has been the massive shift on the part of students since the 1970s from the liberal arts to vocational majors. Even here, however, the precipitating cause of this movement was not the work of employers but a sudden change in the ambitions of entering freshmen. In the space of only a few years in the early 1970s, the percentage of freshmen declaring that their chief aim in college was to develop values and a philosophy of life dropped from 70 to 40, while the share enrolling chiefly to "make a lot of money" rose from 40 to 75 percent.[27] Although the reasons for this shift are not entirely clear, the economic recession of the late 1960s and early 1970s appears to have had a sobering effect on the confidence of college students and strengthened their desire to equip themselves to earn a comfortable living. During the same period, the vocational ambitions of women were increased by the writings of feminist authors and the opening of occupations previously restricted to men. Employers may have benefited from these changes, but they were not necessarily the cause.

The fears of many critics about the impact of corporate demands on undergraduate education also seem exaggerated. The qualities emphasized by employers turn out to be less narrow and less practical than many educators have suspected. In survey after survey chronicling the competencies most desired by business, CEOs have stressed educational priorities that closely resemble those of academic leaders and their faculties.

All in all, therefore, when one examines the influence of corporations on college campuses, what is most striking is how little attention is paid to the views of corporate executives. Although academic leaders may be generally aware of employer dissatisfaction over the preparedness of college graduates, they remain quite confident about the job their own college is doing to ready students for the workforce. Most college seniors are equally satisfied with the quality of their preparation for the workplace and seem blissfully unaware of the contrary views of employers.

The gap between the opinions of CEOs and those of graduating seniors and their college presidents suggests a need for employers to meet with academic leaders and explain their dissatisfaction with many of the graduates who come to them seeking employment. Such an interchange could prove fruitful to all concerned, the more so since business leaders claim to be much more intent on having colleges improve the quality of what they profess to be doing already than on persuading them to adopt a narrow, practical curriculum.

What is most significant, however, about the gulf between the judgments of educators and those of business executives is something more fundamental and consequential. A critical reason for the difference of opinion is the lack of reliable information about the knowledge and competence of graduating seniors. Most college leaders do not collect adequate data on how much their students are learning. Employers have a hard time discovering what graduates know and can do. Today, as in the past, hiring officials can examine SAT scores, take account of how difficult it is to be admitted to the colleges students attended, and observe the grade point averages (GPAs) and course titles listed in their college transcripts. Nevertheless, the proliferation of courses makes a college transcript harder to evaluate than in the past, while grade inflation has robbed the GPA of much of its meaning. The constant growth in the number of colleges makes it harder for employers to draw inferences about the quality of education that job seekers have received by noting the institutions they attended.

In view of these difficulties, one can safely predict that a great deal of time and ingenuity will be expended in the coming years to develop more reliable and informative ways of evaluating the qualifications of recent graduates. In fact, such efforts are already in full swing. Testing organizations are trying to devise better instruments to measure the knowledge and skills of college students.[28] With the emergence of data analytics, many companies are beginning to use sophisticated techniques to collect and analyze large quantities of information in order to discover more about the attitudes and abilities of individual graduates and determine their "fit" for particular jobs.[29] Colleges too are beginning to supply employers with more useful information. For example, in describing the new online program at Southern New Hampshire University, President Paul LeBlanc reports that "employers get a detailed map of the student's [ninety] competencies, excellent third party assessments, and the ability to go [online] and see for themselves the evidence of mastery."[30]

While advances of this kind could eventually prove useful both to educators and to employers, the dangers inherent in such efforts are substantial. Developing adequate measures of a particular competency or body of knowledge is a difficult task in itself, and tests that seem appropriate may later prove to be unreliable. Moreover, a test that is serviceable enough to be useful to a prospective employer often measures only part of what instructors are trying to impart to their students. Tests that cover all or nearly all of the knowledge, capabilities, traits, and values that college educators hope to nurture are well beyond the capability of anything in use at present.

If only certain skills and knowledge can be accurately measured, distortions may arise in college teaching. Once the results of particular tests turn out to be reliable enough to be widely used by employers, many colleges may feel pressure to spend more time teaching students to take these tests instead of trying to convey a deeper understanding of the material involved. In colleges oriented toward preparing students for immediate employment, faculties may begin to concentrate too much on teaching the subjects that can be tested while neglecting other subjects that lack reliable measures. In these ways, the content and nature of a college education could become skewed in favor of measurable competencies at the expense of other values, interests, and qualities of mind and spirit of equal or greater importance.

For many years, concerns of this kind have led educators to resist the use of any tests to measure the effects of a college education. Today, however, such opposition is harder to defend. In any human endeavor where the parties involved have limited knowledge about the results of their efforts, progress is likely to be limited. Thus academic leaders and their faculties will do a disservice to their students and to themselves if they ignore efforts to find better ways of discovering how well their students are progressing. Despite the risks, colleges must either press ahead to discover how to evaluate learning responsibly, or others with less appreciation of the hazards will surely do the job for them.

CHAPTER SIX

෴

Competition, Old and New

EVER SINCE ADAM SMITH'S *THE WEALTH OF NATIONS* appeared in 1776, competition has been lauded as a potent force for bringing the behavior of business enterprises into closer alignment with the needs of their customers. Such beliefs are not confined to the world of commerce. Many informed observers are convinced that competition offers the best hope for improving the quality of our public schools.[1] Can the same be said for higher education, where rivalry has long flourished? Will new forms of competition, fortified by advances in technology, bring changes that enable colleges to raise their graduation rates and increase student learning?

THE PECULIAR EFFECTS OF COMPETITION IN HIGHER EDUCATION

While most colleges and universities are not businesses, they often compete vigorously with one another to attract students. Some institutions have no competitors within easy commuting distance and can count on a steady flow of applicants who value proximity to their home or place of work. Others have a special mission, perhaps resulting from a church affiliation, that assures them of a sufficient number of candidates for admission every year. But well over half of all colleges consider themselves in competition for students.[2] Many of them have to struggle simply to enroll enough paying students to fill their classrooms and balance their budgets.

The competition that exists in higher education has several good effects. It puts pressure on colleges to satisfy the desires of students and provide the kinds of courses and activities to suit their varying needs and ambitions. It reinforces the efforts of universities to produce the very best research they can muster. Nevertheless, competition does not serve the public interest in higher education as well as it does in many parts of the economy. One important reason is that students do not play quite the same role in purchasing a college education as consumers do in helping to allocate resources appropriately, hold down prices, and increase efficiency in many commercial markets.

To begin with, while customers are often regarded as the ultimate arbiters of value in in determining which goods are produced, the public has legitimate interests of its own in the decisions undergraduates make about college, interests that can differ from those of students. For example, as we learned in chapter 2, competition causes colleges to offer programs in subjects that students want to learn. However, the subjects students choose and the incentives markets provide do not always yield the mix of skills the economy requires in order to grow and prosper. Instead, universities may graduate more aspiring novelists, architects, professors, and professional football players than the economy can support, while failing to prepare as many engineers and scientists as employers would like to hire.

Applicants also lack reliable ways of ascertaining which of the colleges they are considering will teach them most effectively and help them learn the most. The various college guides do little to enlighten them on this score. As a result, they cannot make a fully informed choice as to which college offers them the best value for the money. They may even draw dubious inferences, such as assuming that colleges charging higher tuitions must be providing a better education. Under these conditions, colleges do not feel much competitive pressure to improve the quality of their instruction in order to appeal to students.

Once young people arrive at college, they make other choices that do not always match the legitimate interests of the larger society. Many of them do not care very much about improving their knowledge of ethics or learning to become active and enlightened citizens. As a result, the competition for students generates little pressure on colleges to require such courses or even offer them as electives. In addition, as we discovered in chapter 4, many students do not choose to work very hard at their studies, and few press the faculty for more demanding courses. As a result, in spite of society's interest in having undergraduates learn as much as possible, the competition for students places little or no pressure on colleges to demand hard work from students and may actually help to bring about the opposite result.

Such competition as does exist takes other forms. The most prominent version for four-year colleges is a competition for "prestige," an amorphous term that receives its most precise definition in the annual college rankings published by *U.S. News and World Report*. These ratings in turn are based on a variety of measurable factors, of which the most important are the reputation of the college or university in the eyes of officials from other institutions, the number of applicants to the college, the percentage who are admitted and their average SAT scores, and the percentage of freshmen who graduate within a stipulated number of years.

As measures of genuine quality, these factors are widely (and justly) regarded as deeply flawed. They do not reflect how much students learn in college but only how well they performed on SAT exams before they entered. They rely heavily on the views of officials from other colleges even though these sources rarely know much about the educational quality of institutions other than their own. Nevertheless, many colleges take the rankings seriously because they seem to have some influence on high-scoring applicants in deciding where to enroll and because many campus officials worry that prospective donors, trustees, and alumni may pay attention to them as well.

As a result, not only is there little competition for genuine educational quality among colleges; the competition that does take place tends to divert attention and resources away from improvements in teaching and learning toward activities that help determine a college's ranking. For example, many institutions spend large amounts of their financial aid budget on scholarships for students who do not need such help but have SAT scores high enough to boost the average of the entering class. More important, rankings add a powerful incentive to build strong research programs by hiring more professors with impressive publication records, since research, rather than teaching, is the principal factor that determines the reputation of a college in the eyes of officials from other institutions. While research is clearly of great benefit to the nation, the competition over college rankings threatens to distort the delicate balance that universities ought to maintain between scholarship and teaching. The net effect is more graduate (PhD) programs than the nation needs and less attention to teaching than students deserve.

What effect does competition have on graduation rates? Fortunately, the contest over rankings does not work *against* trying to help students stay enrolled. Indeed, one factor used to determine the *U.S. News* rankings is the percentage of entering students who graduate. As it happens, however, graduation rates are chiefly determined not so much by the efforts a college makes to keep its students in school as by the SAT scores of its entering freshmen. Only a small part of a college's ranking reflects its success in achieving a higher graduation rate than the SAT scores of its students would predict. As a result, a college intent on improving its position will accomplish more by offering merit scholarships to attract high-scoring students than it will by spending the same amount of money on better counseling or other steps to prevent students from dropping out.

It is only fair to add that college officials and their faculty members are animated by motives other than a desire for a higher ranking. They care about giving enough financial aid to genuinely needy applicants, helping students learn and develop as much as possible, and keeping them enrolled until they graduate. The point made here is simply that competition does not necessarily reinforce these good motives and sometimes works against them.

NEW FORMS OF COMPETITION

In recent years, new sources of competition have emerged that may affect the behavior of traditional colleges in unaccustomed ways. For-profit institutions have appeared using innovative methods to attract large numbers of students, especially working adults interested in earning more money by acquiring new skills. Unlike traditional colleges, for-profits spend less money per student than the tuition they charge, giving them a strong economic incentive to attract as many applicants as they can. With the aid of aggressive recruiting, the largest among them grew rapidly enough by 2012 to enroll many hundreds of thousands of students, bringing the share of all undergraduates in the for-profit sector to more than 10 percent. Although enrollments have since declined, some analysts predict that they will recover and eventually allow for-profits to take over even larger shares of the total student market.

Meanwhile, a second new form of competition has arisen through the growing use of online education. Attracting additional students to such programs can cost very little once course materials are in place. As a result, institutions that offer such instruction can make money by expanding into student markets wherever they may be found. Some commentators predict that online providers will one day do away entirely with all but the most elite colleges and universities, thus totally transforming the landscape of American higher education.[3]

Finally, aided again by technology, a new breed of entrepreneurs has emerged in the last decade or two offering sophisticated products and services that provide less expensive or more effective ways of performing particular college functions. The services involved range from locating and recruiting promising applicants to advising students and testing seniors and recent graduates in order to give prospective employers more reliable information about their qualifications. A few enterprising pioneers are using cutting-edge technology not merely to perform individual services but to launch entirely new colleges that educate students in cheaper and more expeditious ways.

Together, these new sources of competition are subjecting existing institutions to more intense pressure to adapt than ever before. In time, they could radically change the way colleges and universities do their work and cause the greatest transformation in higher education since the emergence of the modern research university at the end of the nineteenth century. It is therefore worth examining the potential of each of these new competitive forces to increase graduation rates or improve the quality of education.

For-Profits. The recent growth of for-profit universities surprised many people in higher education. Not that offering vocational programs for particular occupations on a profit-making basis was particularly novel. Secretarial schools, cosmetology institutes, and a host of other small proprietary schools had existed for generations. What was new was the creation of profit-making institutions operating in multiple states and enrolling tens of thousands, in some cases hundreds of thousands of students.[4]

The emergence of these mega-universities grew out of an impression that many traditional nonprofit colleges were not adequately serving the needs of working people who wanted to better themselves by learning new skills. Community colleges were ostensibly created to serve this purpose but often failed to do so because they were located in inconvenient places and offered their courses at times that conflicted with the working hours of would-be students holding jobs they couldn't afford to leave.

These conditions created an opportunity to provide vocational education on a profitable basis by scheduling courses during evenings and weekends in classes held in rented space at shopping malls and other convenient locations. For-profit providers could cut costs drastically by refusing to engage in nonessential activities, such as athletics, or to build facilities such as residence halls or even libraries now that reading materials were accessible online. Despite these savings, however, for-profit colleges still had to charge a high enough price to earn an ample surplus for their stockholders while competing against the heavily subsidized public universities and community colleges. The billions of dollars offered by government programs of financial aid provided a solution. By dint of aggressive recruiting, the new for-profits could attract students by offering them a more convenient education tightly aligned with the local job market at a price they could afford with the aid of federal grants and loans.

The advent of online instruction presented an even greater opportunity for making money without having to build new facilities or hire more instructors. The large for-profits were quick to take advantage, and their methods soon proved to be successful. The largest of these institutions, the University of Phoenix, increased its enrollments by 2010 to a total of more than four hundred thousand students.

The rapid rise of the large for-profits was eventually halted, at least temporarily, by a flurry of bad publicity that lowered their share of total college enrollments from 10 to 8 percent. Government investigations revealed shady practices by some recruiters who made exaggerated promises about the jobs and earnings that applicants could obtain by enrolling in the for-profit programs.[5] Attrition rates were also very high, leaving dropouts with large debts and no credential with which to find a well-paid job. Before long, former students from nonprofits accounted for 45 percent of all defaults on government student loans, prompting the Department of Education to develop rules to stop giving federal student aid to students of institutions whose former students were typically unable to earn enough to repay their debts.

Curiously, for-profits as a group have proved to be no more successful than community colleges in preparing their students to obtain good jobs, despite their efforts to work closely with employers to devise effective programs.[6] A recent Public Agenda survey found that human resources executives rated for-profits as no better or even worse than public community colleges as sources of new employees.[7] Moreover, surveys of the employment experience of the graduates of for-profit colleges have found that their earnings are either no greater or lower than those of community college graduates even though they have had to pay much higher tuitions.[*]

Despite these shortcomings, the competition from for-profits has had a useful influence on their nonprofit competitors. Many community colleges have rearranged their schedules to accommodate the needs of working students. A number of them have opened satellite classrooms

---

[*] See, e.g., Kevin Long and Russell Weinstein, *Evaluating Student Outcomes at For-Profit Colleges*, National Bureau of Economic Research, Working Paper No. 18201 (June 2012); Yuen Ting Liu and Clive Belfield, *Evaluating For-Profit Higher Education: Evidence from the Education Longitudinal Study*, a CAPSEL Working Paper (September 2014).

in more convenient locations. Moreover, the example set by for-profits has helped to encourage greater use of online courses and closer ties with employers to understand their needs. The strategy of offering fewer, more highly structured programs, better advising, and more vigorous job-placement efforts has also provided a model for vocational programs that foundations and other reformers are urging on community colleges.

Online Education and Disruptive Competition. At least one observer predicts an even more successful future for the profit-making colleges through the aggressive use of online education. A Harvard Business School professor, Clayton Christensen, has attracted a lot of attention with a theory of "disruptive technology" derived from his prior study of several industries.[8] Christensen explains how new technologies in these industries were first introduced by producers serving the bottom of the market. Their presence was ignored by established higher-end producers who did not take the new competitors seriously. Meanwhile, the "bottom-feeders" gradually improved their products and began invading the markets of established competitors at successively higher and more lucrative levels of the producer hierarchy. By the time the leading companies recognized the threat, it was too late, and they too succumbed and disappeared.

Applying this experience to higher education, Christensen likens the large for-profits to the bottom-feeders and equates online education with the disruptive technologies he examined in his earlier industrial case studies. Eventually, he predicts, as online instruction improves, all but the elite residential universities will have to adapt or give way to the much-maligned and underestimated for-profit companies such as the University of Phoenix.

Although Christensen's theory is intriguing, its applicability to higher education is doubtful at best.* Graduation rates from for-profit univer-

---

*Christensen's theory about disruption has begun to attract a good deal of criticism. In particular, scholars who have looked more closely at the examples from business that he cites claim that many of them do not fully support his theory, and that at least one-third are seriously at variance with his predicted results. See Evan R. Goldstein, "The Undoing of Disruption: Clayton Christensen and His Critics," *Chronicle Review* (October 2, 2015), p. B-6.

sities remain very low by comparison with traditional four-year colleges. Online programs likewise suffer from frequent dropouts.[9] Students, especially eighteen- to twenty-one-year-olds, seem to have difficulty completing a college program on their own without a campus and classmates to support them. Although online courses can provide chatrooms and other devices to connect students with one another, these opportunities do not yet supply the type of supportive community that often sustains students in residential colleges throughout their entire course of study.

There are additional reasons why Christensen's dire predictions may not come to pass. Unlike the industries from which he drew his theory, the most successful nonprofit universities are not ignoring the new technology. On the contrary, they are actively trying to make good use of it by offering online courses of their own or affiliating with separate new organizations, such as Coursera and Ed-X, that are dedicated to online education.

For-profit providers also operate in an environment quite different from that of the ordinary commercial enterprise. Universities such as Phoenix can prosper only so long as they can draw upon the massive subsidies they receive via federal student aid programs. Even with this assistance, they exist in a system filled with public colleges that also benefit from student aid and in addition receive direct support from states and local communities. For-profits have not yet demonstrated that they can threaten the survival of these heavily subsidized institutions.

Even if for-profits did become capable of driving out community colleges and comprehensive universities, public officials might not allow them to do so. Governments have traditionally preferred to create publicly funded schools and nonprofit colleges as the principal suppliers of education rather than relying on commercial enterprises to perform this function. Because it is hard for students to judge the quality of the teaching they receive, policy-makers worry that commercial providers will be able to sell applicants an inferior product that will ultimately leave them with an inadequate education and substantial debts to repay. Recent exposés of the misleading tactics employed by several for-profit colleges in recruiting students, along with their high dropout rates and loan defaults, have intensified these concerns.

Of course, it is still conceivable that Professor Christensen's predictions will eventually be fulfilled. The new administration in Washington may look with greater favor on for-profit providers than the Department of Education did in the Obama years. New advances in technology may bring unforeseen opportunities. At best, however, the current outlook for universities such as Phoenix seems highly uncertain.

The High-Tech Entrepreneurs. A third form of competition that is challenging traditional practice comes from a legion of start-up companies that are developing new and improved ways of providing particular services that universities have heretofore performed themselves. Campus officials have long tried to economize by outsourcing functions that outside firms can provide more cheaply. Food services, campus bookstores, and janitorial work are familiar examples. What is new is the appearance of start-up companies offering high-tech services that are much more central to the academic process than feeding students, selling books, or cleaning classroom buildings.[10]

To enterprising start-ups and the venture capitalists who fund them, universities are bloated, inefficient institutions providing a variety of educational and support services that could be supplied more effectively and inexpensively through the use of new technology. Like hungry wolves eying a flock of plump sheep, these entrepreneurs circle the campus looking for individual services they can split off from the whole and offer more cheaply and effectively.

Among the most publicized examples of the newer high-tech start-ups are Udacity and Coursera, which have created online courses (MOOCs) that other providers can use for instructional purposes. Companies such as StraighterLine produce lower-division courses that colleges can buy. Carnegie Mellon University is marketing a whole series of classes in well-structured subjects featuring computer-driven "tutors" that ask students questions, provide instant feedback, and shift automatically to offer hints and pose additional questions to help students who are encountering difficulty understanding the material.[11]

The list of services that start-ups provide extends well beyond courses of instruction. Some firms have developed computerized advising systems that students with routine questions can access at any time, on any day, instead of having to make an appointment with a faculty adviser. Another company offers a tutoring service that reminds students when papers are due, lets them know what additional courses they must take in order to graduate, and even prompts them in timely fashion when to begin writing term papers and start studying for exams. Still other start-ups offer elaborate programs that mine large quantities of data to help colleges identify students who are at risk of dropping out so that advisers can reach out to help them before it is too late. Half a dozen firms provide "dashboards" based on analyses of student behavior that let professors know how well students are learning the material and where they are encountering difficulty. Several companies sell course management systems, such as Blackboard, that facilitate communication with students via the Internet to inform them of course assignments, readings, and other useful information.

Experimental Colleges. Specific services of the kind just mentioned do not threaten to put colleges and universities out of business. In most cases, the innovations simply allow campus administrators to perform particular functions more cheaply and effectively. Ambitious efforts are underway, however, that could prove to be more disruptive by using technology to create imaginatively conceived new colleges or professional degree programs at a fraction of the usual cost.

One of the oldest examples is Western Governors University (WGU), a nonprofit institution described in chapter 1.[12] WGU offers degrees entirely online in a few vocational fields and allows students to learn at their own pace while also granting them credit for skills they have previously mastered through practical experience. As a result, enterprising students can graduate from WGU more rapidly and at a much lower cost than they could by enrolling in a traditional college or university. Such programs promise to be especially attractive to older working adults who have some college experience but want to upgrade their credentials or acquire new skills to improve their employment opportunities.

Enrollments are increasing rapidly and now exceed eighty thousand. As yet, graduation levels appear to be low, with estimates ranging from a six-year rate of only 26 percent to 40 percent depending on which students are included in the analysis. Even so, at least two states, Indiana and Washington, have agreed to have WGU educate additional students seeking to enter their system rather than having to build new dormitories and classrooms to accommodate them.

The Minerva Project offers an even more radical experiment in undergraduate education. Students are selected from a large pool of applicants strictly on academic grounds. Members of the entering class complete their freshman year in San Francisco, but spend the next six semesters living and studying in different cities throughout the world. All of their first-year courses are prescribed and designed to connect with one another and to build on material previously learned. Classes throughout the four years are taught in the form of online seminars to which students are assigned in order to create a fruitful mix of backgrounds, experience, and intellectual talents.

The conversation in each seminar is recorded in full and analyzed to allow instructors to detect material that individual students are having difficulty understanding or whole sections of a course in which materials and instructional methods need to be modified. Thus the entire college is in a continual state of experimentation, evaluation, and improvement. All this is provided to students for an annual tuition of only ten thousand dollars (plus eighteen thousand for living expenses), a figure that could be revised downward if and when the college grows in size to achieve economies of scale.

THE PROMISE AND PERILS OF THE NEW COMPETITORS

Technology is clearly the elephant in the room as far as competition in higher education is concerned. It is a force more sweeping, more rapid, and more unpredictable than anything previously experienced by colleges and universities. It has inspired unusually apocalyptic visions of the future, from Peter Drucker's prediction of the disappearance of the traditional campus to Clayton Christensen's forecast of the triumph of the "bottom-feeders" armed with steadily improving online education.

As yet, however, though the uses of technology are legion throughout higher education, their effects have been far less revolutionary than these dire forecasts claimed. In undergraduate education, technology has improved access and made many activities and services more efficient and convenient, but it has not yet fundamentally altered the graduation rates of colleges, nor has it transformed the methods and effectiveness of instruction. The impact of technology on the quality of education remains uncertain and may well turn out to vary depending on the type of students involved. For example, one large study of the effects of online courses at a number of community colleges in Washington State found that low-income and minority students learned less and dropped out more frequently than did similar students in conventionally taught courses.[13]

It would be premature, however, to conclude that technology will never bring about fundamental changes in the way students are taught. Already, in other parts of the university, one can find examples of improvements in learning made possible by computers. In graduate schools of architecture, for example, technology has enabled students to complete a host of building plans in a single afternoon instead of the few drawings they could formerly produce by hand. As a result, students can try many different designs, examine them from different angles, and even test the effects of varying environmental conditions. In medical schools, the use of lifelike manikins armed with expert systems has allowed students to ask the "patient" questions and receive instant answers, as well as order tests and obtain the results immediately, thereby honing their diagnostic skills through prolonged practice in a manner not previously possible.

Already, there are signs that comparable technologically inspired advances may be on the way for undergraduates as well.

- At Arizona State University, instructors using adaptive technology have significantly improved the percentage of students who complete remedial math successfully.[14] Instructors can actually observe the way each student is dealing with a problem and offer useful hints and suggestions to help individuals who become stuck.
- Increasing numbers of colleges are analyzing quantities of data about the behavior of undergraduates to identify those who are at risk of dropping out so that they can receive timely help to remain enrolled. Some analysts report that these measures have already had a positive effect on graduation rates in a few public universities.[15] A recent effort on the part of dozens of institutions to share their data could do even more to help participants discover how to lower the dropout rate on their campus.[16]
- In scores of universities, departments have revised large introductory courses to reduce the number of lectures and increase the class time devoted to working on problems with the help of graduate student mentors to assist members of the class who encounter problems they cannot solve by themselves. Most of the classes report increases in learning as well as reductions in cost compared with previous versions of the courses taught by conventional lectures.[17]
- Some instructors are finding it pointless to continue lecturing when MOOCs are available featuring noted experts teaching the same material in professionally crafted productions that students can watch at times of their own choosing. Class time can then be used for more active learning through discussion or with teams of students doing projects and solving problems. Existing research suggests that students tend to learn more under such a format than they can by listening to lectures.[18]

At this point, it is hard to predict how far technology can go in improving student learning and increasing graduation rates. Are the methods used in remedial math capable of being used only in highly structured courses such as mathematics and statistics, or can they be adapted for use in other subjects as well? How large and useful a trove of insights for improving teaching can be gleaned from computer records of student problem solving? How many instructors will abandon lecturing and assign a MOOC in order to use their classrooms for more active student exercises? Most important, what effects will different kinds of online courses have on dropout rates? On costs? On the learning and completion rates of low-income students and minorities?

Another unknown involves the unintended consequences of technology-based innovations. For example, the same online techniques that enable instructors and students to communicate with one another more effectively can also make it easier for students to plagiarize the writings of others or purchase term papers from companies instead of having to write their own. Moreover, consider the use of big-data analytics to examine massive amounts of data about student behavior and patterns of learning. These techniques could improve the admissions process by helping to identify candidates who will learn the most, be least likely to drop out, and provide the "best fit" with the institution. On the other hand, colleges could also use such methods for the dubious purpose of identifying applicants with parents who are especially likely to make large gifts to the university.

In short, technology introduces new elements into the work of colleges and universities that can have good or bad effects while creating more risk and uncertainty than officials in these institutions normally experience. Along with the promise of innovative advances in teaching and learning, the vast reach of computer technology brings colleges into competition with a much wider assortment of rivals than has heretofore been the case, increasing the possibility of disruption. Change can occur quickly, forcing campuses to make decisions more rapidly than traditional forms of campus governance allow.

Under these conditions, the risk of unforeseen results looms large, making the choice of new technologies more hazardous than most of the decisions that campus authorities have traditionally had to make. Even more vexing dilemmas could arise if scientists manage to utilize artificial intelligence to build machines that are smarter than human beings, or develop biological techniques that dramatically enhance the intelligence of students whose parents can afford these methods. Faced with such unsettling prospects, academic leaders seem destined to ponder the future of technology with an uneasy mixture of excitement, uncertainty, and foreboding.

CHAPTER SEVEN

❧

The Major Foundations

PHILANTHROPY, AND LARGE FOUNDATIONS in particular, are a prominent feature of American society and a significant force in shaping the
performance of higher education. By choosing which activities to fund
and what conditions to attach to their gifts, foundations have had much
to do with the success of America's professional schools and the prominent place of our leading private universities in the international rankings of the world's best universities.

While foundations give billions of dollars each year to higher education, they are not universally loved. They are heavily subsidized by the
government as a result of their tax exemption. Yet they are not accountable for their actions to the government or to voters, although they often
seek to influence society, public opinion, and even legislative policy.
Their role in supporting American higher education offers an interesting case study about how they have used their power and, specifically,
how they are currently trying to influence the efforts of American colleges and universities to raise graduation rates and improve the quality
of education.

THE EARLY YEARS

Foundations were a comparatively late arrival in the history of higher
education. Not until the early years of the twentieth century did wealthy
industrialists form charitable organizations with professional staffs to
help them give away large portions of their fortunes. Once created, however, foundations took a particular interest in higher education and soon
became a major force in the development of American universities.

The Carnegie and Rockefeller Foundations were by far the largest of these new philanthropic organizations. Within a few years, they were directing a large share of their gifts to private colleges and universities in amounts great enough to constitute a substantial fraction of their beneficiaries' budgets. Foundation leaders explained this policy on the ground that "neither the federal government nor any one of the states has accepted the responsibility of providing adequately for higher education."[1]

From the beginning, the two foundations not only aided universities; they took an active role in shaping the policies and administrative practices of the institutions they supported. Their first large initiative was a program launched by the Carnegie Foundation for the Advancement of Teaching to finance the growth of pension plans for professors.[2] Over a period of sixteen years, the foundation devoted $118 million to that purpose. This support did not come without strings attached. To qualify, colleges had to institute proper accounting practices, admit only students who had completed the equivalent of four years of high school, and be independent of church control. Since almost every college badly needed the money, most of them accepted the conditions, often to the chagrin of a founding religious organization.

Meanwhile, the two foundations set about to reform medical education.[3] The Carnegie Foundation took the initial step of commissioning a study of medical schools by Abraham Flexner. The Flexner report, issued in 1910, attracted wide attention by documenting the sorry state of medical schools, many of which offered instruction of dubious quality supplied by practicing physicians to supplement their incomes.[4] Dozens of these schools closed down in the wake of the report. Over the next two decades, the Rockefeller-funded General Education Board, having hired Flexner, distributed seventy-eight million dollars to medical schools affiliated with universities. At Flexner's insistence, the board attached conditions to its grants, of which the most important and most controversial required each school receiving funds to agree to hire full-time professors (rather than part-time private doctors) to the key posts in their departments of internal medicine, pediatrics, and surgery.

Over a period of twenty-five years, foundations gave a total of $154 million to medical schools. Their support transformed the quality of medical education. In the words of one historian, "foundations have been the most vital external force in making over 161 nondescript proprietary medical schools into 75 standardized, progressive, and professionally operated institutions."[5]

Not everyone appreciated the way in which philanthropists pressured universities to reform by attaching conditions to their grants. A Methodist minister reacted to the Carnegie Foundation's insistence that its grantees be independent of church control by calling such requirements "a vast scheme for capturing and controlling the colleges and universities of the country."[6] In rejecting a grant demanding that recipients make full-time medical school appointments, Columbia University's celebrated president Nicholas Murray Butler declared, "They [the General Education Board] have already done what I conceive to be so great damage to the cause of medical education by the conditions attached to their several gifts that Columbia will occupy a favored and distinguished position in seeking and securing elsewhere the funds needed for medical school development."[7] Few fellow presidents, however, felt confident enough to follow Butler's example.

Between the two world wars, the priorities of Rockefeller and Carnegie shifted to research, which in those years received little government funding. Much of the money initially went to the health sciences, but foundation interests gradually expanded to include the behavioral sciences and, in the 1930s, the social sciences and humanities as well. Almost single-handedly, Carnegie and Rockefeller provided the funds and financed the supporting organizations that allowed researchers in these fields to pursue their interests in a serious way. In doing so, they helped to pave the way for the remarkable growth of academic research in the decades following the Second World War.

Shortly after World War II, a massive gift of stock made the Ford Foundation the largest of all philanthropic organizations with assets equal to two-thirds of the aggregate endowments of all of America's colleges and universities. Over the next few years, Ford made two huge gifts of more than two hundred million dollars each, one of them to raise faculty salaries at some 630 institutions and the other to build "regional centers of excellence" that could join the ranks of leading research universities. In addition, Ford, along with other foundations, helped build academic programs for emerging subjects, such as area studies and international relations, that would support America's new role in world affairs.

RECENT DEVELOPMENTS

By now, hundreds of charitable foundations have been created. Over 20 percent of their aggregate donations go to higher education. Much of the grant making is quite traditional, consisting of gifts for scientific research, new buildings, professorships, scholarships, and the like. A few foundations have contributed significantly to research on issues of higher education, notably Carnegie, Ford, Mellon, and Spencer. Two relatively recent developments in the foundation world are especially interesting since they depart from the prevailing practice in ways that bear on educational attainment and the quality of undergraduate education.

Conservative Foundations. The first of these is the rise of foundations funded by wealthy individuals to publicize the virtues of the capitalist system and promote other conservative policies and values. One group of these organizations, including the Pacific Legal Foundation and the American Civil Rights Initiative, have opposed affirmative action policies in college admissions and supported lawsuits challenging the use of racial preferences by selective universities. Another advocacy group, the Association of Concerned Trustees and Alumni (ACTA), has sought to improve the quality of education by issuing a series of studies and reports documenting the liberal bias in college faculties, the prevalence of academic writing hostile to American policies, values, and traditions, and the lack of emphasis in college curricula on the Great Books and the history and traditions of Western Civilization.* Still other organizations, including the Madison Center for Educational Affairs and the National Association of Scholars, have issued guides for students and other interested parties comparing colleges on such criteria as the political orientation of their faculties and the treatment of Western history and values in their curricula. Finally, conservative organizations have funded a number of academic centers and programs dedicated to the study of free-market capitalism and other conservative principles by organizing forums, inviting speakers, and arranging a variety of activities to expose campus audiences to conservative ideas.

Organizations funded by conservative sources have sometimes engaged in questionable ventures. An effort by one such organization to publicly list the names of faculty members who were thought to have expressed anti-American views sought to mobilize pressure from donors and other sources to deter professors from expressing their opinions—a practice inimical to ideals of free speech that both true conservatives and liberals hold dear. A center on free enterprise funded by conservative foundations is reportedly planning to offer generous scholarships to students who agree to take a stipulated number of courses created by the center. Such a program seems highly suspect; colleges should never become bazaars where rival political philosophies hawk their wares by paying students to listen.

Despite occasional activities such as these, the efforts of conservative foundations should be viewed against the backdrop of the dominant political orientation of most campuses today. Liberal professors typically outnumber conservatives by a wide margin, sometimes by ratios of 10 or 15 to 1, especially in social science and humanities departments. Although most professors try to keep their political views out of the classroom, the prevailing intellectual environment in the majority of colleges

---

*One such organization, Campus Reform, uses the Web to publicize instances of biased teaching, indoctrination, or suppression of conservatives. As of September, 2015, Campus Reform counted fifteen "victories" in which its reporting resulted in a change of policy or other corrective action by a university. Peter Schmidt, "How the Internet Outrage Machine Berates Higher Education," *Chronicle of Higher Education* (September 11, 2015), p. A8.

and universities has a definite tilt in a liberal direction, as faculty members of all political persuasions acknowledge. Under these conditions, special efforts supported by foundations that expose students to conservative ideas can contribute to the quality of education by adding a greater diversity of opinion on a range of important subjects.

The Mega-Foundations. The second recent development in the world of philanthropy and higher education is the commitment by several new foundations to help increase graduation rates in the United States. Taking the lead in this effort are two huge philanthropic entities, the Gates and Lumina Foundations. Even before President Obama announced the goal of recapturing America's lead in educational attainment, these organizations made it a priority to increase the share of young Americans earning college degrees or certificates (although they have given themselves more leeway by setting their target date at 2025 rather than Obama's 2020).* Following preliminary studies to identify promising policies and practices to achieve their aim, the two foundations have developed comprehensive strategies for encouraging the use of such methods throughout the higher education world.[8]

These efforts are unusual in several respects. For one thing, the mega-foundations are using their impressive resources to reinforce, and indeed to influence, a government-sponsored campaign to increase educational attainment. This policy is a departure from the traditional foundation practice of pursuing goals that have been largely overlooked by public officials. In addition, both Lumina and Gates have devoted much of their funding to marshaling public and political support for their policies. In the words of Lumina's president, Jamie Merisotis, "Lumina will expand its efforts by convening business leaders, lawmakers, higher education groups, and faculty members to build consensus on specific policy measures."[9]

In another departure from traditional practice, the two mega-foundations have directed most of their grants for educational attain-

---

*Lumina's goal is to have 60 percent of Americans between the ages of twenty-five and sixty-four earn "high quality degrees, certificates or other postsecondary credentials" by 2025. Gates's objective is to double the percentage of low-income students who earn a college credential by 2025.

ment, not to universities, but to independent groups, chiefly advocacy organizations and think tanks.[10] For example, in 2010, both foundations gave *six times* as much money to "research-policy" groups as to colleges and universities. The foundations have even directed part of their funding to media organizations for programs that inform the public about the nature and importance of increasing educational attainment.

Finally, of the money they have given to educational institutions, the two foundations have allocated the largest share to community colleges and comprehensive universities rather than the elite universities that have traditionally received the bulk of foundation support. This shift was a natural step to take, since it is community colleges and comprehensives that will educate the vast majority of the additional students needed to achieve the foundations' attainment goals.*

The campaign by the mega-foundations to raise college attainment levels includes a serious effort to improve the quality of undergraduate education. Officials at Lumina and Gates are clearly aware that boosting the number of degree-holders will be worth little if the students involved do not learn a lot in the process. As a result, each foundation has made a series of grants designed to promote learning and avoid sacrificing quality in the effort to raise graduation rates. For example, Gates has backed the efforts of Carol Twigg's National Center for Academic Transformation to improve the effectiveness of introductory and remedial courses, while Lumina has worked with the Association of American Colleges & Universities to enlist hundreds of colleges in an effort to create a clearer understanding of what students should know and be able to do by the time they graduate. Still, it is fair to say that quality has played a secondary role to increasing attainment in the overall program of the foundations.

The strategy just described marks the latest step in the gradual evolution of foundation policy toward higher education. Over the years, the largest and best-known foundations have changed their approach from

---

* This sentence should not be taken to imply that selective colleges have no role in the effort to raise attainment levels and expand opportunities to obtain a college education. For a description of that role, see pp. 19–20.

strengthening colleges and universities through general-purpose grants to using universities as instruments to help achieve specific social goals, and finally, in the case of Lumina and Gates, to directing the bulk of their support to funding independent organizations to help bring about change within colleges and universities.

The novel approach of Lumina and Gates has provoked considerable discussion, much of it critical. Some observers have deplored the efforts of these mega-foundations to shape the philanthropic agenda for higher education according to their own priorities and policies.[11] Yet, large as they are, Lumina and Gates hardly dominate the foundation world to the degree achieved by the Rockefeller and Carnegie Foundations during the first few decades of their existence. Nor are they any more assertive in imposing their policies for reform than the latter two foundations were in funding college pension plans and strengthening leading medical schools. These policies provoked a good deal of criticism at the time. In retrospect, however, it would be hard to deny the immense improvements in higher education that resulted.

Other critics have assailed the policies of Lumina and Gates on the grounds that they amount to an outsourcing of government policy.[12] The point seems to be that the mega-foundations are using their funds to influence the choice of the specific methods used to achieve President Obama's goal of raising educational attainment rates. This criticism seems equally insubstantial. Federal and state officials remain perfectly free to choose their own methods if they disagree with those favored by foundations. Despite the many millions of dollars contributed by Lumina and Gates, their resources are dwarfed by those at the command of the federal government. Their grants make up a much smaller fraction of the total expenditures on higher education than the share allocated by Carnegie and Rockefeller a century ago.

Still, some commentators worry that foundations, which owe much of their wealth to federal tax policy, are trying to shape how the nation goes about achieving higher levels of educational attainment with no accountability to the public for their actions.[13] Again, the same could be said about the early efforts of Carnegie and Rockefeller to influence college admissions policies and accounting practices and to dictate the faculty appointments policies of medical schools. Indeed, the criticism applies not only to the current policies of Gates and Lumina but to the whole tradition of philanthropy in this country. In enacting tax provisions to favor charitable giving, Congress presumably decided that the public good brought about by stimulating private donations was worth the lack of accountability of the donors in choosing the causes they would favor and the activities they would support. In so doing, lawmakers must have been aware that not all philanthropic gifts would reflect the preferences and priorities of the government or the wishes of the American people.

One can press harder and ask whether the added money spent for philanthropy by virtue of the charitable deduction is more valuable to society than the uses to which Congress would put the tax revenues lost to the government. Since no one can be sure how the government would use the increased revenue, however, this question is too hypothetical to yield a definite answer.* Congress appears to have resolved the problem in favor of encouraging philanthropy by enacting the charitable deduction. Given the current distrust of government and its policies, it is unlikely that voters would disagree with that judgment.

It would be especially hard to fault the mega-foundations for choosing to concentrate their higher education funding on the effort to raise current levels of educational attainment. For reasons discussed at length in chapter 1, the issue of attainment is one of the most important challenges facing American higher education. Success in raising completion rates promises to aid economic growth and prosperity, build a stronger,

---

*Gara LaMarche, a former foundation president, has recently posed the issue as follows: "The question is not whether many good things are accomplished with the money excluded from taxation for philanthropy. The standard is whether the record of philanthropy justifies the foregone tax revenue that in our current dire fiscal state could be used to keep senior centers and libraries and after-school programs open, hold tuitions within reach at public colleges and universities, expand Internet access in rural communities, and on and on." "Democracy and the Donor Class," *Democracy: A Journal of Ideas* (Fall 2014), pp. 48, 55. This statement contains an obvious fallacy. In comparing the contributions made by philanthropy with those that might otherwise be supported by the government, one should not only list alternative government uses one favors but consider the full range of government programs—including such measures as financing more wars like the invasion of Iraq and giving even higher subsidies to agribusiness.

more enlightened citizenry, and increase opportunity, especially for minorities and lower-income students. Moreover, through their efforts to strengthen the performance of community colleges and comprehensive universities, foundations are assisting segments of higher education that have long been ignored by philanthropy and underfunded by state governments despite having to pull the laboring oar in expanding college enrollments and increasing educational attainment.

A more telling criticism of the mega-foundations is that they have committed the bulk of their higher education budget to solving a problem that is not sufficiently well understood to devise a successful strategy. As an ex–foundation head has written, "If the theory of change underlying [a foundation's] strategy has not been clearly articulated and rigorously tested, success is unlikely."[14] While Gates and Lumina may have articulated their strategy for raising educational attainment levels, some of their methods were introduced before they had been tested rigorously. Much ignorance still surrounds such basic questions as how much financial aid can affect graduation rates, what colleges can do to keep students from dropping out, and how to improve remedial education. At a still more fundamental level, it is not even clear how much progress colleges can make in raising enrollments and graduation rates in view of the many problems of our public schools, not to mention the prevalence of poverty, drugs, crime, single-parent families, and other conditions that blight the prospects of so many young Americans.

Amid these uncertainties, mega-foundations are gambling on methods carrying a high risk of failure. Both foundations have strongly supported competency-based education without persuasive evidence to show whether all that matters in college can be reduced to a set of capabilities. Both have pressed state governments to adopt performance funding despite repeated failures in the past to raise graduation rates by such methods, not to mention the risk of causing colleges to meet the goals set by their states by relaxing academic standards. Lumina has advocated a series of measures to improve the performance of community colleges, but six years of effort trying out the reforms with a group of these institutions have thus far failed to achieve significant results.[15]

The risks and uncertainties of the completion strategy make it quite unlike the programs of earlier foundations that produced such impressive results. The deficiencies of medical schools were so glaringly obvious that it was relatively easy to perceive how to improve them. The case for investing in university research between the two world wars when governments showed little interest was also compelling and the means of making progress reasonably clear. The same was true of the Ford Foundation decision to support the development of international and area studies at a time when the United States plainly needed to assume a larger role in world affairs.

The methods for increasing the levels of educational attainment are far less obvious, and the risk of failure is hence much greater. At the same time, much of what these foundations are supporting includes research on various ways to increase graduation rates. Granted, many of the pilot programs and the research projects funded by the foundations seem designed more to test their preconceived ideas than to explore a variety of alternatives. One might therefore wish that they were a bit more open to considering proposals that researchers themselves considered important, in addition to projects that matched their own priorities. Still, the scope of the research they have funded is very wide, and it is surely commendable that they are willing to test their policies and practices and to change their methods when subsequent research does not support them. Even if their current campaign falls far short of its goal, modest progress will still be worth having, and much may be learned in the process that will enlighten future efforts.

SUMMING UP

Stepping back to consider more than a century of foundation activity, one must surely admire what these institutions have done for higher education. Not every initiative has succeeded. But the financial strength of our leading private universities, the worldwide eminence of our professional schools, and the distinction of America's academic research are towering achievements that owe much to the encouragement and support provided by the early leaders of our large foundations.

The role of philanthropy in higher education has undoubtedly grown more difficult over the ensuing generations. In the first half century following the creation of the Rockefeller and Carnegie Foundations, the opportunities were more obvious, the relative importance of foundation funding more substantial, and the way forward more clearly marked than has been true since then. In their recent efforts to raise educational attainment levels, the mega-foundations have chosen a much more difficult objective to achieve. The risk of failure is apparent, and the goals set by the foundations may prove to be too ambitious. Yet the intent is admirable, and the community colleges at the center of the foundation effort are the least well funded and the most in need of help of any higher education institutions. In the end, therefore, with all its risks, the enterprise is noble, and one must hope despite the odds that it will eventually be crowned with success.

CHAPTER EIGHT

The Role of Government in Raising Levels of Educational Attainment

No entity can compare with government in the array of instruments at its disposal for shaping the behavior of the institutions subject to its authority. Public officials can issue rules and regulations, offer subsidies and attach conditions to their use, elicit information and publicize it for the benefit of interested audiences, even establish the conditions for the very existence of organizations under its jurisdiction. Armed with such a variety of powers, governments would seem to have all the means they need to induce America's colleges and universities to graduate more students and improve the quality of the education they provide. As it happens, however, the reality is much more complicated.

THE GROWING ROLE OF THE FEDERAL GOVERNMENT

Until the end of World War II, Washington paid little attention to higher education apart from providing federal lands to support universities under the Morrill Acts of 1862 and 1890. In 1944, however, Congress took a major step to help Americans go to college by passing the GI Bill of Rights.[1] Under this law, the government offered sufficient funds to returning veterans to enable them to pay for all or most of the cost of tuition, books, and room and board for up to four years, depending on the length of their military service. By the time the program ended, more than two million GIs had taken advantage of its provisions. Although many of them chose to attend proprietary schools in order to receive some kind of vocational training, enough entered college to boost the share of young people with an undergraduate degree by an estimated 5 or 6 percentage points. Such an increase may seem modest by contemporary standards. However, since relatively few Americans graduated from college prior to World War II, the GI Bill has been estimated to have raised the previous number of students earning degrees by somewhere between 39 and 46 percent.[2]

The next effort to help students go to college took place in 1958 with the passage of the National Defense Education Act, which offered low-interest loans to undergraduates and fellowships to graduate students pursuing subjects related to national security. Seven years later, the Higher Education Act created a broader financial aid program that included grants, loans, and subsidized campus jobs for undergraduates from families of modest means. In 1972, the reauthorization of that act established a massive program of grants for low-income students (later called Pell Grants) that provided a sliding scale of support depending on the family income of the student up to a stipulated level. The maximum grant, given only to individuals whose family incomes were especially low, was originally meant to cover almost all of the average tuition for a public college or university, although the actual amount in real dollars gradually slipped further and further below that goal over the next several decades.

During the ensuing years, Congress enacted a series of other measures extending eligibility for Pell Grants to middle-income students, offering tax deductions for tuition payments, subsidizing jobs on campus, and creating new loan programs for undergraduates and parents. By 2012, the federal government was providing $45 billion per year in grants, $17 billion in tax relief, and $68 billion in student loans.[3]

Surprisingly, the impact of all this money on college enrollments appears to have been quite small. Although the original purpose of the program was to help children from low-income families to attend college, the percentage of students from the lowest income quartile earning a BA degree rose only from 6 to 14 from 1970 to 2012, far below the increase for high-income students.[4] On closer examination, one researcher found that Pell Grant increases could boost enrollments if they were not neutralized by higher tuitions or inflation, although the effect appeared to be quite small.[5]

What accounts for the contrast between the evident success of the GI Bill in raising enrollments and the limited results of subsequent financial aid programs? For one thing, the GI Bill was passed at a time when only about 15 percent of young Americans entered college. As a result, there were many young veterans who were perfectly capable of doing college work and earning a degree if they could find the money to do so. Congress also included monthly stipends for living expenses, unlike most grant programs today. The benefits were not only generous but easy to apply for and well publicized. It is not surprising that so many veterans seized the opportunity.

In contrast, the low-income students whom the newer financial aid programs have sought to help tend to graduate from weaker high schools and have lower test scores. The financial aid they have received over the years has often fallen far short of covering the full cost of tuition, let alone room and board, transportation costs, books, and other living expenses, forcing many recipients to work fifteen, twenty, or even more hours per week. In addition, unlike the GI Bill, the process of applying for Pell Grants and related forms of assistance was very complicated until recently and not well publicized. In order to guard against fraud and abuse, students had to fill out a time-consuming application containing 127 questions. The necessary financial information was often difficult for low-income students to obtain. Advice on completing the form was hard to come by in most of the public high schools attended by students of limited means, since guidance counselors were few and were heavily overworked.

The inhibiting effect of the application process proved to be substantial. One study reported that as many as 850,000 currently eligible college students had not submitted the form or received a Pell Grant.[6] When researchers tested a pilot program in which a sample of high school students received assistance from H&R Block employees in filling out the application form, the percentage of students completing the application jumped by almost 25 percent.[7]

At long last, more than forty years after the Pell Grants were first created, the federal government has finally taken a major step toward simplifying the application procedure. Students are now able to submit much of the necessary financial data in timely fashion using relevant financial information obtained electronically from their parents' previous tax returns.[8] Even if more students apply, however, it is unclear how effective the financial aid program will be in raising levels of educational attainment. Researchers are generally agreed that grants lowering the cost of college by a thousand dollars can increase enrollment by approximately 3–6 percent, provided that the terms of eligibility are easily understood and the application process is simple.[9] Already, however, attracted by a record high earnings premium for college graduates over those with only a high school diploma, more than 85 percent of high school graduates are entering college, either immediately or at some later point. As a result, the chief problem in raising educational attainment is no longer inducing more students to enroll but keeping them enrolled until they earn a degree.

Analysts have doubts about the effects of either grants or loans on the persistence and eventual graduation of recipients.[10] Most researchers believe that Pell Grants by themselves have had little effect on graduation rates.[11] Loans have received less study, but one investigator has even found that borrowing *decreases* graduation rates from community colleges.[12] Whatever the exact answer may be, as Eric Bettinger observed in 2012, "there are few, if any, who claim that current federal financial aid policies have done much to encourage degree completion or to reduce the gaps in attendance between socioeconomic groups."[13]

Why do many students fail to graduate in large numbers even when the financial barriers have been eased? Some are doubtless unable to keep up the struggle to hold two jobs and skimp on recreation, clothes, and even food and medical costs in order to scrape enough money together to stay in school.[14] Fear of not being able to repay large loans is surely another reason.* Nevertheless, there are many causes for leaving

---

* The burden of educational debts and the terms of their repayment are not a major focus of this volume. For more on the subject, see Sandy Baum, *Student Debt: Rhetoric and Realities of Higher*

that are not within the government's power to remove. Some students find that they need to go home to help with family problems. Others receive an attractive job offer. Still others become discouraged when they do poorly in their courses or find that they dislike studying and going to class. Thus even Berea College, which charges no tuition and provides substantial financial aid, finds that many of its students leave without earning a degree.[15]

Colleges have tried a number of strategies to prevent students from dropping out—creating learning communities that keep groups of students together through several initial courses, better advising, and earlier identification of potential dropouts. These measures may help a bit, but the evidence for their success is thin and such studies as exist offer little hope that measures of this kind will make a great difference.[16]

A more important cause of attrition is a widespread lack of preparedness for college. Several analysts have estimated that only about one-third of all high school graduates are actually capable of doing college-level work.[17] At present, up to half of the students seeking to enroll must complete one or more remedial courses for which they typically receive no credit. Of those who enter remediation, fewer than 50 percent complete it successfully, and many more are discouraged and never even try.[18]

One can think of various improvements that could help to overcome the lack of preparedness on the part of so many high school graduates. Colleges might discover more effective methods of remedial education that could allow larger numbers of students to succeed in the regular academic program. If high schools managed to bring their academic standards into a closer alignment with college requirements through the new Common Core curriculum or other means, larger percentages of students might arrive on campus prepared to do regular coursework. Many experts believe that providing better prenatal care and child nutrition would improve academic performance in later years; some have even found that universal access to preschools of good quality could eventually lift college enrollments by 8 or 9 percentage points.[19]

Education Financing (2016); Beth Akers and Matthew M. Chingos, *The Game of Loans: The Rhetoric and Reality of Student Debt* (2016).

The reforms with the most obvious potential for improving gradua-tion rates from college are probably those that help public schools to improve the knowledge and skills of all their students. Nevertheless, ex-perience to date leaves little room for optimism on this score. Over the past thirty years, despite much experimentation and additional funding, the academic capabilities of high school graduates have risen very little. Although almost every racial group has improved slightly, the overall scores have hardly budged because the lower-scoring groups, mainly blacks and Hispanics, have made up a gradually rising share of the total high school student body.[20]

Underlying many of the difficulties of our high schools are a set of social problems that keep low-income students from performing well, such as poverty, single-parent households, and neighborhoods ridden with crime, drugs, and high rates of incarceration among young males. These conditions are so widespread and so expensive and difficult to remedy that they are unlikely to disappear in the foreseeable future.

The obstacles to progress are formidable enough to dampen hopes for any large near-term improvement in the percentage of young Ameri-cans earning college degrees. Many of the problems involved will not be overcome simply through the provision of additional resources. Some-thing more is needed, but progress is hampered by a pervasive lack of essential knowledge about how to accomplish the task. The following recent statements from established authorities in the field illustrate the difficulty.

- According to Andrew Kelly and Mark Schneider, "A lack of good information about which policies and practices help students earn valuable postsecondary credentials, and which do so in a cost-effective manner, is a fundamental handicap to making progress."[21]
- Although the federal government provides more than 170 billion dollars per year for various programs of financial aid, David Mun-del and W. Lee Hansen have concluded that "policy choices, program designs, operational implementation and budget allocations are pri-marily based on hunches, political, and/or personal preferences."[22]

- Notwithstanding a widespread concern about the disparities in educational achievement among different racial and income groups, Sara Goldrick-Rab, Douglas Harris, and Philip Trostes observe that "a failure to account for group differences in responsiveness to [financial] aid is a primary shortcoming of existing research in closing substantial achievement gaps in college completion and requires much more knowledge about the effectiveness of aid in that effort."[23]
- Despite all the controversy over student loans and the amounts that students borrow, Susan Dynarski and Judith Scott-Clayton point out that "almost no evidence exists about the effects of loans on college enrollment and completion."[24]
- Finally, while up to 50 percent of students entering college must first take remedial courses in order to continue, and though roughly one-half fail to complete such courses successfully, Bridget Terry Long observed in 2012 that "the research on remediation and how to improve it is still in its infancy … little rigorous research exists to document best practices in remedial or developmental education."[25]

Without more knowledge than we currently possess about these critical issues, policy making often becomes little more than guesswork, and many seemingly plausible reforms turn out to fail or produce only meager results. It is not surprising, then, that despite the recent efforts of federal officials to increase educational attainment, there is little sign that graduation rates are rising more rapidly or that disparities between rich and poor or whites and minorities have diminished.[26]

THE ROLE OF THE STATES

Unlike the federal government, state and local officials have had a strong hand in shaping American higher education throughout its history. They played a vital role in founding and supporting the nation's first college and have been a constant presence ever since. State legislatures were the dominant source of funding for public colleges and universities throughout most of the twentieth century. They financed the vast expansion of state universities and community colleges that took place from 1945 to 1970 and did so with sufficient generosity that many public universities did not even charge tuition until the 1960s.

Financial Difficulties. In view of their long experience with higher education and their record in underwriting its expansion during the twentieth century, one might have expected states to provide the funds to help colleges and universities respond to the current challenge to increase graduation rates. During the last thirty years, however, the role of the states in financing higher education has gradually diminished, as the amounts of money required have grown, and lawmakers have had to weigh the needs of colleges and universities against those of public schools, Medicaid, prisons, and other expensive programs. After the mid-1980s, appropriations for public higher education ceased to keep up with increasing enrollments. From its peak year in 1987 to 2012, the average state subsidy per full-time-equivalent student fell in forty-eight of the fifty states by an overall average of roughly 30 percent in real dollars.[27]

Public higher education has often lost out in competing for state appropriations, especially in times of economic recession when states struggle to achieve a balanced budget. Legislators know that unlike prisons or public schools, universities can offset cutbacks in public funds by raising tuition, soliciting gifts, and seeking additional research grants to help pay for overhead expenses. Thus as state funding has declined, public universities have raised their tuitions aggressively, especially for out-of-state students, while redoubling efforts to solicit gifts from private donors and to increase their funded research.

The hardships resulting from the decline in state funding have not fallen evenly on all state colleges and universities. While many flagship research universities have enjoyed considerable success in finding alternative sources of support, comprehensive universities and community colleges have had a much more difficult time. Not only have they received less state aid per student; they are far less able to attract large gifts, recruit well-to-do students from out of state, or win research grants from the federal government. Cutting costs and raising tuition are often their only options.

These conditions have made it difficult for states to increase graduation rates while maintaining quality. Cutbacks in per-student funding have weighed especially heavily on the very institutions that must enroll and graduate most of the added undergraduates needed to raise current levels of educational attainment. To make matters even more difficult, most of the new students who will lift attainment levels will come from low-income families and have attended weaker schools, since the vast majority of children with wealthier parents and from better school districts already enroll in college. Educating these new young people properly and helping them to persevere until graduation will require *more* money, not *less.*

New Strategies for Raising Attainment. While presiding over a decline in per-student funding, most governors have professed a commitment to increasing the number of college graduates. After all, success in this endeavor helps to promote economic growth, increase employment, and satisfy the needs of employers for appropriately skilled workers. Because states are hard-pressed financially, however, their officials have often tried to raise educational attainment levels, not by maintaining per-student funding, but by less expensive methods, such as reforms to make the educational system operate more efficiently.

In recent years, more than thirty states have expressed their intention to adhere to a set of measures promoted by a nonprofit advocacy group, Complete College America. These commitments include establishing

---

* Economists John Bound and Sarah Turner found that the failure of state funding to keep pace with enrollment increases led to a *decline* in college graduation rates. This result came about primarily because institutions had to raise faculty-student ratios, and because more students were forced to enroll in community colleges where their chances of graduating were significantly reduced. "Cohort Crowding: How Resources Affect Collegiate Attainment," 91 *Journal of Public Economics* (2007), p. 877. The combination of less funding and increased enrollment is also likely to intensify the pressure to increase online education, which could lower graduation rates. See William Doyle and Michael Kirst, "Examining Policy Change in K–12 and Higher Education," in Michael W. Kirst and Mitchell L. Stevens (eds.), *Remaking Colleges: The Changing Ecology of Higher Education* (2015), pp. 190, 208.

goals to increase the numbers of graduates from each public college, creating statewide plans to achieve these objectives, collecting data and publishing periodic reports on progress toward these goals, linking appropriations for each college to the improvement it makes toward its graduation objectives, and conducting regular reviews of statewide progress to identify problems and take remedial steps to overcome them.[28]

On paper, at least, measures of this kind have the potential to increase graduation rates. Many high school graduates currently arrive at college unprepared for academic work and must enroll in remedial courses, which many of them do not complete successfully. Those who do begin their regular studies in a public two-year or four-year college often receive little guidance in making their way through a bewildering number of programs and courses and typically receive little advice in how to proceed. As a result, many of them accumulate more courses and take longer than they need in order to graduate.[29] For lack of proper advising or coordination among colleges, many other students fail to receive credit for courses they took in community college when they transfer to a public university, forcing them once again to spend more time and money to earn a BA degree.[30] Each of these obstacles takes a toll on graduation rates by causing students to become too frustrated or too burdened financially to stay the course.

In accordance with the Complete College pledge, many states have begun to take steps to address these problems. They have attempted to raise the academic standards of public high schools to align them with the levels of knowledge and skill required in college so that fewer students will have to take remedial courses. Many states have tried to negotiate agreements that will make it easier for students to transfer from community colleges to four-year institutions or from one university to another without losing credits. Many more states have launched efforts to create integrated data systems that will enable officials to track the movement of students from elementary school through high school and college and on into the workforce. Armed with this information, state agencies and educators can follow the progress of students and identify points at which intervention is needed to keep students from dropping out prematurely.

Some states have employed particular methods of their own to help high school students acquire the skills to succeed in college. California and several other states now require high schools to give tests to tenth and eleventh graders to identify skills that students need to improve to avoid having to take remedial courses in college.* Several states have helped high school students test their readiness for college work by allowing them to take college courses for joint credit. Texas has created a high school curriculum geared to college readiness and requires all students to follow it unless they secure the permission of their parents to opt out.

In addition to the steps just mentioned, many states have offered financial incentives for colleges and universities to boost their enrollments and graduation rates. In particular, lawmakers have introduced "performance-funding" schemes whereby the total amount of state appropriations for individual colleges and universities will depend on the fulfillment of specific goals set after consultation between state officials and higher education representatives. By the year 2000, a majority of states had adopted performance funding, and almost all of the agreements they negotiated included goals for enrollment and graduation.[31]

Numerous studies have been conducted to gauge the results of these programs. The clear consensus is that they had virtually no effect on graduation rates.[32] There are multiple reasons why. The amounts of money designated for the purpose tended to be too small to provide an effective incentive. Setting appropriate goals proved difficult because no one was certain how much colleges could do by themselves to graduate more students. In some instances, state officials took too little account of local conditions that affected what individual colleges could accomplish. In other cases, university representatives persuaded state officials to set very modest goals in order to ensure fulfillment. Even when the goals were appropriate, cutting financial support for poorly performing colleges was often not an effective way to bring about improvement.

---

*Preliminary analyses suggest that this measure may reduce the numbers requiring remediation by 2 or 3 percentage points. Michal Kurlaender, "Assessing the Promise of California's Early Assessment Program for Community Colleges," 655 *Annals of the American Academy of Political and Social Science* (September 14, 2014).

In some instances, states reduced performance funding or abandoned it entirely when its legislative champions left office or were replaced by the opposing party. Lawmakers also found it difficult to penalize institutions for failing to meet their graduation goals during times of economic recession when appropriations to all colleges were being cut. For these reasons, performance funding proved too unstable to persuade colleges to invest in costly reforms. In the face of such difficulties, many of the programs were abandoned during the recession of 2000–2001.

In recent years, however, performance funding has returned in more muscular forms.[33] By 2014, some twenty-five states had introduced or were considering schemes of this sort, all of which included goals for graduation rates. The funds subject to performance funding have generally been much larger than those of the earlier programs in order to create a more potent incentive for improvement. Goals have been set with greater sophistication to take more account of local conditions while including bonuses for institutions meeting intermediate targets such as the numbers of students completing remedial courses successfully or the percentages of entering freshmen enrolling for the second or third year.

Notwithstanding these improvements, many of the underlying problems that hold down graduation rates are beyond the power of colleges to resolve—ineffective public schools, insufficient funding for community colleges and comprehensive universities, and inability to figure out how to improve remedial education. In addition to these handicaps, performance-funding schemes rely on several questionable assumptions.

- That it is possible for most colleges to take steps that will lift their enrollment and graduation rates substantially, while maintaining the quality of their educational programs, and accomplish all of this with fewer real dollars per student than they received in the past
- That most colleges will have skillful enough leadership and sufficient determination to institute the reforms needed to achieve ambitious goals

- That few colleges will be able to "game the system" by persuading state officials to set excessively modest goals, or by refusing to admit marginal students, or by lowering the quality of education by eliminating difficult courses or easing grading standards in order to graduate more students
- That lawmakers will continue their performance programs long enough in good times and bad to convince college officials to take them seriously and make the investments needed to achieve success

Because of doubts about these assumptions, few experienced analysts are convinced that this new round of performance funding will be any more successful than the last, although they note that additional time and experience will be needed before a definitive judgment can be rendered.[34]*

THE BOTTOM LINE

How well-conceived are the government policies for helping colleges to achieve more ambitious graduation and attainment goals? At first glance, one might think that the programs of state and federal officials would complement each other nicely. The federal government, with its far greater resources, has concentrated on lowering the economic barriers to higher education by spending billions of dollars on increasing the amounts of financial aid for low- and moderate-income students. State governments, having less money at their disposal, have changed the way they allocate their funding in order to strengthen the incentives of campus officials to increase the number of graduates while taking additional steps to make their educational system more efficient so that students

---

* An early study of Phase Two performance funding in Pennsylvania has found no impact on completion rates. Nicholas W. Hillman, David A. Tandberg, and Jacob P. K. Gross, "Performance Funding in Higher Education: Do Financial Incentives Impact College Completion?" 85 *Journal of Higher Education* (2014), p. 820.

can more easily make their way from high school to community college and then to a four-year college.

In practice, however, the two layers of government, far from complementing one another, have often worked at cross-purposes so as to weaken, rather than strengthen, the overall effort. Instead of reinforcing Washington's attempts to lower the cost of college, state governments have often undermined them by taking advantage of increased federal financial aid to reduce their own support for public colleges and universities. Moreover, while Washington has focused its efforts on helping the community colleges and comprehensive universities that will bear the brunt of educating more students, state budget cuts have weighed most heavily on these same institutions, leaving them little recourse but to cut expenses and raise tuitions, hardly a recipe for encouraging more students to enter college and earn a degree.

Both federal and state officials are also basing their programs to increase the number of college graduates on policies that have done little in the past to lift the levels of educational attainment. The centerpiece of federal policy was to increase Pell Grants for low-income students and to simplify the process of applying for financial aid. While both efforts seem well worth making, there is little solid evidence that either will do very much to increase graduation rates. Meanwhile, state officials have revived and strengthened their use of performance funding notwithstanding the consistent failure of past programs to have any significant effect.

All things considered, then, one can scarcely muster much optimism over the near-term prospects for success at either the national or the state level. Federal initiatives have not yet raised graduation rates nearly fast enough to achieve President Obama's goal, and future progress seems quite uncertain following the election of Donald Trump. The policies of the states seem even more inadequate. Better data, improved coordination, and performance funding may help a little to induce college leaders to operate more efficiently and devote more effort to increasing graduation rates. Nevertheless, it is wildly optimistic to suppose that states can cut their investment per student by almost 20 percent from 2008 to 2016 and still expect colleges to increase their enrollments and graduate more students without sacrificing quality. Such policies hardly constitute a strategy. Rather, to borrow a phrase from Samuel Johnson, they represent "a triumph of hope over experience."[35]

CHAPTER NINE

༄

Government Efforts to Improve the Quality of Education

IN THEIR POLICIES TOWARD HIGHER EDUCATION, both federal and state officials have paid much more attention to increasing educational attainment than they have to improving its quality. At first glance, this tendency seems questionable, since earning a degree does little for graduates or for society unless students learn a lot along the way. Yet there are reasons for the reluctance of officials to impose their judgment on colleges and universities in matters of educational policy. Educators are much more knowledgeable than legislators in making such decisions. Moreover, official rules and regulations are far less effective for improving the quality of education than they are for preventing wrongful acts such as discrimination against minorities or women. Ordering professors to offer certain subjects or to adopt particular methods of instruction rarely works well; instructors must believe in what they are doing in order to teach effectively. Moreover, rules are a poor way to influence a field as diverse as higher education. They impose uniformity on a system with many independent units that need to vary enough in mission and method to serve a vast student population of widely differing abilities and ambitions. Rules can also stifle innovation, a result ill suited for an endeavor that is necessarily imperfect and in constant need of experimentation and improvement.

Considerations such as these must have been in the mind of Supreme Court justice and former professor Felix Frankfurter when he affirmed "the four essential freedoms of a university—to determine for itself on academic grounds who may teach, what may be taught, how it should be taught, and who may be admitted to study."[1] Frankfurter acknowledged that these freedoms could not be absolute; situations would occasionally arise that required government intervention. Even so, he declared, "for society's good, political power must abstain from intrusion into this activity of freedom except for reasons that are exigent and compelling."[2]

As higher education has come to matter more to the nation, governments have become more willing to intervene. But public officials have remained hesitant to interfere directly with the educational process by issuing rules and regulations. Instead, they have resorted to subtler methods to make their influence felt. They have tried to encourage the publication of more factual information about colleges and universities in the hope of influencing students in their choice of college and creating market pressure to persuade faculties to follow the example of the most successful institutions. They have also acted indirectly by ordering accreditation organizations to examine student learning in their periodic inspections of college campuses, a subject explored in detail in chapter 10. Finally, federal officials have tried to encourage academic leaders and their faculties to adopt more effective forms of instruction by offering funds to support such efforts.

These measures all seek to minimize the risks involved in imposing the government's will on the academic policies of colleges and universities. Nevertheless, as the following pages will suggest, each of the methods has problems of its own that limit its effectiveness.

FEDERAL EFFORTS TO IMPROVE QUALITY

During the administration of George W. Bush, the then secretary of education, Margaret Spellings, established a commission on the future of higher education in order to highlight the shortcomings of colleges and universities and suggest ways to improve their performance.[3] In the course of the commission's deliberations, Spellings expressed dissatisfaction with the complacency of academic institutions and their lack of accountability for the outcomes of their educational programs. In an effort to remedy this deficiency, she suggested that all colleges be required to administer the Collegiate Learning Assessment (CLA), a test of writing and critical thinking, and to publish the results in order to reveal how much their students learned during their four years of education. Such publicity, she believed, would motivate college authorities to work harder to increase the quality of teaching in order to improve student performance and thus enhance their reputation. The pressure to improve would be especially strong, she argued, once high school seniors began to take note of the CLA results in deciding where to enroll.

Eventually, cooler heads prevailed and the recommendation was dropped. The idea suffered from multiple problems. As pointed out in chapter 2, CLA results are unreliable since there is no assurance that students taking the test will be motivated to exert their best efforts. For another, the test measures only two of the many valued outcomes of a well-rounded college education. Finally, as a practical matter, it is far from clear that students considering which college to attend would pay much attention to differences in average CLA scores (which are often quite small) or even be aware of their existence.

During the Obama administration, a second effort was made to utilize information and publicity to inform prospective college students and thereby put pressure on poorly performing colleges to improve their academic programs. President Obama proposed the creation of a college scorecard that would include a set of facts about all colleges—their cost, financial aid, graduation rates, level of student indebtedness, and employment records (including earnings) of recent graduates. Based on this information, officials would rank colleges to help students make more enlightened choices about where to enroll.

For many months, the administration published versions of a ranking and solicited comments from college officials and other interested parties. After repeated efforts to amend the model to take account of objections and suggestions, the Department of Education quietly abandoned the project. The intellectual difficulties of transforming the available information into a sufficiently reliable metric with which to compare thousands of different colleges simply proved to be insurmountable.

In addition to these unsuccessful efforts to use publicity to improve performance, lawmakers have provided money to encourage colleges and universities to experiment with innovative methods of instruction and evaluate their effects on student learning. One of the earliest examples of the latter approach was the Fund for the Improvement of Postsecondary Education (FIPSE), created by Congress in the 1970s. FIPSE began by funding promising initiatives in curriculum design and instructional methods. Over time, however, members of Congress could not resist earmarking the funds to pay for pork-barrel projects in their own district, many of which involved the construction of new buildings and other facilities. Before long, the volume of earmarks grew sufficiently large that it sometimes consumed all of the funds appropriated for FIPSE, leaving no money to spend on innovative programs.

Not all federal funds for improving teaching have suffered the same fate. Over the past twenty years, for example, the National Science Foundation (NSF) has spent hundreds of millions of dollars to bring about improvements in the way schools and colleges teach courses on STEM subjects (science, technology, engineering, and mathematics). The intent has been not only to make science instruction more effective but to help it become more interesting and engaging in order to reduce the number of students who come to college intending to major in science but subsequently shift to other fields. Researchers have shown that dissatisfaction with the teaching of these subjects is a leading cause of the attrition.[4]

The STEM initiatives provide an intriguing contrast to federal efforts to increase graduation rates and educational attainment levels. The latter policies suffer from a lack of knowledge about how colleges can achieve the government's goals. In the case of STEM education, however, much more is known about how to improve teaching, since it is relatively easy to measure how much students have learned, at least in introductory and intermediate courses. Yet here too, the federal government has had only limited success.

By now, a consensus has developed, based on impressive empirical support, that the traditional forms of teaching STEM subjects, featuring extensive lecturing, are less effective than more active methods of instruction.[5] Using class time to have students apply material in the assigned readings to solve new problems, or forming small groups to work collaboratively on challenging projects, or allowing undergraduates to participate in doing research with professors instead of merely watching instructors perform experiments all appear to produce more learning than teachers achieve by conventional methods. In one large-scale experiment by Richard Hake involving sixty-two semester-long classes averaging one hundred students each, active methods of instruction resulted in learning gains more than twice those achieved through extensive lecturing.[6] Subsequent experiments by Nobel physicist Carl Wieman, along with work by other investigators, have arrived at similar results.[7]

Emboldened by these findings, the National Science Foundation has spent large sums helping to promote the use of active teaching and learning. Numerous workshops, conferences, demonstration projects, and other supporting activities have taken place. Some progress has certainly occurred through these efforts. Scores of instructors have begun to use the new methods in their classes. Nevertheless, despite convincing evidence of the superiority of active teaching and learning, and even though these results are well known to many STEM instructors through articles in leading science journals, the President's Council of Advisors on Science and Technology declared in 2012 that "scientifically validated methods of improving the teaching of science and math simply have not found widespread adoption at American colleges."[8]

The reasons for the glacial pace of reform in STEM instruction have already been described in chapter 3—the time and effort required to learn a very different method of teaching, an incentive structure that rewards research far more than effective pedagogy, and a frequent lack of institutional support and technical help for instructors wishing to use technology to enhance student learning.[9] Even professors who have read the literature reporting on the advantages of active learning can easily find reasons to justify sticking with their tried-and-true teaching practices. Many of those who lecture most of the time receive favorable student evaluations and hence see no problem with their performance despite their reliance on passive methods of teaching. If members of their class do poorly on exams, instructors can easily blame the students for not working harder or the admissions staff for accepting applicants with little aptitude for science.

These inhibitions and rationalizations do not forever doom the effort to improve STEM teaching. Most professors want to help their students learn, and their efforts to do so form an important part of their professional identity. Once they become aware that they are not teaching as effectively as they thought, the realization will usually rankle and eventually cause them to revise their methods.* Still, the pace of change can be very slow, and federal officials do not yet appear to have had much success in speeding up the process even though the known facts clearly call for reform.

STATE EFFORTS TO IMPROVE QUALITY

State lawmakers have seldom taken direct steps to try to enhance the quality of education at public colleges and universities. Occasionally, a legislature enacts a law prescribing the minimum number of hours professors must spend per week teaching classes. But faculties have usually found ways to get around such requirements without actually changing their behavior.[10] This pattern is unlikely to change. Laws handed down from above commanding instructors to change their ways rarely do much good.

A number of states have tried to improve the quality of undergraduate teaching by including educational outcomes among the goals of their performance-funding program. Legislators have used a variety of outcome measures for this purpose. Some have relied on scores on

---

*The rise of civil rights for minorities and equal opportunities for women provide useful examples of this process. For generations, minority groups and women suffered from discriminatory practices that were in conflict with the deeper beliefs of Americans in equal opportunity for everyone. All manner of rationalizations were used to paper over the inconsistencies. Eventually, however, as more and more people called attention to these conflicts, behavior and policy changed to bring behavior into closer alignment with the deeper values of Americans. For a prescient analysis of how this process would eventually bring about more equal treatment of minorities and women, see Gunnar Myrdal, *An American Dilemma: The Negro Problem and Modern Democracy* (1944), pp. 997–1026, 1073–79.

standardized tests of student learning in general education courses, specific majors, or entrance exams for graduate schools. Some have looked to the percentage of the university's academic programs that are accredited. Still others have used surveys of student and alumni satisfaction, or levels of success achieved by recent graduates in finding jobs and earning good salaries.

Performance funding has had no more effect on the quality of education than it has had on graduation rates. There are plenty of reasons why. The measures used to estimate success are very crude. The amounts of money available to reward progress have been too small and have usually gone to the institution rather than to the professors whose behavior needs to change in order to improve the quality of instruction. Surveys show that few department chairs and still fewer faculty members have even known about the existence of performance funding, let alone modified their teaching as a result.[11]

A serious handicap in setting goals for educational quality is the lack of accurate ways to determine how much student learning has taken place. Undergraduate surveys are unreliable. As previously noted, standardized test scores, such as the Collegiate Learning Assessment (CLA), are suspect. Employment records of recent graduates are even more questionable, since they are often influenced more by local economic conditions or by the ability of the entering students than by the skills and knowledge acquired in college. Beset by such difficulties, efforts to reward or penalize institutions on the basis of such measures seldom improve the quality of instruction but merely divert the effort and attention of campus officials from more important pursuits.

It is even possible that performance funding will do more to hurt educational quality than to improve it. The predominant emphasis on graduation rates in most state performance schemes could lead some colleges to meet their goals by lowering academic standards to flunk fewer students. There is already scattered evidence of colleges counseling weaker students not to take courses that are likely to be too difficult or even discontinuing such courses altogether.[12]

Any appraisal of the effects of state policies on the quality of education must also take account of legislative funding patterns over the past several decades. Cuts in appropriations have subjected most community colleges and comprehensive universities to severe economic pressure. Many of these institutions have had to take steps that threaten academic quality, such as increasing class sizes, hiring more part-time instructors at meager rates of pay, and raising tuition sufficiently to force lower-income students to work longer hours to earn enough money to stay enrolled. Particularly damaging has been the long-standing tendency of most state legislators to provide the lowest amount of funding per student to community colleges and comprehensive universities even though their students tend to be the least prepared for college classes and the hardest to teach.

THE TROUBLE WITH GOVERNMENT

Government efforts to enhance the quality of education as well as attempts to increase attainment levels have both had disappointing results. Neither financial inducements, nor efforts to inform the public, nor rewards and punishments to hold institutions accountable seem to have had much success. Further reflection on this experience reveals a variety of problems that limit the effectiveness of public policy in trying to reform higher education.

As federal officials have discovered, although financial incentives may seem the best available tools to achieve the government's purposes, money can be a leaky bucket with which to bring about reform. There are several ways in which public funds can be diverted or offset before they reach the individuals for whom they are intended. For example, increases in Pell Grants for needy students have often been offset by for-profit colleges raising their tuition, by selective private colleges reducing their financial aid, and by state governments lowering their subsidies to public four-year colleges and community colleges.

The fragmented system of government in the United States helps in other ways to frustrate the efforts of the administration to fashion a coherent educational program. Congress can fail to appropriate funds requested by the president, as it did by agreeing to only a small part of the thirteen billion dollars requested by President Obama in 2009 to strengthen community colleges. Public universities have sometimes capitalized on increased federal student aid to reduce their own scholarship funds for low-income students and thereby gain more money to spend on other activities they favor. Even separate offices within the executive branch may pursue independent policies that conflict with one another, as when the generous support that the National Science Foundation gives for summer research weakens the incentives created by the more modest sums provided to encourage professors to adopt more effective methods of instruction. Bringing all the parts and levels of government into a unified effort to improve higher education is often more than public officials can manage.

The problems associated with fragmented government have been exacerbated in recent years by the polarization of the two dominant political parties. Ideological divisions have made it much harder to enact legislation while subjecting measures that do pass to awkward compromises that limit their effectiveness. In addition, polarization tends to bring larger swings in policies and priorities when control of government changes hands, thus limiting the success of government initiatives and making it harder for universities to plan.

Even in more stable times, political considerations often undermine well-intentioned initiatives to help students and strengthen colleges and universities. In providing financial aid, neither presidents nor members of Congress have been able to resist giving costly tax credits and deductions to benefit wealthier parents even though these benefits do nothing to increase the already high enrollments and graduation rates of students from well-to-do families. For years, Congress gave banks a windfall of several billion dollars for providing unnecessary services in the student loan program until the practice was finally discontinued in 2010. In appropriating money to improve the quality of education, Congress has sometimes been stymied by individual members who have used earmarks to divert the funds to pay for politically popular projects in their own districts.

In addition to these handicaps, crucial gaps in existing knowledge often blunt well-intentioned government efforts to raise the level of educational attainment or improve the quality of education. When pressure builds for public officials to deal with a problem, lawmakers sometimes feel compelled to act even though too little is known about the subject to construct a successful program. Thus Department of Education officials have approved the use of federal financial aid for programs awarding college credit for competencies gained outside of college without sufficient evidence about the effect on the quality of education, while President Obama announced his ill-fated plan to rank the performance of colleges without adequate assurance that such an effort was truly feasible.

To minimize the risk of wasting money on ineffective programs, the federal government would have been well-advised to begin decades ago to mount a vigorous program of research to build a body of knowledge that could help lawmakers spend tax dollars wisely. But Congress has never provided much support for education research. As a result, to quote a 1999 report by a committee of the National Academies of Sciences, Engineering, and Medicine: "One striking fact is that the complex world of education—unlike defense, health care, or industrial production—does not rest on a strong research base. In no other field are personal experiences and ideology so frequently relied on to make policy choices, and in no other field is the research base so inadequate and so little used."[13]

Since 1999, the situation has improved a bit. Funding has edged upward. Congress has given responsibility for research to a new organization, the Institute of Education Sciences (IES), which is charged with examining the effectiveness of new ideas for improving education. The IES is widely credited with producing more rigorous research with greater insulation from political pressure. Even so, funding for this work remains extremely low in comparison with other fields, such as health and medicine, space exploration, or national defense. For every one hundred dollars that the federal government spends on all forms of research, education receives a mere forty-three cents, most of which goes to studies having to do with K–12 education. As a result, since the Institute of Education Sciences was founded in 2002, it has managed to fund only a handful of studies per year evaluating ways to improve the quality of education. In contrast, the National Institutes of Health has sponsored as many as *twenty-seven hundred* clinical trials in a single year for testing new medicines and medical procedures.[14]

There is a price to be paid for creating such a limited stock of useful and reliable knowledge. Congress continues to appropriate vast sums each year for student aid with insufficient knowledge of the effect on enrollments or graduation rates. Political leaders have recently proposed new programs costing billions of dollars per year to make public colleges free without solid evidence of their likely impact on graduation rates or the survival of small, independent colleges.

State lawmakers encounter many of the same difficulties in devising policy as their counterparts do in Washington. But there are two additional tendencies unique to the states that carry additional risks and disadvantages. The first results from the prohibition in almost all states against incurring a budget deficit. This restriction forces states to make draconian spending cuts during economic recessions when tax revenues drop. For reasons already mentioned, these cuts tend to fall especially heavily on public colleges and universities, causing a degree of financial instability that makes academic planning difficult.

A second practice affecting higher education is the preferential treatment that state officials give to their research universities. These institutions have long benefited from the fact that they are most likely to claim state legislators among their alumni, most likely to field athletic teams that gain national attention and attract local support, and most likely to have students and alumni from the kinds of prominent, well-to-do families with above-average political clout. These advantages have been reinforced in recent years by the attempt in many states to develop the next "Silicon Valley," replete with successful high-tech companies, well-paid jobs, and increased tax revenues. The result is a rivalry among states featuring tax concessions to attract new businesses, merit scholarships to enroll talented students in the hope that they will remain in the state to supply the skilled workforce coveted by high-tech companies, and financial support for flagship universities to help them build the kinds of research programs that attract successful entrepreneurs.

These policies work to the disadvantage of the comprehensive universities and community colleges that will enroll most of the additional students needed to boost educational attainment. Once again, as with the growing use of merit scholarships and the tax benefits the federal government offers well-to-do parents, the political process allocates too much money to those who need it less while awarding too little to students who depend on aid in order to stay enrolled and earn a degree. The result is one more impediment to achieving the national goal of graduating larger numbers of college graduates and providing greater opportunities for racial minorities and low-income students to acquire the education to achieve success in later life.

The limitations of government policy making do not render successful initiatives impossible. State and federal programs have sometimes produced great achievements in higher education, such as the growth of an impressive research establishment after World War II and the transition from an elite to a mass and ultimately a universal system. In these instances, however, the needs of the country and the interests of colleges and universities were closely aligned, a growing economy provided ample resources for the task, and academic leaders and their faculties knew how to accomplish what public officials wanted done. Today, unfortunately, money for the task is not so readily available, and knowledge of how to achieve the desired ends is often insufficient. Under these conditions, the likelihood of ineffective policies and harmful unintended consequences is substantial. Success may not be impossible, but it is clearly harder to achieve than it was in the earlier periods of massive change.

CHAPTER TEN

༱

Accreditation

ALL ADVANCED COUNTRIES WANT TO MAKE sure that their universities offer an education of sufficient quality. As pointed out in chapter 6, the academic marketplace, despite its vigorous competition for students, offers no guarantee of good teaching, because it is too difficult for applicants to judge the quality of education in the colleges they are considering before they decide where to enroll. Consequently, almost every nation has created some system of oversight to protect students from shoddy programs of little or no value. In the United States, this task has been performed by accreditation.

Of all the external forces that seek to influence colleges and universities, accreditation is the only one that has devoted most of its efforts to improving the quality of education. Until recently, no one paid much attention to accreditors other than campus officials awaiting their periodic inspection, who grumbled about the quantity of paperwork involved. Within the past ten years, however, the process has begun to attract much closer scrutiny—from the Department of Education, from Congress, from innovative entrepreneurs seeking to introduce new methods of educating students, and from commentators discussing the reform of higher education.

This flurry of attention has produced a paradox. Over the past decade, no outside group has had as much success as accrediting organizations have achieved in persuading colleges to devote more effort to evaluating and improving the quality of teaching and learning. Over the same period, however, accreditation has been subjected to unrelenting criticism.[1] Almost no one has a good word to say about it, and almost everyone has a strong opinion about what should be done to improve the system.

THE COMMON CHARACTERISTICS OF QUALITY ASSURANCE PROGRAMS

Systems of quality assurance and enhancement in advanced industrialized countries tend to share several basic features.[2] They provide for some sort of periodic inspection, preceded by the submission of extensive information by the institution being evaluated. These reviews are normally conducted by a small team composed of individuals with ample experience in higher education. Following the visit, the team submits a written report to the overseeing authority containing its findings and recommendations. The authority then decides to approve the accreditation, or deny it, or approve it provisionally, subject to certain specified improvements.

While sharing these characteristics, systems for maintaining and enhancing quality can differ along a continuum from voluntary procedures administered by universities themselves to systems devised and operated by the government. Experience has shown that neither a wholly voluntary nor an entirely government-run effort is likely to work well. Systems that are run by the government can become adversarial so that universities and their faculties try to satisfy the state inspectors by appearing to comply without actually doing so. On the other hand, wholly voluntary systems can be too weak to bring about much improvement, let alone inspire much confidence among audiences outside the universities themselves. For example, a number of higher education associations in the United States agreed several years ago to have their member universities conduct and publish assessments to show how much their students learned. In the end, however, not all of the colleges involved produced reports, and many of those that did gave incomplete and confusing information that could not help students or anyone else to compare one institution with another.[3]

In light of this experience, systems in advanced industrialized nations tend to be a blend of the state-run and voluntary models. They seek to combine enough government involvement to cause universities to take the periodic inspections seriously with evaluators who possess enough knowledge of higher education to elicit the cooperation and respect of campus officials and their faculties.

THE AMERICAN ACCREDITATION SYSTEM

The United States has traditionally inclined toward more voluntary forms of accreditation. The system for inspecting degree-granting colleges is operated by seven private organizations operating in six different regions of the country, each governed by a board largely composed of university representatives.* Every institution is evaluated at least once every ten years by a team made up of faculty members and administrators from other colleges and universities who serve without pay. The teams submit reports to the accrediting body's board, which then decides whether to renew accreditation, deny it, or renew it with qualifications (often accompanied by a provision for follow-up visits in the next year or two to determine whether the problems causing the qualifications have been corrected).

This system has some obvious advantages. Because it relies on volunteer evaluators, it is inexpensive, requiring a paid staff in the nation as a whole totaling scarcely more than 150 full-time employees. The use of professors and academic leaders on inspection teams helps to spread useful ideas for improvement to other colleges. Moreover, since the volunteers are peers from other institutions, the process is more likely to inspire trust and less likely to become adversarial than would a system staffed by paid professional inspectors.

---

*These organizations accredit more than 3,000 institutions. Other bodies accredit an additional 3,719 institutions, including professional schools as well as for-profit vocational schools that do not offer degrees. The problems associated with the latter accreditation system are too varied and complicated to be discussed in this chapter. States also have their own regulations for licensing colleges and universities. These laws vary greatly from one state to another and will likewise not be discussed. See Andrew P. Kelly, Kevin Janes, and Rooney Columbus, *Inputs, Outcomes, Quality Assurance: A Clear Look at State Oversight of Higher Education*, American Enterprise Institute (August 2015).

In the Veterans' Readjustment Act of 1952, Congress decided to make accreditation a prerequisite for receiving federal financial aid. This requirement was retained in the Higher Education Act of 1965 and remains in force to this day. Because few colleges can afford to do without federal student aid, this delegation of authority has given added clout to the accrediting organizations, but it has also made these organizations dependent upon the government and more subject to its wishes.

Over the years, Washington has gradually expanded its influence over the accreditation process.[4] In 1992, Congress made its reliance on accrediting organizations conditional on their willingness to review each item on a list of subjects during their periodic campus inspections. The list included a requirement that accreditors examine how much students are learning in each college they review. In the same year, Congress took the further step of establishing a National Advisory Committee on Institutional Quality and Integrity composed of government appointees who advise the department on the competence of the accrediting organizations to carry out their functions, the subjects accreditors must consider in evaluating institutions, and other matters involving the effective operation of the system.

SETTING MINIMUM STANDARDS

From their inception, America's accrediting organizations have assumed responsibility for protecting students from weak and ineffective colleges. Those who study the system almost all agree that accreditors have not performed this function well. Even defenders of the existing system would concede that a substantial number of colleges have been allowed to exist despite graduating only a small percentage of their students and offering a very poor quality of education. From October 2009 through March 2014, accreditors denied approval to less than 1 percent of the colleges subject to their oversight. More than two hundred institutions have been allowed to continue operating even though they graduate fewer than 20 percent of their entering students.[5]

Eventually, the Department of Education grew concerned over having to provide large quantities of federal aid to students attending colleges with poor records of performance. The problem came to a head with the rapid growth of for-profit colleges, many of which received almost all their revenue from financial aid while having persistently low graduation rates, large student debt loads, and unusually high default rates in repaying educational loans. The Department of Education consequently announced its intention to deny aid to colleges that allowed their students to incur greater debts than they could repay in view of the jobs their education prepared them to fill.

The jury is still out on how successful the department will be in denying aid and effectively closing down colleges that fail to meet its standards. Institutions threatened with such a fate typically mount a fierce resistance. In keeping with this tendency, the draft rules that the department issued for comment met with determined opposition and lawsuits from for-profit institutions, causing further deliberation by officials followed by concessions and compromises before the rules were eventually approved by the Federal Court of Appeals for the District of Columbia.[6] Meanwhile, few colleges as yet have been disqualified for federal student aid.* With the advent of a new administration in Washington that is openly critical of regulation, it is possible that this latest attempt at government intervention will be abandoned or amended to affect only a small number of institutions.

Who Should Establish Minimum Standards? Despite the difficulties involved, the Department of Education had good reasons for deciding to formulate its own minimum standards. The purpose of accreditation is to improve the quality of instruction offered by colleges and to protect students and society from institutions that provide an education of little value. The rules issued by the Department of Education have a slightly

---

*A front-page story from the *New York Times* on October 13, 2015, proclaimed, "For-Profit Colleges Fail U.S. Rules but Get Billions." According to this article, "the continuing flow of money illustrates the quandary facing federal education officials. On the one hand, they have moved forcefully to try to protect taxpayer funds and prevent students from falling deeply into debt without anything to show for it. On the other, they must avoid running roughshod over private for-profit schools that have not been found guilty of wrongdoing."

different aim. Their purpose is to protect the government from responsibility for loans that carry excessive risk of not being repaid. This task involves financial judgments that seem most appropriate for the government to make.

A number of critics have gone further and argued that private accrediting bodies should be deprived of all responsibility to decide which institutions should be disqualified from receiving federal financial aid. Instead, such decisions should henceforth be made by the Department of Education.[7*] Such a change would have several advantages. It would relieve accrediting organizations of a task they have not performed especially well and allow them to concentrate exclusively on improving the quality of education in the colleges within their region. It would also take care of the recurring criticism that accreditors have a conflict of interest in deciding whether colleges should remain eligible for federal aid, since the boards of accrediting organizations, which ultimately decide whether to grant or deny accreditation, are largely made up of college representatives.

Although a complete decoupling of financial aid from accreditation is conceivable, it seems unlikely. Accrediting organizations would oppose the change because of a fear that many colleges might not cooperate with campus evaluators or even seek accreditation at all if they would no longer lose student aid funds as a result. Colleges would resist such a move rather than face the prospect of an additional set of campus inspections by the Department of Education. The government itself might shrink from the prospect of having to decide whether individual institutions should be eligible to receive financial aid. The task is difficult and

---

* Current federal efforts to increase educational attainment accentuate the need to have the government decide which institutions should be eligible for federal student aid. Under present federal policies, millions more high school graduates are being encouraged to enroll in college. Because a great many of these students will be unprepared for college work and will fail to finish, some colleges may have very low graduation rates even though they are doing all they can to help their students succeed. In such cases, the issue is not primarily a matter of whether these colleges are doing an adequate job; it requires a judgment about the appropriate trade-off between the desire to increase the number of college graduates and the desire not to spend tax dollars on colleges with excessive numbers of federally aided students who are unable to succeed and thus drop out and eventually default on their loans. This is a judgment of federal financial policy that should arguably be made by the government, not by accreditors.

contentious, and could entail costly investigations of many colleges, which would be burdensome for the department as well as for colleges forced to undergo another round of inspections in addition to those of accrediting organizations. Besides, as matters now stand, accreditation gives the department a convenient way to influence the nature of under-graduate education indirectly by issuing requirements for accreditors without having to undertake the more controversial and politically sensitive task of trying to impose its will directly on the academic policies of colleges and universities.

One possible outcome is that Congress will allow the department to establish detailed rules and outcome measures that accreditors must apply in deciding whether colleges deserve accreditation. A bill to this effect has already been introduced in the US Senate.[8] Passage of this legislation would greatly expand the federal government's power over higher education and would have the added effect of diverting the attention of accreditors from improving the quality of education to enforcing minimum requirements issued by the department for retaining eligibility to receive student aid funds.

Facilitating Innovation. At a time like the present, when new ideas abound for improving on existing methods of education, it is especially important that accreditation not become an impediment to promising innovations. Several critics insist that current practices have precisely this effect.[9] Their chief complaint is that existing procedures create a catch-22 situation for would-be innovators. The federal government requires that a new college become accredited before the students can receive financial aid. But accreditation typically takes several years to obtain since accreditors understandably prefer to judge a new entity on the basis of substantial operating experience. Unless the innovative college has unusually patient investors, it cannot afford to wait that long to qualify for financial aid.

This is not an impossible problem to resolve. The obvious solution is to grant provisional approval for the receipt of financial aid to new institutions whose plans satisfy a set of preliminary requirements and seem to have a substantial chance of success, provided that the institution obtains final accreditation within a prescribed period of years.[10]*

Some critics may still complain that accreditors are blocking innovation if they deny approval to new programs offering inexpensive ways of teaching valuable job-related skills not only by utilizing online courses and competency-based methods but by eliminating requirements that force students to take courses that do not contribute directly to performance on the job. The question such cases pose is whether completion of a strictly vocational course of study should entitle a student to a college degree. Accrediting organizations will argue that a bachelor's or associate degree has long required a breadth of study beyond strictly vocational instruction—typically, a minimum set of courses in the sciences, humanities, and social sciences—even though these courses may not contribute directly to workplace skills. Proponents of this requirement defend the practice on the grounds that a traditional college education has important long-term benefits unrelated to success in the workplace, such as greater participation in civic activities, better health, lower rates of incarceration and of drug and alcohol abuse, and higher levels of education among their children. They may also assert that a broad education will have greater long-term value by enabling graduates to adapt more easily to changes in the economy, citing figures showing that liberal arts majors often earn more money in the long run than graduates of narrowly vocational programs.

Not everyone will agree with these claims. The governors of several states have indicated that only job-related courses benefit the taxpayer.[11] The governor of Kentucky even suggested recently that taxpayer money should subsidize the cost of instruction only in science, technology,

---

* Many critics who allege that accreditors are hampering innovation do not seem to appreciate the nature of the judgments involved in such cases. Most educational innovations fail. In the case of innovative colleges, failure can often mean disappointment and wasted money for students and a loss of federal financial aid funds for the government. As a result, it is not enough that an organization has an interesting new idea; accreditors evaluating a new way of educating students have to decide whether the innovation's promise is sufficient to justify the risk of failure, with the losses that this will entail for the government and the students. Prudence may well require disapproval of some intriguing proposals.

engineering, and mathematics, since only these courses provide real value for the economy.[12] Officials of this persuasion may see no reason not to award traditional degrees to students who acquire a designated set of vocational skills as quickly and inexpensively as possible.

There is a simple solution to such an argument. As organizations created by colleges to maintain academic standards, accrediting organizations should have the power to determine the minimum requirements of content for the awarding of college degrees, including the right to insist on a broad curriculum of the kind traditionally associated with an undergraduate education in America.[*] At the same time, the department should have authority to decide whether to provide federal financial aid for students enrolled in innovative, expeditious programs to acquire vocational skills. Graduates of these programs may then receive certificates or similar indicia of their accomplishment, which can acquire the recognition from employers that their value in the marketplace deserves.

IMPROVING TEACHING AND LEARNING

For many years, accreditors have devoted the bulk of their efforts not to enforcing minimum requirements but to the larger task of trying to improve the educational quality of *all* colleges and universities. This role was a natural one for accreditors to fill. Had they not done so, and merely denied their stamp of approval to the weakest colleges, most of their

---

[*] While accrediting organizations should retain the power to establish basic minimum requirements for BA and AA degrees, they should not go to the other extreme by heeding the suggestion of some staunch supporters of liberal education and insisting that colleges adopt a lengthy list of specific learning outcomes, such as those proposed by the Association of American Colleges & Universities, as prerequisites for a college degree. E.g., Carol Geary Schneider, "Learning at Risk," *Liberal Education* (Fall 2015/Winter 2016), pp. 24, 25. By requiring such a detailed set of competencies, proposals of this sort would inhibit innovation and prohibit legitimate differences of educational philosophy among the many hundreds of colleges offering a liberal arts education and a BA degree.

campus visits would have been pointless, since accreditation would have been a foregone conclusion.*

Over the years, the methods of evaluating colleges have evolved. Accreditors have shifted from emphasizing "inputs," such as the percentage of faculty members with PhDs or the number of books in the library, to "outcomes," and, in particular, to the amount and quality of learning acquired by the students. In doing so, accreditors have insisted on certain basic requirements that are essential to the awarding of a BA or associate degree, but they have generally refrained from imposing detailed curricular requirements or a specific list of essential goals that undergraduate education must pursue. Instead, they have wisely given considerable latitude to colleges, realizing that there is no single ideal curriculum. What accreditors do is to examine the efforts by each college to ascertain how much progress its students are making toward the institution's own learning objectives, and to address any weaknesses revealed by its assessments.

Because of prompting by accreditors, more than 80 percent of colleges have now defined their learning objectives, and most have begun to use some method or methods to assess how much their students are learning.[13] As yet, however, there are few, if any, ways to measure learning that experienced educators consider truly reliable, let alone an effective, comprehensive test to determine mastery of all the subjects and competencies included in a liberal education. Thus accreditors have wisely refrained from insisting that all colleges utilize some designated way to assess student learning.

---

* Some critics have argued that accreditors should concentrate their efforts on weak institutions and pay only cursory attention to colleges of obvious good quality. E.g., Peter T. Ewell, *Eleven Reform Proposals for Accreditation*, NCHEMS (April 2015). While there is something to be said for such a policy in view of the heavy workload of most accrediting organizations and the complexity of the inspection process, there are at least two powerful reasons for not making this change. To begin with, many selective and well-endowed institutions have done relatively little to evaluate the quality of their educational programs or to introduce more effective methods of instruction and hence need the encouragement to do so that the accreditation process provides. In addition, because there is a strong tendency among colleges to emulate the best-known institutions, it is especially important that the latter be encouraged to maintain a high standard of educational quality.

Making Accreditation Reports Public. A persistent source of controversy is whether accreditation bodies should make public the reports they receive from the volunteer teams that inspect individual colleges. Advocates have repeatedly argued that releasing the reports would increase public confidence in the accreditation process and provide valuable information for students wondering which college to attend.[14] If campus officials knew that prospective students would be scrutinizing the reports, they would arguably work harder to improve the quality of their educational programs in order to avoid receiving criticism in a published report that might discourage capable students from applying.

Those who defend the status quo have a ready response to each of these assertions. They argue that releasing inspection reports that pinpoint deficiencies will hardly build public confidence in the nation's colleges. As for informing prospective students, supporters of the current system contend that few applicants would read the reports. Instead, they would continue to make their decision on other grounds, such as the evaluations in college guides, or the academic programs, location, and cost of different institutions, or even the records of their athletic teams.

More important, publicizing reports could easily change the character of campus inspections for the worse. Campus officials and their faculties would no longer be so willing to cooperate with inspection teams to discuss ways of getting better. Faced with the threat of an unfavorable public report, colleges would attempt to "game the system" and turn it into a public relations exercise by hiding problems and emphasizing strengths. Since campus inspections usually last only two or three days and are carried out by volunteers, such efforts might well be successful, making the accreditation reports unreliable.

This controversy reveals a deeper, more pervasive difference of opinion that runs through all discussions about the purpose of accreditation. Should the process be treated chiefly as a useful source of good advice accompanied by sustained but gentle pressure to induce colleges to improve themselves? Or should accreditation place more emphasis on providing accountability and putting pressure on reluctant colleges to reform?[15]

The opposing views reflect fundamentally different conceptions of the nature of universities. To those sympathetic to the existing system, the leaders and faculties of most universities have a genuine desire to educate students properly and welcome insights from fellow educators about existing weaknesses and how to overcome them. Using pressure to force professors to change their ways threatens to bring about covert resistance rather than voluntary compliance. In contrast, those more critical of higher education believe that most universities are complacent, weighed down by inertia, and interested more in raising money, doing research, and gaining greater visibility and prestige than in the hard work of giving students a first-rate education. Such critics are convinced that universities will rarely reform themselves unless they feel great pressure to do so.

On reflection, it probably makes little difference which opinion is correct, as far as publishing the reports is concerned. The results of compelling disclosure would probably be neither as dire nor as beneficial as opponents and supporters suggest. Knowing that their report would be published, inspection teams would take great care to avoid being unfair in drafting their conclusions lest they unjustly damage the institution they were evaluating. Findings would become tentative, conclusions qualified, and criticisms muted. The final reports would be too bland either to compel universities to change or to convey much useful information to the outside world, thus removing most of the value critics hoped to gain by having the documents published.

Grading Colleges and Universities. If publishing inspection reports would be ineffective, some observers who believe in putting pressure on colleges suggest that accreditors should at least find a way of letting the public know which institutions are doing a particularly good job of giving their students a first-rate education. Accrediting bodies should therefore characterize colleges as "Excellent," "Satisfactory," "Approved Provisionally Subject to Modifications," or some similar set of evaluations. In this way, even college officials who know that their institution will be accredited will still try hard to improve their graduation rate and their educational programs in order to obtain the highest rating and thereby gain an official recognition of quality that could please alumni and attract larger numbers of exceptional applicants.

Despite these advantages, the proposal also carries a risk of losing much that is valuable about the current system. Campus inspections, which should ideally be a cooperative process for achieving educational improvement, could degenerate into a determined effort on the part of universities to obscure their difficulties and exaggerate their successes in order to impress the evaluators.

Only experience can show whether a revised rating system will do more harm than good. However, the dangers involved are sufficient to suggest that accreditors proceed with caution. Rather than adopt such a change wholesale, accrediting organizations would be well advised to experiment with a limited number of colleges and observe the effects carefully before deciding whether to go further.

Another set of complaints about the current accreditation process is that the campus visits are too brief, too infrequent, and too amateurish to accomplish all they might.[16] Such concerns clearly have substance. Congress has required accreditors to inspect a daunting list of subjects: curricula; student achievement; quality of faculty; fiscal and administrative capacity; facilities, recruiting, and admissions; program length and objectives; student complaints; and compliance with federal rules and regulations. A two- or three-day inspection of an entire college carried out by lightly trained volunteers is far too brief to allow a careful review of more than one or two of these items.

Inspecting Each Department and Program. To overcome this problem, some critics have suggested that separate reviews be conducted of each department and program in the college.[17] Such a process would allow the accrediting organization to choose evaluators who are experts in the particular program or department being reviewed and have them examine the quality of the education provided in much greater depth than they could if they had to review an entire college.

Separate departmental inspections have actually been used in a few countries, such as Denmark and Germany. Even in the United States, accreditation procedures for individual departments already exist for a number of vocational programs. The visits are typically organized under the auspices of professional bodies, and inspection teams are made up of a mixture of professors and practitioners belonging to the profession involved. By most accounts, such procedures have been effective in bringing about useful reforms in programs for educating schoolteachers and engineers.[18]

To use such a model for all undergraduate education, however, with its several thousand colleges and community colleges, each with a wide array of separate departments and programs, seems quite impractical. Finding teams of competent accreditors to visit tens of thousands of different programs and departments and preparing them to conduct their reviews would be an enormous task. The cost to colleges preparing for all these visits would be an extraordinarily heavy burden. These problems have apparently proved insurmountable in other nations that have tried a department-by-department approach. According to David Dill, a leading observer of accreditation systems overseas, "because universal external assessments or accreditations at the subject level in other countries have proven costly and exhausting, most countries are now adopting institutional reviews focused on ensuring and improving academic quality at the collective faculty level within institutions."[19]

Employing Trained Evaluators. If visits to each individual department and program are impractical for the United States, using trained professionals in place of volunteer professors and academic leaders might seem to offer a useful way to improve matters.[20] Through training and extensive experience, professional inspectors could surely acquire skills that would help them get the most out of their brief campus visits.

Even professionals, however, could not attend properly to all of the tasks envisaged under the current published rules. Moreover, paid inspectors would cost far more than current volunteers. They would almost certainly lack the credibility possessed by volunteer professors and would have a harder time gaining the trust and confidence of the institutions they inspected.[21]

Narrowing the Focus of Campus Visits. While using trained inspectors may not be wise, accreditation organizations still need to consider how to construct a more effective system of evaluation. At present, the list of subject areas that Congress has mandated for accreditors to study is far too long for the two or three days that visiting teams currently spend on a campus. If the visits are to be of real use, teams must be free to concentrate their efforts on a few areas of particular concern rather than try to inspect everything and risk rendering a superficial assessment of no use to anybody.*

Except in unusual cases, accreditation teams would do well to confine their efforts to the two issues of greatest importance at present: access and graduation rates, on the one hand, and the quality of education, on the other. At the very least, Congress should remove responsibility for monitoring compliance with federal regulations; this is a task that the government itself should perform, since inspection teams composed of academic personnel are normally much less qualified than federal officials to provide such oversight. As for other subjects included by Congress in its prescribed accreditation standards, such as facilities, admissions, or student complaints, Congress should make clear that accreditors need to examine such matters only to the extent that they appear to have a significant effect on access, graduation rates, or the quality of education.

Since inspection teams cannot possibly review every program and department in the institutions they inspect, it is also important that accrediting organizations narrow the subjects to be evaluated with the aid of the self-study and the consultations between accrediting staff and campus officials that regularly precede campus visits. Inspection teams might also be freed from ceremonial or routine meetings with groups of trustees, deans, professors, students, and the like in order to concentrate on talking with the individuals directly responsible for the issues and

---

* For example, in the instructions given this author in chairing an inspection of a large research university, the visiting team was supposed to evaluate compliance with such standards as the following: "the institution demonstrates an effective system of academic oversight, assuring the quality of the academic program wherever and however it is offered" and "degree programs have a coherent design and are characterized by appropriate breadth, depth, continuity, sequential progression, and synthesis of learning." No inspection of two or three days' duration can possibly produce reliable judgments about a list of standards of such breadth and complexity.

practices of greatest importance to graduation rates and the quality of education.

A campus inspection focusing on retention and quality of education needs to pursue a number of specific questions. For example, teams investigating retention should examine the completion rates for students assigned to remedial programs, and inquire whether there are plans for improvement. They should likewise determine how well the overall graduation rate compares with those of carefully chosen peer institutions. If the comparisons reveal that the college being inspected lags behind, are its peers using methods that deserve a try? More important still, does the college being visited have a plausible plan for increasing graduation rates in the future?

In reviewing the quality of teaching and learning, inspection teams need to examine the efforts being made to evaluate student progress toward the college's learning objectives. How reliable are the measures of learning used? Have the results been discussed with the faculty and are steps being taken to devise reforms to improve areas of weakness? The inspection team might also try to discover whether the teaching of courses is aligned with the learning objectives established by the college, and whether examinations in a random sample of courses reflect the learning objectives of the programs and departments involved. Finally, evaluators could examine the steps taken by the administration to encourage innovation and improvement by supporting and rewarding efforts by faculty members to introduce new methods of instruction.

For visits of this kind to succeed, it is essential to select visiting teams possessing the competence and experience to deal with the questions just described. The issues involved can be complicated, and accreditation teams should include individuals with the expertise to evaluate what colleges are doing and offer advice that commands respect on further steps that campus leaders and their faculties need to consider. Experience as a faculty member or even as a dean or chief academic officer provides no guarantee that volunteer evaluators will possess the specific knowledge to do this job well. If accrediting organizations cannot find enough volunteer evaluators with the requisite knowledge, they should presumably consider hiring additional staff with the relevant expertise in order to assist inspection teams in narrowing the questions for review, formulating appropriate questions, and evaluating the answers received.

The point that cannot be emphasized too strongly is that accreditation is entering a new and more demanding phase in its development. Now that most colleges and universities have identified their learning objectives, compiled their graduation rates, and reported on their retention efforts, any serious effort to help them improve will require considerable expertise in order to evaluate such specialized activities as online programs or remedial education, and to offer constructive suggestions for improvement. Assembling evaluators and staff members with the necessary knowledge and experience may well be the greatest challenge facing accrediting organizations in the coming years.

FINAL REFLECTIONS

Since accreditation has recently become a favorite target for criticism, it is appropriate to end this chapter by emphasizing a few important points.

First, accreditation is the only source of outside influence of the many discussed thus far that is primarily focused on improving student learning. This function is especially important today when public officials are trying to encourage more underprepared young people to enter college and obtain degrees at a time when many colleges are being given less money per student to do the job.

Second, under these conditions, it is important that accreditation focus on accomplishing its mission of improving quality and increasing graduation rates. Public officials should not divert the energy of accreditors by calling for "reforms" designed to achieve other purposes, such as trying to boost public confidence in the system by appointing more public members to inspection teams (unless such members possess genuine expertise in retention and student learning), adding still more subjects that accreditors must inspect, or making accreditation reports public on the doubtful premise that they will assist students in choosing colleges and thus put pressure on campus leaders to improve their educational programs.

Third, it is important to recognize the gains that accreditors have already made over the past two decades. Their emphasis on student learning during campus visits has given college leaders a credible reason to raise questions about the quality of instruction without stirring up resistance from members of the faculty who might otherwise resent presidential interference with their teaching. In response to prodding from accreditors, the vast majority of colleges have now clarified their learning objectives and begun to use a variety of methods to measure how much improvement students are making.[22]

According to chief academic officers, the accreditation process has been the single most effective factor in bringing about such progress.[23] Campus officials also observe that accreditors have achieved these results while retaining the support of colleges and gaining increased acceptance by faculties for using assessments to measure how much students are learning.[24] In a recent independent survey of academic leaders, 74 percent of respondents stated that accreditation had resulted in curricular changes, while 47 percent reported changes in instructional methods.[25] It is hard to identify any other source of influence that has accomplished as much in nudging colleges to improve the quality of their educational programs.

It is true that many academic leaders have still not shared the results of their assessments with the faculty or engaged in serious discussions about needed improvements. Yet some of them are doing so, and much has been accomplished to prepare the ground for others to follow. As George Kuh and his collaborators from the National Institute for Learning Outcomes Assessment pointed out in 2014, in their latest review of assessment in US colleges and universities, "higher education may be on the verge of an inflection point where what comes next is a more purposeful use of evidence of student learning outcomes in decision-making—which in turn has the potential to enhance academic quality and institutional effectiveness."[26]

In short, this is hardly the moment to endanger the gradual progress that accreditors are making by pressing for drastic changes out of impatience with the slow pace of reform. The next phase of campus visits will be more difficult and will require more focused effort and expertise, but accrediting organizations deserve an opportunity to succeed. If further improvement stalls and unused assessments and useful ideas for improvement gather dust in administrative offices, the moment may come to consider a thorough overhaul. But such a time has not arrived yet.

PART THREE

The Way Forward

CHAPTER ELEVEN

∾

Increasing Educational Attainment

EIGHT YEARS HAVE PASSED SINCE PRESIDENT OBAMA announced that America would regain its global lead in the educational level of its workforce by 2020. The goal was ambitious, requiring an increase in little over a decade of more than 40 percent in the number of Americans earning college credentials. Yet the environment for such a change seemed promising. The financial incentives to get a degree were exceptionally strong, since the average earnings premium of college graduates over those with only a high school education or less had reached its highest level in a century. Many state governors had already recognized the need to raise graduation rates and set explicit goals for their colleges and universities.[1] Academic leaders too had accepted the challenge. In a survey of college presidents conducted by the *Chronicle of Higher Education*, "Improved Retention and Graduation Rates," ranked below only "Having a Balanced Budget" and "Strengthening the Institution's Reputation" as a way to define success.[2] Eighty-four percent of provosts listed "improving retention and degree completion" as one of the top five challenges facing their campus, while 90 percent agreed that the national campaign to increase attainment levels "focused needed attention on retention and graduation rates in higher education."[3]

Despite these auspicious beginnings, now that two-thirds of the allotted time has passed for recapturing our global lead in educational attainment, the effort seems doomed to failure. Enrollments surged for the first year or two as the bleak job prospects following the 2008 financial crisis caused many young people to enter college rather than look for work. Thereafter, however, total college enrollments declined, losing almost half of their postrecession growth. Over the next decade, the numbers of high school graduates are expected to grow very slowly. As a result, enrollments will not receive the population boost that they have had in the past, making the president's goal even harder to reach. Meanwhile, college graduation rates for the country as a whole have risen only slightly, the gap separating rich and poor has continued to widen, and racial differences have not narrowed appreciably.[4] Far from leading the world in the education of young adults, we still lag behind a number of other advanced nations.[5]

REASONS FOR THE SLUGGISH RESPONSE

What accounts for this disappointing record? One reason, surely, is that the support of key actors turned out to be weaker than one might have anticipated. Congress did not appropriate nearly as much money for community colleges as the president requested, and state officials had already blunted much of the added federal funding by the cuts they made in financial aid and per-student support for their public colleges and universities. The latter responded by raising their tuitions by larger percentages than usual to compensate for the loss of state support, hardly a helpful step for raising attainment rates. Thus both the funding and the shared commitment were lacking for such a massive increase in college graduates.

It is unlikely, however, that attainment rates would have risen nearly fast enough even if more money had been available for the purpose. As the number of college-educated employees the economy needs continues to grow, increasing the supply of graduates depends more and more on educating students from underfinanced, poorly staffed high schools, many of them in neighborhoods struggling with high unemployment, crime, drugs, and single-parent families. The handicaps suffered by young people growing up in such conditions are an important reason why American seventeen-year-olds do not perform very well on tests of basic competencies and rank below their counterparts from many other nations in international assessments of reading and quantitative literacy. These results have not improved markedly in the past thirty years despite repeated efforts at reform in the wake of the influential commission report *A Nation at Risk*, which spoke of "a rising tide of mediocrity" and a "unilateral educational disarmament" in America's public schools.[6]*

Because of these deficiencies, up to half of the students who come to college must take an average of 3.5 remedial courses before they can even begin working toward their degree. Many students assigned to remediation are discouraged and leave immediately. Among those who begin these courses, fewer than half complete them successfully. Of those that do, only 28 percent earn a degree or certificate within eight and a half years compared with 43 percent of those who do not need remediation. Overall, according to James E. Rosenbaum, "our high school graduates with low grades who are unprepared for college have an 86 percent chance of dropping out (often with zero credits)."[7]

Once students begin their regular courses, more than two-thirds of those who enroll in four-year colleges manage to earn a degree within eight years, quite a high figure by international standards. The problem lies chiefly in community colleges, where barely one-third of the entering students earn any kind of diploma within six years. Most of those who leave without a degree have a low enough aptitude for college study that their chances of graduating were never very high to begin with.[8]

Given these difficulties, the efforts of government officials to raise educational attainment hardly seem adequate. President Obama deserves credit for focusing attention on low-income students and the oft-overlooked community colleges that enroll so many of them. The strategy the president used to achieve his goal, however, is much more problematic. The federal government devoted most of its effort to reducing the cost of college by increasing financial aid. While there is evidence that larger Pell Grants can modestly increase college enrollments, enrollments are not the problem. More than 85 percent of American high school graduates already seek to enter college at some point. Some of them have to work too many hours each week to pay the costs and

---

* The peak year for the scores of seventeen-year-olds on national tests of competence in mathematics and reading was 1999 for both tests. US Department of Education, *The Nation's Report Card: Trends in Academic Progress* (2015).

eventually drop out. They might conceivably stay in college if the cost of doing so were lowered. But many simply lack the academic skills they need to earn a degree. Financial aid cannot do much by itself to remedy that problem.

State governments have also chosen money as their principal means of boosting educational attainment by making a substantial portion of their higher education budget dependent on the success or failure of each public college in meeting a negotiated goal for the number of graduating students. The premise underlying this approach is that college officials will increase the number of college graduates substantially if they are given a stronger incentive to do so. This assumption has not yet been borne out in the states where it has been tried. Since most states have gradually reduced their per-student funding of public higher education over the past few decades, they have scarcely made the task of college leaders any easier.

In fairness, financial aid and performance funding are not the only policies that governments are using to increase educational attainment. In an effort to improve the preparation given by high schools, both state and federal officials have also devoted much effort to promoting a new Common Core curriculum with higher standards and richer subject matter content more closely aligned with the requirements for successful college work. Forty-six states initially agreed, at least in principle, to adopt the Common Core. The hope is that the new curriculum will lift the achievement of high school graduates and reduce the number having to take remedial courses before they can start their college studies.

The Common Core project at least addresses the principal problem hampering efforts to increase educational attainment. Unfortunately, however, analyses of past school reforms have found that new curricula and higher standards have not succeeded in increasing student learning. These findings led a team of analysts from the Brookings Institution to conclude in 2012: "The empirical evidence suggests that the Common Core will have little effect on American students' achievement. The nation will have to look elsewhere for ways to improve its schools."[9]

Opposition to the new curriculum has also been growing and may intensify if large numbers of high school students cannot cope with the material and fail to receive a passing grade. Past experience suggests that such a result will lead to vocal protests by parents and teachers, followed by "adjustments" that water down the curriculum in order to increase the rate of student success. Should that occur, there will be even less reason to expect the Common Core to increase the number of freshmen capable of succeeding in college.

It is also not clear how much schools and colleges can do to overcome the handicaps of poorly prepared students, who have grown up in low-income families, often in high-poverty neighborhoods. As Robert Putnam points out in his recent study of unequal opportunity in America: "Our contemporary public debate recognizes this problem but assumes that it is largely a school's problem. On the contrary, we have seen that most of the challenges facing [these] kids are not caused by schools."[10] Instead, as Putnam explains in detail, they arise from underlying social and economic conditions that are far more difficult to overcome. The United States stands at or near the top of advanced industrialized nations in levels of child poverty, single-parent families, violent crime, and incarceration rates for young males, while ranking below many other nations in the percentage of children enrolled in preschool programs. In light of these problems, regaining our leadership in the percentage of our workforce holding "quality degrees" seems a very tall order indeed.

NEW POSSIBILITIES

While major increases in educational attainment have yet to occur, politicians have recently indicated support for several new ways to improve matters. While it is still too early to be sure exactly how the Trump administration plans to address this issue, the path it seems to be taking is to increase competition and student choice by easing restraints on for-profit colleges. This is an uncertain strategy at best for raising attainment rates. In the past, for-profits have managed to enroll many working adults in vocational programs by offering courses at more convenient times and places and by vigorously promoting online education. Yet these successes have been diminished by high dropout rates and the inability of most graduates to find jobs that pay more than those obtainable by attending a much cheaper community college. Unless for-profits can find a way to overcome these problems, they are unlikely to do a great deal to raise the number of college graduates with quality degrees. Weakening regulations threatens to make it easier to attract new students by exaggerated promises of higher pay and better jobs instead of by improving the quality of education to make the promises come true.

In 2015 and 2016, prominent Democratic officials proposed their own policies for enrolling and graduating more students. President Obama began by suggesting that community colleges become tuition-free for all students who maintain a 2.5 grade point average and are enrolled at least half-time.[11] Under the president's plan, the federal government would pay three-quarters of the cost of doing away with tuition, and states would contribute the rest. Students receiving Pell Grants would continue to do so and use the money to pay for books, transportation, and living costs. The total cost to Washington would be an estimated six billion dollars per year. Although it seems unlikely that a Republican president and Congress will accept such a proposal, several states and cities have already enacted their own version for making community college free or are actively considering ways of doing so.[12] In time, the idea may spread further and even be enacted nationwide.

In 2016, Hillary Clinton announced an even bolder, more expensive plan to lower the cost of college. Under her proposal, the federal government would give large sums to states that agreed to pay the additional cost of making *all* their colleges and community colleges tuition-free for in-state students from families with incomes up to $125,000 per year. This plan appeared to be a response to an even more sweeping scheme put forward by her political rival, Senator Bernie Sanders, that would have made all public colleges free to students regardless of their family income. Expensive proposals of this kind seem even less likely than President Obama's plan to be enacted by Congress any time soon. Still, Governor Cuomo has recently proposed a somewhat similar plan for New York State, and other states could do likewise in the years to come.

While many students may welcome having to pay less money for their college education, it is not at all clear that any of these plans would raise graduation rates substantially. Granted, many low-income students struggle to pay for their college education, and some of them find the sacrifice too great and drop out before earning a degree.[13] Doing away with tuition could enable these students to remain in school. Nevertheless, no one knows how many would remain and eventually graduate. There are some indications that the numbers would not be large. Berea College charges no tuition but still has dropout rates of 40 percent despite giving additional amounts of financial aid to defray the living costs of needy students.[14] An experiment in West Virginia that offered free tuition to first-time, full-time students who maintained a minimum grade point average managed to raise graduation rates but by only 4 percentage points.[15]

President Obama's plan could actually dampen completion rates by causing more students to enroll in community colleges rather than four-year institutions where their odds of graduating would be substantially better. Clinton's plan did not have that disadvantage, since it would give free tuition at all public colleges to students from families with incomes below $125,000. Nevertheless, both her plan and that of Bernie Sanders were much more expensive and would have subsidized many families that could surely pay something toward the college tuitions of their children. Their proposals could also have had drastic consequences for private colleges—not for the highly selective institutions with their flood of applications and large endowments but for the hundreds of small, independent colleges in precarious financial condition that struggle to attract enough students to survive.

Both plans sought to halt the erosion of state funding for public colleges and universities by conditioning their new subsidies on the willingness of states to maintain their existing levels of support. At the same time, both plans threatened to extend Washington's influence over higher education by giving its officials a powerful new role in college affairs. Once the federal government agreed to pay the largest share of college costs, it would naturally insist on having a lot to say about what these costs should be. Whether such a move would be wise depends on one's political philosophy. In view of the current political polarization in Washington, however, and the frequent deadlocks in Congress, this prospect could scarcely seem appealing to most colleges and universities.*

ALTERNATIVE POSSIBILITIES

Before investing heavily in strategies of uncertain efficacy, government officials might be well-advised to test prospective remedies to see how effective they are in practice. Already, there are a number of promising new ideas being proposed or actually in use at one or more colleges that deserve such an evaluation to determine whether they can be made to work successfully on a larger scale. With respect to remediation, for example, Arizona State University seems to have achieved considerable success using online adaptive tutoring to increase the completion rates in remedial or introductory mathematics.[16] Judith Scott-Clayton and colleagues have suggested new ways of deciding which entering students should be required to complete remediation, since existing assignment methods may force many individuals into remedial courses who are actually capable of doing college work.[17] Several states are using a variety of ways to give high school students early warning of their need to improve particular skills so that they will be ready to take regular college courses when they arrive on campus.[18] Finally, recent studies have found that while increased financial aid alone may do little to raise graduation rates, such assistance coupled with ample support services, such as better orientation, mentoring, and peer advising, can produce results significant enough to make such a program more than pay for itself.[19]

---

*A *state* program to make public colleges free would not increase federal influence over tuitions. But it would diminish the ability of public colleges to get their state to approve higher tuitions to cushion the effect of cuts in their state subsidy, since the state would now have to pay for much of the increase.

These ideas and others like them should be evaluated carefully to determine whether they can be used more widely. If they prove to be successful, each may help to improve graduation rates by only a small amount. Together, however, they could conceivably make a substantial difference. In addition, there are at least two other ideas that could turn out to have a greater impact on attainment levels.

Toward Simplifying Community College Programs. One proposal that many experts consider especially promising is to replace the daunting array of different programs and courses offered by most community colleges with a few well-structured pathways, each leading to a good job or transfer to a four-year college. At present, students are bewildered by having to choose among a long list of courses and programs with little guidance or supervision. As a result, they often take unnecessary courses, delay their progress toward a degree, become discouraged, and eventually drop out. Under the recommended new program, students would receive increased counseling and mentoring to help them select one of a handful of simplified programs and stay on track until graduation. In addition to having far fewer choices and much better advising, students would be required to enroll on a full-time basis and would receive enough financial aid to enable them to stay in school without experiencing financial stress or having to work so many hours as to interfere with studying and going to class.

Similar reforms have recently been tried on a pilot basis in New York City with considerable success.* Whether the new approach can be spread

---

* The City University of New York has already created pilot programs of this kind in six of its community colleges. Students received enough money to cover tuition and fees and were also given free use of textbooks and Metrocards to cover the cost of public transportation. All students were required to attend on a full-time basis. One study by the Society for Benefit-Cost Analysis in 2014 compared students who did not require remedial education with a control group in the six colleges and found that 54.9 percent of the students in the new program graduated within three years compared with only 24.1 percent of the control group. Henry M. Lewin, Emma Garcia, and Donna Linderman, *Benefit-Cost Analysis of Accelerated Study in Associate Programs (ASAP) of the City University of New York: A Study Informing the Expansion of the Program* (March 14, 2014). In another study of this proposal involving three of the colleges, students requiring remedial education were almost twice as likely as students in a control group to have earned a degree within three years (40 percent vs. 22 percent) and were 50 percent more likely (25 percent vs. 17 percent) to be enrolled in a four-year college. Susan Scrivener et al., *Doubling Graduation Rates: Three Year Effects of CUNY's Accelerated Study in Associate Programs (ASAP) for Developmental Education Students,* MDRC (February 2015).

widely enough to lift system-wide graduation rates, however, is still uncertain. Faculty members and their unions may balk at the prospect of abandoning many of the courses they are used to teaching in order to construct a few new pathways. State governments may be unwilling to pay the extra costs involved even though the added expense could be more than counterbalanced by sharply reduced dropout rates, thus lowering the *cost per graduate* below existing levels. Nevertheless, the results from pilot programs that tested these reforms seem promising enough to warrant larger trials to discover whether the approach truly has the potential to increase completion rates substantially.[20]

A Cheaper, Faster Way to Acquire Useful Workforce Skills. Another promising way to increase attainment might be to concentrate on individuals who are already employed, especially the more than thirty million adults who have attended college in the past but never graduated. For these workers, along with many others in today's economy, changes in employment opportunities are occurring more rapidly and unpredictably as a result of technological innovation and global competition. Fewer young people can expect to spend the bulk of their careers with a single employer. Many will experience half a dozen or more job changes during their working lives. In such a world, most college students cannot know what skills they will need to master over their lifetimes, nor can they obtain all the preparation they will require by the age of twenty-one or twenty-five. Instead, they will need periods of additional education lasting from a few days to a year or more at various points in their careers. Already, universities have experienced large increases in the number of older students returning to campus for further education, either to prepare themselves for an entirely new job or simply to continue to succeed in their present field of work.

Meeting these needs has become much easier through the use of online teaching, self-paced learning, and the awarding of credit for skills already mastered whether or not they were learned in college. Online teaching permits working adults to gain the added education they need without leaving their homes or their jobs. Self-paced learning lets learners progress at their own speed and complete vocational training whenever they can demonstrate mastery of the skills being taught. Competency-based education enables students to avoid having to take instruction for skills they can prove they have already acquired in other ways. Together, these innovations allow determined individuals to finish a desired course of study more rapidly and inexpensively than is possible in traditional programs that require students to complete a prescribed number of college courses and classroom hours.[21]

If these convenient ways to prepare for a better job become widely available, many more working adults may make the effort to obtain the additional education they need. It is possible that those who take this route will not obtain all of the nonmarket benefits that result from a traditional BA degree, but they will acquire new skills and with them greater opportunities for a better life and a bigger boost to the productivity of the economy.*

In order to realize the full potential of these methods, however, ways must be found to award credentials for completing programs that give a reliable enough indication of the recipient's knowledge and skills to be widely accepted by employers throughout the area or industry involved.[22] At present, the American labor market has a long way to go to achieve this result. In the words of a recent report issued by the Corporation for a Skilled Workforce, the United States is currently made up of "a chaotic patchwork of sub-degrees, certificates, licenses, and other credentials ... offered by a confusing array of industry and occupational groups, third party validators, and educational providers and systems.... In most cases, there is little clarity about what these credentials mean—their value, their quality, and how they connect."[23]

---

* It does not follow that students who complete a competency-based, self-paced education without having taken general education courses will receive a quality *undergraduate* education sufficient to warrant the award of a BA degree. While career and employment needs may be met through the acquisition of a particular set of skills, it is doubtful that all the advantages of a good undergraduate education can be reduced to a list of work-related competencies. Attempts to do so may well sacrifice important benefits of a traditional college education, such as helping young students discover what they want to do and achieve in life, and providing valuable nonmarket effects, such as better health, more civic involvement, and lower rates of suicide, crime, drug abuse, and other harmful behaviors. It would be premature to encourage such a substantial change in the traditional requirements for a college degree without first taking care to ascertain the effects on these important outcomes.

Under current conditions, then, adults seeking further education to upgrade their skills are often confused, misled, and disappointed by the training programs they enter, while employers complain of difficulty finding the employees they need or judging what applicants for jobs can actually do. By using their convening power and offering financial inducements to bring the interested parties together, government officials may be able to help employers and educators to agree on necessary competencies and establish reliable accrediting mechanisms to verify that the needed skills have been mastered.

A successful system of this kind should be attractive to all concerned. For employers, a cheaper, more flexible education aligned with current workforce needs offers abundant possibilities for overcoming the skills gap described in chapter 1. For policy-makers struggling to raise the educational levels of America's workforce, online education and competency-based, self-paced programs create efficient, inexpensive ways of acquiring additional skills, especially for working adults who entered college in the past but did not graduate. These older students may prove to be more capable of demanding study and more motivated to improve their knowledge and skills than many of the poorly prepared young high school graduates who will otherwise make up most of the new undergraduates needed to regain America's global lead in educational attainment.

Despite the efforts described in the last few pages, it is still unlikely that America will regain the global lead in the education of young adults by 2020 or even 2025. Nevertheless, various ideas for improvement that are already circulating offer promise for the future. If they survive a careful evaluation, they may help to raise rates of attainment significantly above their present level. Such progress will be well worth having even if more ambitious goals elude our grasp.

᠍

CHAPTER TWELVE

Improving the Quality of Education

INCREASING GRADUATION RATES AND LEVELS of educational attainment will accomplish little if students do not learn something of lasting value. President Obama acknowledged as much in 2009 by defining his objective in terms of an increase in "quality degrees." Economists have confirmed that how much students learn matters far more than whether they graduate.[1] Yet federal efforts over the last several years have focused much more on increasing the number of Americans who go to college than on improving the education they receive once they get there. The same could be said about the work of state officials.

By concentrating so heavily on graduation rates and attainment levels, policy-makers are ignoring danger signs that the amount students learn in college may have declined over the past few decades and could well continue to do so in the years to come. The reasons for concern have been discussed in earlier chapters and can be summarized as follows.

- College students today seem to be spending much less time on their coursework than their predecessors did fifty years ago, and evidence of their abilities suggests that they are probably learning less than they once did and quite possibly less than their counterparts in many other advanced industrial countries.[2]
- Employers complain that many graduates they hire are deficient, not so much in job-specific knowledge as in basic skills such as writing, problem solving, and critical thinking that college leaders and their faculties consistently rank among the most important goals of an undergraduate education.[3]
- Most of the millions of additional students needed to increase educational attainment levels will come to campus poorly prepared for

college work, creating a danger that higher graduation rates will be achievable only by lowering academic standards.

- More than two-thirds of college instructors today are not on the tenure track but are lecturers serving on year-to-year contracts. Many of them are hired without undergoing the vetting commonly used in appointing tenure-track professors. Studies indicate that extensive use of such instructors may contribute to higher dropout rates and to grade inflation.[4]

- Finally, the quality of education is at risk because of the substantial cuts in state support per student over the past thirty years for the public colleges and community colleges that will bear most of the burden of increasing educational attainment levels. Existing research suggests that failing to increase appropriations to keep pace with enrollment growth tends to reduce learning and even lower graduation rates.[5]

While some college leaders are making serious efforts to improve the quality of teaching, many others seem content with their existing programs. Presidents and chief academic officers tend to have a much more favorable impression of their students' readiness for the workforce than do the employers who hire their graduates.[6] They are also much more confident about their success in training students to write and think critically than tests of these skills would seem to indicate.[7] Although they recognize the existence of problems affecting higher education as a whole, such as grade inflation or a decline in the rigor of academic standards, few of them seem to believe that these difficulties exist on their own campus.[8] If they do acknowledge problems in student learning, they tend to attribute most of the difficulty to the poor preparation of students before they enroll. In fact, however, several of the deficiencies exhibited by undergraduates persist throughout their college years even though they could be improved by appropriate changes in existing practices.[9]

SOME IMMEDIATE IMPROVEMENTS

Although the most substantial ways to improve educational quality may take a number of years to carry out, there are a few useful initiatives that could be implemented immediately. To begin with, many colleges present their students with a formidable array of courses, majors, and extracurricular opportunities but do little beyond offering broad generalities to describe what students can gain from their undergraduate education, and how the classes they take can further these aims. Yet firsthand accounts of student life at various colleges indicate that many undergraduates do not feel that the material conveyed in their readings and lectures has much relevance to their lives, either now or in the future.[10] Sentiments of this kind suggest either that the courses involved do not in fact contribute much to the ultimate goals that colleges claim to value, or that instructors are not taking sufficient care to explain the larger aims of their courses and why they should matter to students. In either case, remedial action is needed, since the motivation of many undergraduates appears to be suffering and with it the effort they devote to their courses.

Other studies suggest that many instructors do not teach their courses in ways best calculated to achieve the ends that faculties themselves consider vitally important. For example, one investigator studied samples of the examinations given at elite liberal arts colleges and research universities. Although 99 percent of professors consider critical thinking an "essential" or "very important" goal of a college education, fewer than 20 percent of the exam questions actually tested for this skill.[11] A large majority of the questions simply called for lower-order competencies such as recall of information or comprehension of written material. While some improvement may have occurred since these studies were published, such practices still appear to be commonplace.*

---

* One recent study reports that 89 percent of California professors regarded critical thinking as a fundamental goal, but "only 9 percent were able to explicate how they taught to encourage critical

Now that faculties on most campuses have defined the learning objectives of their college and its various departments and programs, it should be possible to review recent examinations to determine whether individual professors, programs, and departments are actually designing their courses to achieve these goals instead of merely seeking to "cover" the relevant subject matter. As a further indication, college authorities could examine their student evaluation forms and modify them where necessary to ask students whether they believe that the stated goals were emphasized in the courses they took.* Since faculty members themselves have chosen the objectives, they should be moved by the results to consider whether they need to take steps to bring their teaching (and their exams) into closer alignment with their goals.

Another problem deserving immediate attention is the limited time many undergraduates spend on coursework and the modest demands often made on them for reading, working on problem sets, and writing papers. Since the average time devoted to studying varies widely among different colleges, there should be ample room for many campuses to require more of their students. Colleges lacking evidence about the study habits of their undergraduates can inform themselves through confidential surveys. Faculties can then review the findings and consider whether homework assignments should be increased and other steps taken to encourage greater student effort and improve learning.

Finally, the evidence presented in chapter 5 indicates quite convincingly that large numbers of college seniors have a greatly exaggerated notion of how much they have learned at college in mastering skills such as writing, critical thinking, and problem solving that are central to un-

---

thinking." The same study also stated that 70 percent of faculty at nonselective colleges rely on multiple-choice tests supplied by textbook publishers, even though multiple-choice exams usually test for recall rather than critical thinking. Thomas R. Bailey, Shanna S. Jaggars, and Davis Jenkins, *Redesigning America's Community Colleges: A Clearer Path to Success* (2015), pp. 85–86.

* In one highly selective college where the principal aim of the general education program was expressly declared to be fostering critical thinking, student evaluation forms were revised to ask undergraduates whether they felt that the general education course they were evaluating had helped to improve their ability to think critically and reason carefully. Although students expressed great satisfaction with many of the courses, less than 10 percent of the offerings were thought by members of the class to have helped them to think critically.

dergraduate education.[12] Such overconfidence leaves students ill-prepared for their careers and weakens their motivation to work harder in college at increasing their knowledge and skills.

The vast difference between how well seniors *think* they can perform and their *actual* proficiencies (according to tests of basic skills and employer evaluations) suggests that many colleges are failing to give students an adequate account of their progress. Grade inflation may also contribute to excessive confidence, suggesting a need to work with faculties to restore appropriate standards.˙ Yet tougher grading alone is unlikely to solve the problem. Better feedback on student papers and exams will be even more important in order to give undergraduates a fuller, more accurate sense of how much progress they have actually made and what more they need to accomplish before they graduate.

MORE SUBSTANTIAL REFORMS

In addition to the immediate steps just described, there are more fundamental changes that will take longer to achieve but could eventually yield even greater gains in the quality of undergraduate education.

Improving Graduate Education. One important reform would be to reconfigure graduate programs to give aspiring professors a better preparation for teaching. The current model for educating PhDs is, and always has been, heavily oriented toward research. As late as two or three generations ago, that model may have seemed defensible. Much less was then known about how students learn and how much they learned in college. Moreover, large majorities of new PhDs, at least in the better graduate programs, found positions where research was primary, either in major universities or in industry or government. Today, however, fewer PhDs obtain tenure-track appointments in research universities;

˙Now that a majority of faculty serve on short-term contracts, deans and department chairs seeking to take such steps will have to convince instructors that they will not be penalized when their reappointment is under consideration because of student complaints about tougher standards and stricter grading practices.

many find employment in colleges that are chiefly devoted to teaching, or work as adjunct instructors and are not expected to do research.

There is also much more now that aspiring college instructors need to know in order to teach effectively. A large and increasing body of useful knowledge has accumulated about learning and pedagogy. Numerous studies have been done on the design and effectiveness of alternative methods of instruction. Meanwhile, the advent of computers and other technologies has given rise to new methods of teaching that require special training for effective use. As evidence accumulates about promising ways of engaging students actively, identifying difficulties they are having in learning the material, and adjusting methods of teaching accordingly, the current gaps in the preparation most graduate students receive become more and more of a handicap.

Universities have already taken rudimentary steps to prepare their graduate students to teach by giving them opportunities to assist professors in large lecture courses and by creating centers where they can get help to become better instructors. More departments are beginning to provide (or even require) a limited amount of instruction in how to teach. Nevertheless, it is no longer possible to equip students adequately for a career in the classroom simply by allowing them to serve as largely unsupervised teaching assistants. Nor is it sufficient to create centers where graduate students can receive a brief orientation and attend a semester-long class or a few voluntary sessions on teaching. Useful as these opportunities are, a more substantial preparation is required and will become ever more necessary as the body of relevant knowledge continues to grow. Like other attempts to improve the quality of education, programs to accomplish this result should be evaluated carefully to determine whether they actually enable participants to teach more effectively. If successful, however, such training could have far-reaching effects in sustaining the current interest in teaching and encouraging young faculty to engage in a continuing process of experimentation to find better ways to help students learn.

It is curious that most departments have done so little along these lines. With all the talk in graduate school circles about preparing doctoral students for jobs outside academia, one has to wonder why departments would spend time readying PhD candidates for entirely different careers before they have developed adequate programs for the academic posts that graduate schools are supposed to serve, and that most of their students continue to occupy.

It is possible that faculties have reacted as they have because they are not equipped to teach the kinds of material about teaching and learning that are needed today to prepare graduate students as teachers. Most professors of management or medieval history know little about learning theory or the extensive literature on the undergraduate curriculum. Provosts and deans, who could easily enlist competent teachers for such instruction from elsewhere in the university, may hesitate to do so since graduate education has always been the exclusive domain of the departments. Whatever the reason, enterprising funders might consider giving grants to graduate schools or departments willing to make the necessary reforms. If even a few leading universities responded to such an invitation, others would probably follow suit.

Creating a Teaching Faculty. Another promising way to improve undergraduate education would be to encourage efforts to create well-trained, full-time teaching faculties to staff lower-division college courses. The seeds of such a change already exist through the proliferation of instructors who are not on the tenure track but are hired on a year-to-year basis or a somewhat longer term to teach basic undergraduate courses. Such instructors now constitute as much as 70 percent of all college instructors. At present, many of them are paid less than four thousand dollars per course and receive little preparation or support for their teaching. Often, they work part-time, are hired haphazardly by department chairs or their designees, receive little supervision, and lack adequate office space, health benefits, and other conditions routinely provided to tenure-track professors.

The multiplication of adjunct instructors, especially in community colleges and comprehensive universities, has largely been an ad hoc response to the need to cut costs in order to cope with severe financial pressures resulting from reductions in state support and larger student enrollments. The current situation, however, seems highly unstable. Already, adjuncts are beginning to join unions.[13] Meanwhile, researchers are discovering that relying on casually hired, part-time teachers can have adverse effects on graduation rates and the quality of instruction, and can contribute to grade inflation.[14] Sooner or later, the present practices seem bound to give way to more satisfactory arrangements.

While the end result is uncertain, one plausible outcome would be to create a carefully selected, full-time teaching faculty whose members lack tenure but receive appointments for a significant term of years with enforceable guarantees of academic freedom and adequate notice if their contracts are not renewed. Such instructors would receive opportunities for professional development to become more knowledgeable and proficient as teachers. They would not be expected to do research of a traditional kind but instead would teach more hours per week than the tenured faculty. In return, they would receive adequate salaries, benefits, and facilities and would share in deliberations over educational policy, though not in matters involving research and the appointment and promotion of tenure-track professors.

A teaching faculty created along these lines would have marked advantages from the standpoint of improving undergraduate education.* Instructors would be better trained in teaching and learning than the current research-oriented faculty. Being chiefly engaged in teaching, they might also be more inclined to experiment with new and better methods of instruction if they were encouraged to do so.

Members of the tenured faculty with a flair for teaching large undergraduate courses could still be free to do so if they wished. Such profes-

---

* Some faculty members may fear that such a proposal will lower the quality of undergraduate education. Since large majorities of undergraduate instructors are already off the tenure track, such concern plainly lacks substance. Moreover, what little research exists does not support such fears with respect to a teaching faculty of the kind described above. For example, the president of Northwestern University and a faculty colleague measured the effects of full-time non-tenure-track instructors in introductory economics and political science courses on the tendency of students to take advanced courses in the same field and the grades they received in such courses. The authors found that these instructors were more effective than their tenure-track colleagues. David Figlio, Morton O. Schapiro, and Kevin B. Soter, *Are Tenure Track Professors Better Teachers?* National Bureau of Economic Research, Working Paper 19406 (September 2013).

sors add much to the quality of the college experience, and their partic-ipation should be welcomed. However, many of their colleagues prefer to concentrate on mentoring future scholars and teaching advanced un-dergraduate courses and seminars while reserving ample time to pursue their research. They would find it easier to do so in a university with a corps of full-time instructors devoted entirely to teaching introductory and general education courses.

The creation of a teaching faculty for lower-division courses is not a new idea. It was tried at one time with foundation support but aban-doned because few doctoral students preferred a role that was widely regarded as a second-class alternative.[15] Today, however, more graduate students claim to be interested in positions largely devoted to teaching. Moreover, the existence of such a faculty is now an established fact on most campuses; the only open questions have to do with the terms and conditions of employment given its members. The arrangements de-scribed above would represent a considerable improvement over the sta-tus quo. They would also seem far more appropriate to a world in which teaching has become more challenging and important than it seemed a few decades ago.

A reform of this sort would undoubtedly cost more than most uni-versities currently pay their non-tenure-track instructors (though less than having tenured faculty teach the lower-level courses). Even so, the shabby treatment of many part-time instructors is hard to justify, and higher costs seem inevitable once adjunct faculties become more orga-nized and use their collective strength to bargain for better terms. As knowledge accumulates about the adverse effects on the quality of edu-cation resulting from the hiring of large numbers of underpaid and badly treated part-time instructors, many colleges may eventually find it advantageous to begin the process of providing better terms of employ-ment and better training for a full-time teaching faculty.

Progress may have to come gradually as finances permit. But the tran-sition to a full-time teaching faculty, coupled with a greater emphasis on teaching and learning in graduate schools, could eventually do a lot to improve the quality of undergraduate education. Instead of today's legions of casually hired, underpaid, and insecure adjunct instructors, a substantial segment of the college faculty would possess the time, the training, and the job security to participate in a continuing effort to develop more effective methods of instruction to engage their students and help them derive more lasting value from their classes.

Rethinking the Undergraduate Curriculum. The changes just described could also help to bring about useful reforms in the undergraduate curriculum of four-year colleges. As pointed out in chapter 2, the familiar division into fields of concentration, electives, and general education leaves too little room for students to pursue all of the objectives that professors themselves deem important for a well-rounded college education. This tripartite structure, with its emphasis on the major and its embrace of distribution requirements and extensive electives, was introduced by research universities and designed more to satisfy the interests of a tenured, research-oriented faculty than to achieve the various aims of a good undergraduate education. However appropriate the arrangement may have been half a century ago when the tenure-track faculty did the great bulk of undergraduate teaching, it hardly seems justified now that such professors make up only a minority of college instructors and are often more interested in advanced courses and research than in teaching introductory classes or general education courses.

Imperfect as it is, the existing structure is unlikely to change so long as decisions about the curriculum remain under the exclusive control of the tenure-track professors who benefit from the status quo. By now, the standard curriculum has become so firmly rooted that during the periodic reviews conducted in most universities, the faculty rarely pause to examine the tripartite division and its effect upon the established goals of undergraduate education. Instead, the practice of reserving up to half of the required number of college credits for the major is simply taken for granted along with maintaining a distribution requirement and preserving an ample segment of the curriculum for electives. The only serious discussion that typically occurs involves a Procrustean effort to fit the remaining aims of undergraduate education into the limited space that remains.

The most promising way to encourage a genuine debate over the existing structure is by changing the nature of curricular reviews so that all those who play a substantial part in trying to achieve the goals of undergraduate education can participate in the process. It is anomalous to allow the tenure-track faculty to enjoy exclusive power over the curriculum when they provide such a limited share of the teaching. The obvious remedy is to expand the discussions to include the non-tenure-track instructors who currently make up a majority of the teaching faculty. Such a reform might be difficult under current conditions in many colleges where most undergraduate instructors serve part-time, are often chosen haphazardly, and frequently lack either the time or the interest to participate fully in a review of its undergraduate program. If adjunct instructors achieve the status previously described, however, their prominent role in teaching undergraduates should entitle them to a seat at the table to discuss the educational program, including its current structure.* There is even some evidence that tenure-track faculty would be receptive to such a change.[16]

Amending the process of review to include these additional voices does not guarantee that the basic structure will be altered or even discussed. The tripartite division and the allocation of course credits among the three segments are now so well established that they may continue to be taken for granted in most colleges and universities. But opening the discussion to instructors whose self-interest is not so closely linked to the status quo should at least increase the likelihood of a serious discussion of the existing curricular structure to determine whether it truly serves the multiple aims of undergraduate education. The progress

---

* A further change in existing procedures appropriate for most four-year colleges would be to allow some meaningful participation by members of the administrative staff who are prominently involved in college life, such as deans of student affairs and directors of admission. The current division between formal instruction and the extracurriculum is arbitrary, since many goals of undergraduate education, such as moral development and preparation for citizenship, are influenced significantly by the policies for admitting students, the administration of rules for student behavior, the advising of undergraduates, the nature of residential life, and the extracurricular activities in which many students participate. If each of the several traditional aims of undergraduate education is truly important, representatives from all groups responsible for the policies and practices that affect these goals should have something to contribute to reviews of undergraduate education.

already made by accreditors in having faculties define the goals of education should also inspire a closer look at whether the goals are being pursued effectively and whether the current structure interferes with their achievement.

The Need for Education Research. There is an urgent need for more and better research both to improve the quality of undergraduate education and to increase the number of students who complete their studies. Among the many questions deserving further exploration, four lines of inquiry seem especially important.

- How can remedial education be improved? At present, low rates of completion in remedial courses are a major impediment to raising levels of educational attainment. The use of computer-aided instruction in remedial math provides one promising example of the type of improvement that could yield substantial benefits. There are doubtless other possibilities that need to be discovered and carefully evaluated.

- A second important question about which far too little is known involves the kinds of courses or other undergraduate experiences that contribute to such noneconomic benefits in later life as better health, greater civic participation, and lower incidence of substance abuse and other forms of self-destructive behavior. Yet ignorance persists about which aspects of college contribute to these results. Better understanding of these connections could help educators increase the lasting value of a college education while providing a stronger empirical basis for the sweeping claims frequently made about the lifelong benefits of a liberal education. Such understanding would also reduce the risk of inadvertently eliminating valuable aspects of a college education in the rush to find quicker, cheaper ways of preparing students to obtain good jobs of immediate value to economic growth.

- A third subject of importance to raising attainment levels involves the additional steps that should accompany financial aid in order to achieve more substantial increases in graduation rates. Existing research suggests that better advising and other forms of student support may substantially enhance the effect of increased financial aid in boosting the numbers of students who complete their studies. With billions of dollars already being spent on student grants and loans, and the announcement of costly new proposals to further reduce the costs of college, it would clearly be helpful to know more about how to maximize the effects of such subsidies on graduation rates.

- Finally, more work is needed to develop better ways for colleges to measure student learning, not only for critical thinking and writing but for other purposes of undergraduate education, as well as for individual fields of concentration and even single courses.

The importance of this last point can scarcely be overestimated.* Without reliable measures of learning, competition for students can do little to improve the quality of instruction, since applicants have no way of knowing which college offers them the best teaching. Provosts, deans, and departments will have difficulty identifying weaknesses in their academic programs in need of corrective action. Academic leaders will be handicapped in trying to persuade their professors to change the way they teach if they cannot offer convincing evidence that alternative methods will bring improved results. Faculty members will do less to improve their teaching if they continue to lack adequate ways to discover how much their students are learning. Imagine the effect on the

---

*This does not mean that testing and evaluation should play the same role in colleges as it has in public schools. Three guiding principles are especially important. *First*, faculty members should take part in reviewing and adapting the evaluation instruments used. Otherwise, they are much less likely to have confidence in the results. *Second*, evaluations should be used only to help faculty members identify weaknesses and make improvements in their teaching and educational programs. The results should not be used for purposes of salary and promotion or for helping students to decide which college to attend. Existing methods of assessment are not yet reliable enough to be a basis for penalizing and rewarding colleges or their professors. *Third*, evaluations should not be used so often as to interfere with student learning. Where possible, moreover, they should be embedded in regular tests and papers in order to ensure that students will be motivated to try their hardest.

If the principles listed above are not observed, faculties will be much less willing to accept assessment. Instead of making a voluntary effort to improve the quality of teaching, they are likely to resist and to try to ignore or discredit assessment and the instruments used to carry it out.

quality of research and on the very motivation to engage in scientific inquiry if investigators could perform any experiments they chose but were somehow unable to ascertain the results.

The reforms discussed in this chapter could do a lot to improve the quality of undergraduate education (as well as increase levels of attainment). Other useful ideas will doubtless continue to appear. As yet, however, too little attention has been paid to the process by which improvement occurs. How do useful reforms originate? Why has change occurred much more rapidly in some periods than in others? How can the process be encouraged and, if possible, speeded up? These questions have important implications for the effort to meet the current demands on our colleges and universities. They will occupy the next and final chapter in this volume.

CHAPTER THIRTEEN

Encouraging Reform

ONE OF THE MOST NOTEWORTHY DEVELOPMENTS in higher education today is the amount of activity underway to meet the challenges treated in this book. A host of new approaches are being tried in one college or another to increase graduation rates and improve student learning—accelerated remediation, learning communities, computer-based advising, big-data analytics to identify potential dropouts, new ways to assess student learning, adaptive online tutorials, "flipped" classrooms, competency-based education—the list goes on and on. Meanwhile, accreditors are urging college authorities to measure how much their students are learning, states are providing stronger financial incentives to boost enrollments and graduation rates, foundations are making grants to colleges willing to try new methods of remedial instruction, and venture capitalists are bankrolling start-up firms offering innovative ways to improve teaching and increase the efficiency and effectiveness of college services.

Despite all this activity, progress toward raising graduation rates and enhancing teaching and learning has been disappointingly slow. The number of young people earning college degrees has not been rising significantly faster than it did prior to President Obama's challenge to regain America's preeminence in the education of its workforce. Nor have the gaps in graduation rates between rich and poor or whites and minorities narrowed perceptibly. While some progress has occurred in using improved methods of teaching, there is no reliable evidence yet that college students as a whole are learning more; in fact, various indicators suggest that they are learning less today than they did several decades ago. Overall, American higher education shows disquieting signs of resembling our health-care system, boasting some of the finest universities in the world and the highest per-student expenditures of any nation, while exhibiting levels of competency on the part of college graduates as a whole that are below those of many other countries and leaving large percentages of lower-income students and minorities without a college degree.

WHY THE SITUATION TODAY IS DIFFERENT

Why has the response of our colleges to the challenges they face been so much less successful than it was during previous times of transformation, such as the emergence of the modern university in the late nineteenth century or the vast expansion of college enrollments and academic research following World War II? Some observers might point to the lack of university leaders like the "giants" who helped build new universities after the Civil War and led the fight to change the outmoded classical curriculum. Since then, much of the influence over academic affairs has shifted from college presidents to the faculty, while the initiative for expanding access to higher education has moved to the federal government and the Lumina and Gates Foundations. The growing dependence on donors and other influential groups has also caused many academic leaders to pay more attention to their university's reputation and hence become more hesitant to undertake bold reforms that might cause controversy or irritate important constituencies. Meanwhile, the need to raise ever greater sums of money and manage a much larger bureaucracy has taken a toll on the time that even the most conscientious presidents can spend on academic matters.[1]

These trends, however, real as they are, can hardly be the principal reason for the slow rate of progress. Chief academic officers and deans may not fully take the place of reform-minded presidents, but they can still exercise some leadership in matters of teaching and research. Moreover, none of the influential groups that matter most to university presidents—be they government officials, business leaders, or major foundations—are opposed to raising graduation rates or enhancing student learning. On the contrary, all enthusiastically support increasing the numbers of college-educated Americans and helping them to learn more. Some professors may not relish teaching growing numbers of underprepared students with the same enthusiasm they display for working with bright, motivated undergraduates. Even so, most instructors in the community colleges that will absorb the bulk of the additional students believe strongly in opening doors to young people who have had few opportunities heretofore. Professors in research universities may be slow to embrace new methods of teaching, but they too profess a strong desire to help their students gain the knowledge, skills, and other attributes to live fulfilling lives. It is doubtful that many faculties would refuse to change if they knew what they could do to help their students learn more.

Could a simple lack of resources be the reason for the sluggish response of colleges and universities? Certainly, money is a big problem for many institutions. Over the past thirty years, most public community colleges and universities have received diminishing funds per student from their states. Private colleges other than the most selective have had to give larger and larger discounts from their published tuitions to attract enough students to fill their classrooms and balance their budgets. Meanwhile, the public resists almost any proposal to raise taxes while condemning colleges for their constantly rising tuitions.

Although these financial difficulties are real, one can exaggerate their importance. The federal government currently devotes more than $170 billion each year to helping larger numbers of students go to college. In 2016, leading Democratic politicians called for additional billions to reduce the cost of college and encourage more high school graduates to enroll and earn a degree. Several governors have recently done the same. Granted, the polarization of politics dims the prospects for enacting such proposals into law. Still, given the support of the business community for increasing the number of college graduates and improving the quality of their education, it is hard to believe that lawmakers would resist for very long if they were convinced that added dollars would actually raise graduation rates and help students become more productive employees.

All things considered, then, though insufficient academic leadership and financial resources undoubtedly play a role, a strong case can be made that the principal reason for the weak response of so many colleges and universities is a pervasive lack of knowledge about how to proceed— how to remediate underprepared students successfully, how to keep students from dropping out, and how to inspire undergraduates to work harder and learn more during college. Without sufficient knowledge, even money and leadership will not succeed in achieving the desired results.

In this respect, the contrast with earlier periods of successful transformation is striking. During the decades at the close of the nineteenth century, not only were the needs of an industrializing society becoming clear; there were prominent academic leaders who knew what universities had to do—train aspiring faculty members for research, loosen the requirements of the traditional curriculum to provide more practical courses and greater student choice, and build stronger professional schools, especially in law and business, to support the new economy. The generosity of wealthy individuals and foundations gave universities the money they needed to accomplish these goals. Following World War II, the needs for reform were likewise clear—strengthening campus-based research, educating many more students, and expanding graduate programs to train the professors to staff a rapidly growing higher education system. Once again, academic leaders knew how to respond. With generous government support, they had little difficulty in getting the job done. If today's educators and public officials knew as much about how to increase graduation rates and improve the quality of education, they might well have achieved similar success.

THE CURRENT PREDICAMENT

The dilemma facing government officials in trying to bring about a massive growth in educational attainment reveals itself in the strategies they have chosen to achieve their goal. President Obama concentrated on trying to increase access to college by lowering its cost. If successful, the effect of this policy would be to increase the enrollment of marginal students, since the vast majority of well-prepared high school graduates already attend college. Officials in many states have elected to reinforce the federal effort by increasing their appropriations to public colleges that achieve an agreed-on increase in the number of graduates while cutting their funding for colleges that fail to reach their goal. However, since more of the entering students will not be adequately prepared for college work, stronger incentives could well cause campuses to lower academic standards in order to meet their graduation goals. Moreover, the arrival of larger cohorts of poorly prepared, low-income students will tend to increase the number of college students who rely on government-backed loans to pay for college but fail to repay their debts, either because they drop out without earning a degree or because they graduate without the knowledge and skills required to find and retain a well-paid job. Eventually, the government may find it necessary to deny aid to colleges whose former students have exceptionally high default rates. Such a policy, however, will tend to discourage colleges from accepting the very high-risk students that government officials hope to educate in order to raise attainment levels to meet the needs of the economy.

The only way to resolve this dilemma and still increase attainment levels substantially will be for high schools and colleges to discover better ways of preparing low-performing students to succeed in the classroom and graduate with the knowledge and skills to become productive employees. Thus far, attempts to meet this challenge have not been successful. Over the past twenty-five years, repeated efforts to improve our public schools have not produced significantly higher levels of achievement or reduced the numbers of graduates who require remedial courses before they can begin their regular college studies. Neither community colleges nor for-profits have yet managed to increase the percentage of students who complete remediation successfully or to raise their graduation rates to anything like the levels required to lead the world in the education of our workforce. Even at current levels of attainment, employers complain that many college graduates are deficient in basic skills such as writing, speaking, critical thinking, and problem solving.

It would be unfortunate to abandon efforts to increase attainment and enhance quality. Achieving this goal will improve our ability to compete successfully in the world economy. It will give new life to the American Dream by offering greater opportunities to millions of citizens who are currently unable to enjoy better jobs and more fulfilling lives. It will strengthen our society by multiplying the many civic and other non-pecuniary benefits associated with a quality college education.

The difficulties involved, however, are formidable. Proven ways to graduate large numbers of additional students possessing the skills required to flourish both in the workplace and in life either do not yet exist, or, if they do exist, are not in widespread use. For this reason, success is not likely to occur without a good deal of innovation and advancement over existing educational practices. It is therefore important to take a closer look at how new ideas for improving education emerge, get tested, and eventually become widely adopted.

THE PROCESS OF IMPROVEMENT

For purposes of analysis, the current process can be divided into several stages. The first step involves the discovery of a new way to improve higher education by making it more accessible, more effective, or less expensive. The second stage calls for testing and evaluating the new idea to make sure it actually works. The third phase consists of early adoption—the willingness of a few educational institutions to take a chance on a promising proposal and invest the money, time, and effort to put it to use and set an example for others to follow. The final step is marked by a widespread embrace of the new idea so that it becomes the normal practice, and failure to use it comes to be viewed as a problem requiring explanation.

Discovery begins with someone who recognizes a problem with existing practice and tries to find a way to improve it. Such recognition may not come automatically. Problems can go undetected for long periods of time. Even when they are perceived, they may be considered beyond the capability of human beings to rectify or ignored because they are thought to be the responsibility of someone else.

In many respects, higher education seems an ideal setting for identifying opportunities to improve educational programs. The system is composed of countless centers of initiative through its thousands of separate colleges and universities, each with many highly intelligent, independent instructors who profess a genuine interest in teaching and helping their students learn. On closer scrutiny, however, the prevailing environment is not as ideal as it first appears. Some problems go largely unrecognized by college leaders and their faculties for long periods of time; the deficiencies of lecturing for promoting student learning provide a recent case in point. Other problems receive little attention for extended periods because they are assumed to be the responsibility of others. High dropout rates, for example, were long regarded as the result of insufficient ability or motivation on the part of students, not as a condition that colleges should try to improve.

Fortunately, recent developments have increased the likelihood that problems involving graduation rates or the quality of education will be identified and possible remedies discovered. Under pressure from accreditors, campus authorities are doing more to try to assess how much students are learning and identify where weaknesses exist. Researchers have acquired new insights about motivation and cognition that can suggest better ways to teach. Advances in technology are yielding fresh ideas about how to enhance learning and prevent dropouts. Finally, entrepreneurs with financial backing have started to look for deficiencies in higher education that can be overcome or alleviated with the aid of new technologies.

To be sure, conditions are not perfect. One can always wish for more funding for the research from which new insights about learning will emerge. It would also be helpful if more faculty members tried to identify problems in their teaching and search for ways to overcome them. Still, it is fair to say that the current environment has begun to produce more potentially useful ideas for improving higher education than have appeared for a very long time, if ever.

The second stage—involving the testing of promising ideas—is especially important because so many attractive possibilities for improving education fail when closely evaluated. During the first decade after the

Institute for Education Sciences was created and began using rigorous methods to discover which reforms actually "worked," only eleven proposals out of ninety reviewed survived the test of random-assignment evaluation.[2] With such a low rate of success, careful assessment is essential to avoid wasting a lot of time and money on intriguing ideas that prove to be ineffective.

Support for testing and assessment has been growing in recent decades. The National Science Foundation has invested heavily in evaluations to prove the superiority of active forms of instruction over lecturing in the teaching of large STEM courses. Major foundations such as Gates, Lumina, and Mellon have all spent goodly sums on testing promising ideas for increasing graduation rates, measuring student learning, and improving remedial instruction and the effectiveness of public schools.

Despite these favorable trends, the current process for testing new ideas is far from ideal. Compared with sectors such as health care, national defense, and numerous other industries, the funding available to evaluate proposals for improving education continues to be paltry. Granted, the field lacks the successful track record of research in the physical and biomedical sciences, and its findings are more vulnerable to politicization and ideological controversy. Nevertheless, while these reasons help to explain the neglect of educational research, they do not justify it.

The third stage in bringing about reform requires a decision by a few potential users to try a promising new idea. Early adoption "breaks the ice" by subjecting innovations to a further test and inspiring others to follow suit. Users will sometimes test a new method on their own initiative. At other times, early adoption is brought about by an outside entity such as a foundation or a government agency that enlists colleges to try a promising proposal in order to evaluate its potential. In such cases, testing and early adoption are combined in a single project.

Adoption requires some kind of communication that informs potential users about a new way of doing things and tells them how to proceed. Scholarly periodicals often perform this function. Professors Eric Mazur and Uri Treisman each developed important improvements in teaching and published descriptions of their work in discipline-based journals.[3] Fortunately, both men not only had a good idea; they had tested their methods themselves in convincing ways and achieved dramatic results. Within a decade, scores of other college instructors were using these methods to improve their own teaching.

Effective communication can also occur through various other channels. Firms such as Eduventures, and periodicals such as the *Chronicle of Higher Education*, perform this function. Think tanks, foundations, and other nonprofit organizations publish reports of new ideas and disseminate them widely by putting them on the Web. Higher education associations often discuss promising ideas at meetings of their members and persuade member colleges to try them. For example, with foundation assistance, the Association of American Colleges & Universities has enlisted several hundred member colleges to join in helping to develop and test a set of common goals for undergraduate education, including an extensive array of competencies and knowledge together with rubrics for evaluating student progress.[4]

Are current efforts of this kind sufficient for the purpose? Or are there promising ideas "born to blush unseen" like the flowers in Gray's "Elegy Written in a Country Churchyard"?[5] One can think of one or two such examples. Critics have complained for over a century about the failure of graduate programs to prepare aspiring PhDs as teachers and educators as well as researchers. The need for such preparation has continued to increase, yet no university has launched a truly comprehensive program to serve the purpose, nor have funding sources given them much encouragement to do so. Whether such examples are commonplace, however, or merely rare exceptions is unknown, at least to this author.

The final stage in the development and use of new ideas is the adoption of successful improvements by a majority of potential users. Ideally, spreading of this kind should occur quite rapidly once a significant number of early users have tried a proposal and achieved clear-cut success. A striking example in higher education and elsewhere is the computer, which has found so many helpful applications that it is a rare campus that does not employ some of them. More than six million current students have taken at least one course online, while e-mail, along with other uses, such as online registration, course scheduling, and course management systems, exist almost everywhere. These improvements are sufficiently valuable in terms of convenience, speed, and occasionally lower costs that it would be difficult for colleges to explain why they did *not* take advantage of them.

Progress occurs less swiftly for the spread of new and improved methods of instruction. The decentralized nature of colleges with their corps of largely autonomous instructors offers fertile ground for the discovery of new ideas but tends to impede their rapid diffusion. Inventive professors such as Mazur and Treisman may have had their methods adopted by hundreds of instructors, but thousands more continue teaching as before. Nobel physicist Carl Wieman, after years of speaking and writing in behalf of active methods of teaching and learning backed by substantial funding and support from the National Science Foundation, has been disheartened by the sluggish response. Studies of the adoption of Wieman's proposals reveal that even scientists who are well aware of his writings and familiar with evidence of the successful use of active teaching often fail to use the new methods in their own classes.[6]

Why does the diffusion of good ideas for improving classroom teaching frequently stall or proceed very slowly? For one thing, since few colleges use reliable methods of assessment, no one may be aware that there are problems with the amount that students are learning. The competition among colleges to attract more and better students creates little incentive to improve teaching, since applicants have no way of knowing which institutions will give them the best instruction. In most colleges and universities, there is no constituency clamoring for innovations in teaching. Students, who have most to gain from better methods, do not realize that they could be learning more, and tend to be content with the status quo. They often give good evaluations to engaging lecturers and initially resist efforts to introduce more effective forms of instruction.

The incentives for professors to improve their teaching are also remarkably weak. As pointed out in chapter 3, new methods of instruction seldom bring tangible advantages to the adopter. Interviews with scientists who know of Wieman's writings on the drawbacks of lecturing reveal that many of them are deterred by a concern that learning to use his ideas would take time away from research, which brings much greater recognition within the profession, along with prizes, invitations to speak, attractive job offers, and other signs of respect seldom accorded to innovative teachers. In most four-year colleges, surveys of professors repeatedly find that the number of pages of published research is the single most important factor in making tenure and promotion decisions.[7] Other studies covering a wide variety of four-year colleges have shown that research is routinely rewarded when salaries are set, while the number of hours spent on teaching is negatively correlated with compensation.[8] Even faculty members who do wish to try new instructional methods are often discouraged by a lack of technical support or financial help to cover the costs involved.

The environment for adopting better techniques of instruction is least favorable in community colleges—the institutions that need them most in order to improve remediation and increase graduation rates. Less money is available to support innovation than in other types of college. Most teachers are adjunct instructors who seldom receive opportunities for professional development and lack the time or the job security to experiment with new methods of teaching. Moreover, as an Aspen Institute study discovered, few community college presidents are chosen or encouraged by trustees to undertake major improvements in teaching or student outcomes.[9]

In summary, then, the process of reform and its diffusion throughout higher education presents a mixed picture. The system is currently doing quite well at producing innovative ideas. It also does reasonably well at identifying and publicizing proposals that show promise of lowering costs, improving learning, or reducing dropout rates. It is less effective, however, at supplying funds for evaluating new ideas, especially for testing them to see whether they can be made to work "at scale."[10]

The greatest obstacles to progress occur at the final stage when proven reforms need to spread throughout the system. Diffusion can occur if the new idea promises to yield a tangible result such as additional revenue, greater convenience, or lower costs. That is why a number of useful administrative applications of computer technology have spread so rapidly. The speed of adopting promising ideas also tends to be greater for changes that are easy to implement or initiatives that do not require persuading the faculty to alter their accustomed ways. Thus large numbers of colleges in the 1970s were quite quick to introduce simple changes in the freshman year such as the addition of small seminars, learning communities, and "how to succeed in college" courses once academic officers became aware that large numbers of students were dropping out before they began their sophomore year. On the other hand, changes in accustomed teaching methods are much harder to achieve, since instructors have complete power to decide how to conduct their classes and receive little encouragement to change.

Overall, given the prevailing incentives and priorities in most non-profit colleges and the independence enjoyed by their faculties, one would expect good ideas to spread more slowly than in industry and commerce, where employers have more power over their workforce and competition and the desire for profit provide a potent motive for improvement. Sure enough, twenty-five years ago, Malcolm Getz, John Siegfried, and Kathryn Anderson reviewed a large number of useful changes and confirmed this hypothesis: new ideas in higher education took up to three times longer to spread than improvements in for-profit industries.[11] In view of the sluggish response of most colleges to the challenges currently before them, there is little reason to believe that the situation has changed fundamentally in the last quarter of a century.

SPEEDING UP THE PACE OF PROGRESS

How might the process of reform be improved, and who can improve it? Responsibility must clearly begin with colleges and universities themselves. There are plenty of opportunities for progress, but too few are currently recognized because most colleges have done very little, at least until recently, to discover how much their students are learning or why so many of them leave before earning a degree.

Having seldom engaged in rigorous self-scrutiny, many college leaders and their faculties are excessively optimistic about the performance of their own institution. As earlier chapters have revealed, surveys find that most presidents and chief academic officers are much too confident about such matters as the preparedness of their graduates for the workforce or the extent of grade inflation on their campus.[12] Instructors are likewise more satisfied than they should be about their proficiency in the classroom. Surveys have shown that the vast majority of professors consider themselves better-than-average teachers.[13]

The key to overcoming complacency is to obtain better evidence of how each college is performing. Fortunately, there are simple ways of doing so. Several hundred colleges are already receiving much useful information from the National Survey of Student Engagement (NSSE). Every college can compare its dropout rates with those of carefully selected peer institutions to learn why some of these colleges do better at remediating and graduating students. Course evaluation forms can ask students to estimate how much time they spent per week preparing for class, how much of the assigned reading they completed, and the extent to which they think that the objectives of the college (such as improving critical thinking) were actually achieved. Since student evaluations are not especially reliable, more rigorous methods are also needed to ascertain how much students have learned, not simply overall but in individual courses and majors. The successful innovations developed by Treisman and Mazur both began with convincing evidence from a particular course that revealed a serious deficiency in student learning. Academic leaders could multiply such discoveries by working with their faculty to devise short before-and-after tests in individual courses, beginning with subjects such as science, mathematics, statistics, and foreign languages where student progress can be measured relatively easily. Further evidence of student learning may become increasingly available from analyses of information recorded in online courses to discover how students go about solving problems and applying the knowledge conveyed by their assigned readings.

College officials could also try to increase awareness of successful new methods of teaching developed elsewhere. A member of the staff could be tasked with scanning the voluminous literature to identify promising ideas that might be worth trying. Descriptions of the improvements could then be widely disseminated on campus.

A bolder step for colleges to consider would be to follow the lead of other large organizations by using new ways to elicit imaginative ideas for improvement from their own communities. Universities are filled with highly intelligent, creative people who are seldom, if ever, asked to participate in volunteering solutions to educational problems on their campus. There are several ways by which to solicit such suggestions— crowdsourcing, where faculty members, students, administrators, and even selected alumni are invited to submit ideas for lowering dropout rates, inducing students to do more of their assigned readings, or halting grade inflation, just to mention a few of the problems in need of creative remedies. Alternatively, task forces could be assembled composed of members of diverse backgrounds and talents to consider particular problems. Competitions could be held among different teams to think about ways to address still other questions. Panels of interested faculty and academic leaders could then be appointed to decide which of the proposals elicited by these methods deserve to be evaluated for possible use. While success is not guaranteed, experience in other large organizations suggests that expanding the number and diversity of participants in thinking about challenging problems can often yield surprisingly imaginative solutions.

In addition, most colleges could do much more to encourage faculty members to try new methods of teaching by offering them released time, technical assistance, and funds to cover the cost of implementation. Successful innovations could be taken into consideration in setting salaries and recognized in other ways. Such actions would not only be useful in facilitating change; they could also help to convince the faculty that the administration is truly serious about reform.

Finally, graduate schools could make greater efforts to equip their PhD candidates with the knowledge and skills of teaching and learning while colleges begin to replace their part-time adjunct instructors with a full-time, better-trained teaching faculty as described in chapter 12. These changes would eventually create a corps of undergraduate teachers possessing the knowledge, the job security, the incentive, and the encouragement to participate actively in an ongoing quest for new and better ways to help their students learn.

Campus leaders are often hesitant to take the steps just outlined. They worry that the faculty will resent administrative initiatives that could appear to suggest a criticism of their teaching. If they did take action, instructors might resist efforts to measure what their students have learned, either from an instinctive apprehension over what may be discovered or out of fear that the evaluations will be crude and unreliable yet used against them when salary increases and promotions are considered. Beset by such concerns, academic officers and deans often feel that they cannot take the time or risk the controversy that serious attempts at reform might entail.

Trustees could help to overcome this inertia and launch a systematic program of self-scrutiny by asking the president for reliable information about dropout rates, the progress students are making in the classroom, the quality and effectiveness of teaching, and the steps college officials have taken to encourage and support improvements. While some boards will take such action, however, many others will not. They may protest that they are not competent to evaluate the material they are given, or they may be unwilling to risk antagonizing the president or causing controversy that could interfere with fund-raising or other pressing matters. As a result, forces from outside the college or university will often have to supply the necessary encouragement.

Accreditors are a natural body to turn to, since they have been asking for information about student outcomes for the past twenty years and have achieved some degree of success. As yet, however, they have largely confined their work to urging college authorities to disclose their graduation rates, define their learning objectives, and apply some method to assess the overall progress of their students without inquiring more deeply into the adequacy of campus efforts to improve performance.

Having come this far, accreditors could begin to urge the colleges they visit to evaluate learning in individual classes and departments, at least in subjects where such measurements can be readily carried out. They could suggest (not demand) new methods of instruction, new steps to improve remediation, and other innovations that have proved successful in comparable institutions. They could urge deans and department chairs to examine the syllabi and exams used in randomly selected courses to determine whether instructors are aligning their teaching with the learning objectives they claim to be pursuing.

Corporate leaders and human resources executives, who often express dissatisfaction over the competence of the recent college graduates they hire, could likewise play a constructive role. They could first consult with their human resources staff to be sure that all those involved in hiring are consistent and clear about the qualities they are seeking. They could then initiate meetings with campus officials either individually or in concert with other employers in order to make sure that their criticisms are being heard. They could also use such occasions to arrive at a better understanding with college authorities on how to allocate responsibility for workforce preparation.

Finally, governments (along with interested foundations) could do a lot to strengthen the process of discovering and implementing useful new ideas for improving teaching and learning. In particular, they could invest more heavily in the search for new and better ways of reducing dropout rates, deeper understanding of the noneconomic effects of education and what accounts for them, and more reliable methods of measuring the progress students are making toward each of the principal objectives of a college education. Such support could range from increased funding for fundamental research in cognitive science and psychology to testing promising ideas at scale, such as the methods used by

Arizona State University to improve remedial math or the CUNY experiment in reorganizing community colleges described in chapter 11.

Similar assistance could be useful in persuading leading universities to undertake significant changes in their graduate programs in order to prepare future faculty properly for their role as teachers and educators, as well as researchers. Added funds could be provided for research and experimentation on improved methods of measuring student learning, since many faculty members will not be receptive to reform unless they see convincing evidence that their current teaching or that of their department is not achieving the results they previously assumed. Recent federal initiatives to support innovation, such as the First in the World fund for research and experimentation to increase access and college completion and the Department of Education's fund to develop and test better methods of remedial education are promising steps in the right direction.

If lack of knowledge is the principal impediment to raising levels of attainment and increasing educational quality, support of this kind seems eminently sensible. Over past decades, the United States has spent more per student on our public schools than almost any other nation while obtaining very modest results. America also spends more per full-time college student than any other country, yet both our attainment rates and the competencies of our college graduates appear to be mediocre in comparison to our peers. In light of this record, it surely makes sense to invest millions of dollars in discovering and testing new ways to graduate more students and improve the quality of their education before spending billions more on making college free and other speculative ventures of uncertain efficacy.

In all the ways just outlined, government officials, foundations, employers, accreditors, trustees, and, most of all, academic leaders themselves could do a lot to create a more productive environment for reform.[14] Even so, impatient critics of higher education may dismiss the efforts just described and call for more muscular ways to bring about immediate improvement. State legislatures have already promised to cut their appropriations to colleges that fail to graduate enough students.

Federal officials may try again to summon market forces to force faculties to improve the quality of their educational programs by publishing the reports from their last accreditation inspection or the scores of their students on tests of critical thinking. Another recent proposal that has generated traction in some quarters would make colleges accountable for the defaults of former students on their educational loans by requiring them to pay a share of the resulting losses.

Although the aims these reformers seek may be admirable, the methods they propose are dubious at best. As pointed out in earlier chapters, pressure tactics rarely succeed. Neither stiff financial penalties nor market forces can induce colleges to increase their graduation rates or improve student learning if campus leaders and their faculties do not know how to accomplish these results. In fact, such methods could easily do more harm than good. For example, the proposal to require colleges to share the losses resulting from student loan defaults could easily lead campus officials to refuse admission to the very high-risk, underprepared applicants who must be educated if the United States is to achieve significantly higher attainment rates.

In short, trying to reform the educational practices of colleges by bringing strong external pressure to bear is much like playing a pinball machine. Giving a little push or a gentle, well-directed nudge may help a bit. But if one shoves too hard, the screen flashes "TILT," the game comes to an abrupt halt, and the money to play the game is lost. In education, as in pinball, patience and informed trial and error are more likely to be rewarded than resorting to more forceful measures.

Critics who remain unconvinced might pause and ponder the huge sums of money that have been spent over the years on largely unsuccessful educational reforms. Such a record calls to mind the fable of the tortoise and the hare. Given the challenges facing higher education today and the growing supply of ideas to overcome them, encouraging the tortoise and supporting the search for knowledge to light its path may well bring success more quickly than continuing to place large bets on seemingly plausible, politically popular, but still untested remedies.

While Aesop's fable seems apt, college leaders and their faculties need to grasp its full import. Like wayward hares, expensive government programs to reform education frequently go astray. At the same time, the tortoise can prevail only if it emerges from its shell, examines the terrain, and moves ahead with all deliberate speed. On all too many campuses, the current environment tends to inhibit rather than encourage the self-scrutiny, experimentation, and innovation needed to meet the most important problems of undergraduate education. This condition does not serve the best interests of our colleges or the nation.

Because of the importance of higher education in expanding opportunity and promoting growth, the federal government has come to spend vast amounts on student aid. By doing so, it has acquired a huge stake in achieving higher levels of educational attainment together with effective teaching and learning. Yet graduation rates from colleges have risen only gradually over the past several decades, and there are multiple signs that the amounts undergraduates are learning have not increased and may have actually declined. This state of affairs is not tenable. Any notion that colleges can keep on indefinitely raising their prices without improving the services they provide seems patently unrealistic, especially when their services are as important to the nation as a good college education. If past trends continue, the government is bound to intervene more and more intrusively, if not in this administration, at some point thereafter.

Judging from past experience with educational reforms, the ensuing interventions are likely to have frustrating results. Money will be wasted, unanticipated side effects will materialize, red tape will proliferate, and bureaucracies will grow. Meanwhile, the effect on graduation rates will be either meager or achieved only by lowering academic standards, a Pyrrhic victory indeed.

Rather than risk such disappointing results, colleges and public officials, with the help of foundations, employers, and accreditors, could join in a vigorous collaborative effort to strengthen the process of innovation and discover more effective ways to improve remedial education, reduce dropout rates, and increase student learning. Such a process will not bring immediate progress. The problems to be solved are very difficult. Many intriguing new ideas that emerge will not survive rigorous testing, and those that do may not be adopted overnight. In the end, however, a robust process of continuous self-scrutiny, experimentation, and evaluation offers the safest, surest, and least expensive way to graduate millions more students with the education they need to live more successful and fulfilling lives.

NOTES

CHAPTER ONE   GRADUATION RATES AND EDUCATIONAL ATTAINMENT

1. Claudia Goldin and Lawrence F. Katz, *The Race between Education and Technology* (2008).

2. White House, *Remarks of President Barack Obama—Address to Joint Session of Congress* (February 24, 2009).

3. Arthur M. Hauptman, "Increasing Higher Education Attainment in the United States: Challenges and Opportunities," in Andrew P. Kelly and Mark Schneider (eds.), *Getting to Graduation: The Completion Agenda in Higher Education* (2012), p. 17.

4. Ibid., p. 36.

5. T. Alan Lacey and Benjamin Wright, "Occupational Employment Projections to 2018," 132 *Monthly Labor Review* (2009), p. 82.

6. Anthony Carnevale, Nicole Smith, and Jeff Strohl, *Help Wanted—Projections of Jobs and Education Requirements through 2018* (2010).

7. See, e.g., David Autor, "Skills, Education and the Rise of Earnings Inequality among the Other 99 Percent," 344 *Science* (2014), p. 843.

8. *Closing America's Skills Gap: A Business Roundtable Vision and Action Plan* (December 2014), p. 4.

9. "New Bayer Survey: Is There a STEM Workforce Shortage" (October 22, 2013).

10. Paul E. Harrington and Andrew M. Sum, "College Labor Shortages in 2018?" (unpublished paper, March 3, 2015).

11. E.g., Richard Dobbs, James Manikya, and Jonathan Woetzel, "No Ordinary Disruption," McKinsey Global Institute (2015); Stephen Vaisey, "Education and Its Discontents: Overqualification in America, 1972–2002," 85 *Social Forces* (2006), p. 835.

12. Paul Beaudry, David A. Green, and Benjamin Sand, *The Great Reversal in the Demand for Skill and Cognitive Tasks*, National Bureau of Economic Research, Working Paper No. 18901 (March 2013). Other economists respond that the halt in the earnings premium of college graduates after 2000 was due to a surge in the numbers of students graduating from college. E.g., David Autor, note 7, p. 847.

13. Peter Capelli, *Skill Gaps, Skill Shortages, and Skill Mismatches: Evidence for the U.S.*, National Bureau of Economic Research, Working Paper No. 20382 (August 2014).

14. Ibid., p. 10.

15. E.g., Hal Salzman, Daniel Kuehn, and B. Lindsay Lowell, *Guest Workers in the High-Skill US Labor Market*, EPI Briefing Paper No. 359 (April 24, 2013).

16. Peter Capelli, *Why Good People Can't Get Jobs: The Skills Gap and What People Can Do* (2012).

17. Ibid., p. 32.

18. Carl B. Frey and Michael A. Osborne, *The Future of Employment: How Susceptible Are Jobs to Computerization?* (2013), pp. 38, 42.

19. Martin Ford, *The Rise of the Robots: Technology and the Threat of a Jobless Future* (2015), p. 252.

20. Daron Acemoglu and David Autor, "What Does Human Capital Do?" A review of Goldin and Katz's *The Race between Education and Technology*, 50 *Journal of Economic Literature* (2012), pp. 426, 458; Enrico Moretti, *The New Geography of Jobs* (2012).

21. E.g., David Autor, note 7, p. 845; Raymond Sin-Kwok Wong, "Understanding Cross-National Variation in Occupational Mobility," 55 *American Sociological Review* (1990), p. 560.

22. Martha J. Bailey and Susan M. Dynarski, *Gains and Gaps: Changing Inequality in U.S. College Entry and Completion*, National Bureau of Economic Research, Working Paper No. 17633 (December 2011).

23. William G. Bowen and Michael S. McPherson, *Lesson Plan: An Agenda for Change in American Higher Education* (2016), p. 39.

24. National Center for Educational Statistics, *Educational Attainment of Young Adults* (May 2016), pp. 2–3.

25. William G. Bowen and Michael S. McPherson, note 23, pp. 29–30.

26. See generally, Walter W. McMahon, *Higher Learning, Greater Good: The Private and Social Benefits of Higher Education* (2009); Philip Oreopoulos and Kjell G. Salvanes, "Priceless: The Nonpecuniary Benefits of Schooling," 25 *Journal of Economic Perspectives* (2011), p. 159.

27. *Gallup-Perdue Index Report: Great Jobs, Great Lives* (2014).

28. See, e.g., Thomas Dee, "Are There Civic Returns to Education?" 88 *Journal of Public Economics* (2004), p. 1697.

29. Edward L. Glaeser, Giacomo A. M. Ponzetto, and Andrei Schleifer, "Why Does Democracy Need Education?" 12 *Journal of Economic Growth* (2007), p. 77.

30. Walter W. McMahon, note 26, p. 208; Juan Botero, Alejandro Ponce, and Andrei Schleifer, *Education and the Quality of Government*, National Bureau of Economic Research, Working Paper No. 181119 (June 2012). See also Michael Hout, "Social and Economic Returns to College Education in the United States," 38 *Annual Review of Sociology* (2012), pp. 379, 392 et seq.; Sandy Baum and Jennifer Ma, *Education Pays: The Benefits of Higher Education for Individuals and Society* (2007).

31. S. Murdock et al., *The New Texas Challenge: Population Change and the Future of Texas* (2003).

32. H. B. Brady, Michael Hout, and J. Stiles, *Return on Investment: Educational Choices and Demographic Change in California's Future* (2005).

33. For a discussion of this and other research on the independent efforts of higher education, see Walter W. McMahon, note 26, pp. 331–46.

34. J. D. Angrist and A. B. Krueger, "Does Compulsory School Attendance Affect Schooling and Earnings?" 106 *Quarterly Journal of Economics* (1991), p. 979; Philip Oreopoulos and Uros Petronijevie, *Making College Worth It: A Review of Research on the Returns to Higher Education*, National Bureau of Economic Research, Working Paper No. 19053 (2013), p. 21.

35. *First State of the Union Address* (January 25, 1994). President Obama has echoed this statement. "I think the big challenge that we've got on education is making sure that from kindergarten through your 14th or 15th year of school, or 16th year of school or 20th year of school, that you are actually learning the kinds of skills that make you competitive and productive in a modern, technological economy." David Leonhardt,

"After the Great Recession: An Interview with President Obama," *New York Times Magazine* (May 3, 2009), pp. 36, 39.

36. Rick Scott, "Politicians Then and Now on Liberal Education," *Chronicle of Higher Education* (January 30, 2015), p. A21.

37. Editorial, "Gov. Walker's 'Drafting Error,'" *New York Times* (February 7, 2015), p. A16.

38. No one has put the matter more eloquently than Thomas Jefferson: "I look to the diffusion of light and education as the resource most to be relied on for ameliorating the conditions, promoting the virtue, and advancing the happiness of man." (E.g., Thomas Jefferson, quoted by Robert Darnton, "Google and the Future of Books," *New York Review of Books* [February 12, 2009], p. 9.) More recently, Harry Truman remarked, "Among the greatest dangers to free government in this country are lack of knowledge, lack of civic responsibility—ignorance and apathy and perversion of truth." (Harry Truman, *Public Papers of the Presidents: Harry S. Truman* [1952–53], p. 579.) President Eisenhower looked to higher education to prepare America to exercise enlightened leadership for an expanded role in world affairs. (Christopher P. Loss, *Between Citizens and the State: The Politics of American Higher Education in the 20th Century* [2012], pp. 156–60.) President Johnson fought to expand access to school and college not only as a means of increasing opportunity and overcoming poverty but to preserve freedom. As he put it: "Every child must be encouraged to get as much education as he has ability to take.... We want this not only for his sake—but for the nation's sake. Nothing matters more for the future of our country ... for freedom is fragile if citizens are ignorant." (Lyndon Johnson, *Public Papers of the Presidents: LBJ* [1965], pp. 1102–5.)

39. Kevin Eagan, Jennifer P. Lozano, Sylvia Hurtado, and Matthew H. Case, *The American Freshman: National Norms* (Fall 2013), p. 40. Much the same pattern appears in a New America Foundation survey of college students in 2015. Ninety-one percent of students listed "improving employment opportunities" as an important or very important reason for going to college, and 90 percent did likewise for "make more money," but 85 percent listed "to learn more about a favorite topic or interest" as an important or very important reason. Rachel Fishman, *2015 College Decisions Survey: Part I: Deciding to Go to College* (2015), p. 4.

40. Kevin Eagan et al., note 39.

41. Ibid.

CHAPTER TWO   THE QUALITY OF EDUCATION

1. See, e.g., Rachel Fishman, *2015 College Decision Survey, Part I: Deciding to Go to College* (2015), p. 6.

2. Sylvia Hurtado, Kevin Eagan, John H. Pryor, Hannah Whang, and Sarge Tran, *Undergraduate Teaching Faculty: The 2010–2011 HERI Faculty Survey* (2012), p. 26.

3. Susan M. Barnett and Stephen J. Ceci, "When and Where Do We Apply What We Learn? A Taxonomy for Far Transfer," 128 *Psychological Bulletin* (2002), p. 612; Douglas K. Detterman, "The Case for the Prosecution: Transfer as an Epiphenomenon," chapter 1 in Douglas K. Detterman and R. J. Sternberg (eds.), *Transfer on Trial: Intelligence, Cognition, and Instruction* (1993), p. 1, and D. F. Halpern, "Teaching Critical Thinking for Transfer across Domains," 53 *American Psychologist* (1998), p. 449.

4. Quoted in Frederick Rudolph, *The American College and University* (1962), p. 304. See also Roger L. Geiger, *The History of American Higher Education: Learning and Culture from the Founding to World War II* (2015), p. 321.

5. Frederick Rudolph, note 4, p. 305.

6. See, e.g., Roger L. Geiger, note 4, pp. 414–15.

7. See, e.g., Eric A. Hanushek and Ludger Woessmann, *How Much Do Educational Outcomes Matter in OECD Countries?* National Bureau of Economic Research, Working Paper No.16515 (2010). According to the authors, a one standard deviation in standardized test scores in math and reading is associated with an increase in annual growth rates of 2 percent.

8. Organization of Economic Cooperation and Development (OECD), *OECD Skills Outlook for 2013: First Results from the Survey of Adult Skills (2013)*, pp. 234–44.

9. Ernest T. Pascarella and Patrick T. Terenzini, *How College Affects Students: Findings and Insights from Twenty Years of Research* (1991).

10. Ernest T. Pascarella and Patrick T. Terenzini, *How College Affects Students*, vol. 2, *A Third Decade of Research* (2005).

11. Sylvia Hurtado, Kevin Eagan, John H. Pryor, Hannah Whang, and Sarge Tran, note 2, p. 12.

12. For a detailed discussion of the development of the College Learning Assessment (CLA), see Richard Shavelson, *Measuring College Learning Responsibly: Accountability in a New Era* (2010).

13. Richard Arum and Josipa Roksa, *Aspiring Adults Adrift: Tentative Transitions of College Graduates* (2014), pp. 37–46; *Academically Adrift: Limited Learning on College Campuses* (2011).

14. See John Etchemendy, "Are Our Colleges and Universities Failing Us?" in *The Big Picture: Assessing the Future of Higher Education*, Carnegie Corporation of New York (2014), p. 44.

15. Compare Susan M. Barnett and Stephen J. Ceci, note 3, p. 612, with Douglas K. Detterman, note 3, p. 1, and D. F. Halpern, note 3, p. 449.

16. Ou Lydia Liu, Brent Bridgeman, and Rachel M. Adler, "Measuring Learning Outcomes in Higher Education: Motivation Matters," 41 *Educational Researcher* (2012), p. 352; David Glenn, "Scholar Raises Doubts about the Value of a Test of Student Learning," *Chronicle of Higher Education* (June 2, 2010). http://www.chronicle.com/article/Scholar-Raises-Doubts-About/65741/.

17. E.g., Ernest T. Pascarella and Patrick T. Terenzini, note 10, p. 129. Still another longitudinal study reached an almost identical result concerning student improvement in critical thinking. Charles Blaich and Kathleen Wise, *From Gathering to Using Assessment Results: Lessons from the Wabash National Study*, Occasional Paper No. 8 (2011), p. 9.

18. *National Assessment of Adult Literacy, A First Look at the Literacy and America's Adults in the 21st Century* (2006).

19. E.g., Ernest T. Pascarella and Patrick T. Terenzini, note 10, p. 158.

20. Organization of Economic Cooperation and Development (OECD), note 8, p. 97.

21. Ibid., pp. 74–75.

22. Martin West, *Education and Global Competitiveness: Lessons for the United States from International Evidence* (n.d.), p. 6.

23. Organization of Economic Cooperation and Development (OECD), note 8, p. 204. The import of this finding, however, is not entirely clear. It could mean that America's low rankings are not the fault of college but result from experiences in high school or even earlier. On the other hand, our performance could also be the result of an unusually large and growing difference in America between the average academic ability of students who go to college and those who don't.

24. Philip S. Babcock and Mindy Marks, "The Falling Time Cost of College: Evidence from Half a Century of Time Use Data," 93 *Review of Economics and Statistics* (2011), p. 468.

25. E.g., Ralph Stinebrickner and Todd R. Stinebrickner, "Time-Use and College Outcomes," 121 *Journal of Econometrics* (2004), p. 243; Marcus Crede, Sylvia G. Roch, and Urszula M. Kiesczynka, "Class Attendance in College," 80 *Review of Educational Research* (2010), p. 272.

26. Stephen Brint and Allison M. Cantwell, "Undergraduate Time Use and Academic Outcomes: Results from the University of California Undergraduate Experience Survey," 112 *Teachers College Record* (2010), pp. 2441, 2442.

27. See, e.g., E. Ashby Plant, K. Anders Ericsson, Len Hill, and Kia Asberg, "Why Study Time Does Not Predict Grade Point Average across College Students," 30 *Contemporary Educational Psychology* (2005), p. 96.

28. National Survey of Student Engagement, *Promoting Student Learning and Institutional Improvement: Lessons from NSSE at 13* (2012), p. 18.

29. E.g., John Hattie and Gregory C. R. Yates, *Visible Learning and the Science of How We Learn* (2014): "Overall, the message is that multitasking is the wrong option any time you expect to learn, acquire knowledge, or think deeply," p. 193; Reynol Junco and Sheila Cotton, "No A-U," 59 *Computers and Education* (2012), p. 505; Evan Risko, Dawn Buchanan, Srdan Medimorec, and Alan Kingstone, "Everyday Attention: Mindwandering and Computer Use during Lectures," 68 *Computers and Education* (2013), p. 275.

30. For a sample of opinions on grade inflation, see Lester H. Hunt (ed.), *Grade Inflation: Academic Standards in Higher Education* (2008). An oft-cited article on the subject is Stuart Rojstaczer and Christopher Healy, "Where A Is Ordinary: The Evolution of American College and University Grading, 1940–2009," 114 *Teachers College Record* (July 2012), p. 1.

31. Philip Babcock, "Real Costs of Nominal Grade Inflation? New Evidence from Student Course Evaluations," 45 *Economic Inquiry* (2010), p. 983.

32. See, e.g., Michael Prince, "Does Active Learning Work? A Review of the Research," 93 *Journal of Engineering Education* (2013), p. 327.

33. George D. Kuh, Natasha Jankowski, Stanley O. Ikenberry, and Jillian Kinzie, *Knowing What Students Know and Can Do: The Current State of Student Learning Outcomes and Assessment in U.S. Colleges and Universities*, National Institute of Learning Outcomes and Assessment (January 2014), p. 14.

34. Eric A. Hanushek and Ludger Woessmann, "The Role of Education Quality in Economic Growth," World Bank Policy Research Working Paper No. 4122 (February 2007).

35. Organization of Economic Cooperation and Development (OECD), note 8, pp. 223–46.

36. Ibid., p. 246.

CHAPTER THREE   CAN COLLEGES MEET THE CHALLENGES
BY THEMSELVES?

1. Byron G. Auguste, Adam Cota, Kartik Jayaram, and Martha C. Laboissiere, *Winning by Degrees: The Strategies of Highly Productive Higher Education Institutions* (2010).

2. Clayton M. Christensen and Henry J. Eyring, *The Innovative University: Changing the DNA of Higher Education from the Inside Out* (2011).

3. Robert W. Mendenhall, "Western Governors University," in Diane Oblinger (ed.), *Game Changer: Education and IT* (2012), p. 115.

4. Estimates of WGU's graduation rates vary widely because of differences in which students are counted. The government's calculation excludes 57.6 percent of the entering students because they are part-time or previously entered another college. Calculated in this way, the six-year graduation rate is only 6.5 percent. WGU calculates its graduation rate at a much higher figure, 40 percent, by including the categories of students that the government excludes. See Steve Kolowich, "Model of the Moment," *Inside Higher Ed* (May 9, 2011). Moreover, the effectiveness of online teaching, especially for less academically proficient students, is also a matter of dispute. See, e.g., Di Xu and Shanna S. Jaggars, "The Impact of Online Learning on Students' Course Outcomes: Evidence from a Large Community and Technical College System," 37 *Economics of Education Review* (2013), p. 46; Community College Research Center, "What We Know about Online Course Outcomes," *Research Overview* (April 2013), pp. 3, 4.

5. E.g., Paul D. Umbach, "How Effective Are They? Exploring the Impact of Contingent Faculty on Undergraduate Education," 30 *Review of Higher Education* (Winter 2007), p. 91; M. Kevin Eagan, Jr., and Audrey J. Jaeger, "Closing the Gate: Part-Time Faculty and Instruction in Gateway Courses and First-Year Persistence," in John M. Braxton (ed.), *The Role of the Classroom in College Student Performance* (2008), p. 39.

6. See, e.g., Di Xu and Shanna S. Jaggars, note 4, p. 46.

7. Kevin Eagan et al., *The Undergraduate Teaching Faculty: The 2013–2014 HERI Faculty Survey*, Higher Education Research Institute (2014), p. 6. See also Regan A. R. Gurung, Nancy L. Chick, and Aeron Haynie (eds.), *Exploring Signature Pedagogies: Approaches to Teaching Disciplinary Habits of Mind* (2009).

8. Quoted in Jeffrey Brainard, "The Road to Better Science Teaching," *Chronicle of Higher Education* (August 3, 2007). For a discussion of teaching methods in a wide range of disciplines, see Nancy L. Chick, Aeron Haynie, and Regan A. R. Gurung (eds.), *Exploring More Signature Pedagogies: Approaches to Teaching Disciplinary Habits of Mind* (2012).

9. Jack H. Schuster and Martin J. Finkelstein, *The American Faculty: The Restructuring of Academic Work and Careers* (2006), p. 89. According to one recent faculty survey, approximately 80 percent of faculty across all types of institutions think that "promoting the intellectual development of students is a "high" or "the highest" priority. Kevin Eagan et al., note 7.

10. Jack H. Schuster and Martin J. Finkelstein, note 9, p. 469.

11. E.g., Lion Gardiner, *Redesigning Higher Education: Producing Dramatic Gains in Student Learning* (1994), p. 57.

12. James S. Fairweather, "Beyond the Rhetoric: Trends in the Relative Value of Teaching and Research in Faculty Salaries," 76 *Journal of Higher Education* (2005), p. 401.

13. George D. Kuh, Natasha Jankowski, Stanley O. Ikenberry, and Jillian Kinzie, *Knowing What Students Know and Can Do: The Current State of Student Learning Outcomes Assessment in U.S. Colleges and Universities*, National Institute for Learning Outcomes Assessment (2014), p. 3.

14. See, e.g., Charles Blaich and Kathleen Wise, *From Gathering to Using Assessment Results: Lessons from the Wabash National Study*, Occasional Paper No. 8 (2011), pp. 3, 11.

15. Wei Sung and Harold V. Hartley, *Presidents of Independent Colleges and Universities*, Council of Independent Colleges (2011).

16. E.g., Ernest T. Pascarella and Patrick T. Terenzini, *How College Affects Students*, vol. 2, *A Third Decade of Research* (2005), pp. 168–70.

17. Jeffrey L. Selingo, *What Presidents Think: A 2013 Survey of Four-Year College Presidents* (2013), p. 14.

18. Ninety percent of presidents believe that their institution is "somewhat effective" or "very effective" at developing writing skills. Poll of Presidents by Gallup and *Inside Higher Ed* (2014).

19. Kenneth C. Green, *The 2011–12 Inside Higher Ed Survey of College and University Chief Academic Officers* (2012), p. 12.

20. Project on Governance for a New Era, *Governance for a New Era: A Blueprint for Higher Education Trustees* (2014), p. 5.

21. *Aspen Institute and Achieving the Dream: Crisis and Opportunity: Aligning the Community College Presidency with Student Success* (2012).

22. Ibid., p. 13.

23. Ibid., p. 12.

24. Ibid.

25. Ibid., p. 15.

26. Association of Governing Boards, *Governing Board Oversight of College Completion* (2015).

27. John Immerwahr, Jean Johnson, and John Rochkind, *Still on the Sidelines: What Role Will Trustees Play in Higher Education Reform?* (2011).

28. Association of Governing Boards, *How Boards Oversee Educational Quality: Report on a Survey of Boards and the Assessment of Student Learning* (2010), p. 6.

29. Ibid., p. 7

30. E.g., José A. Cabranes, "Myth and Reality of University Trusteeship in the Post-Enron Era," 76 *Fordham Law Review* (2007), p. 955.

31. George D. Kuh et al., note 13, p. 5.

32. Association of Governing Boards, note 26.

33. Public Agenda, *A Difficult Balance: Trustees Speak about the Challenges Facing Comprehensive Universities* (2015), p. 4.

34. Ibid., p. 16.

35. Ibid., p. 17.

CHAPTER FOUR   THE INFLUENCE OF STUDENTS

1. E.g., Steven Brint, "The Rise of the 'Practical Arts,'" in Steven Brint (ed.), *The Future of the City of Intellect: The Changing American University* (2002), pp. 231, 235. See also W. Norton Grubb and Marvin Lazerson, "Vocationalism in Higher Education: The Triumph of the Education Gospel," 76 *Journal of Higher Education* (2005), p. 1.

2. Rachel Fishman, *2015 College Decision Survey, Part I, Deciding to Go to College* (May 2015).

3. See Nancy W. Malkiel, *"Keep the Damned Women Out": The Struggle for Coeducation* (2016).

4. Mary Grigsby, *College Life through the Eyes of Students* (2009), p. 54.

5. See, e.g., Peter Sacks, *Generation X Goes to College: An Eye-Opening Account of Teaching in Postmodern America* (1996); Professor X, *In the Basement of the Ivory Tower: Confessions of an Accidental Academic* (2014); Mary Grigsby, note 4; Rebekah Nathan, *My Freshman Year: What a Professor Learned from Becoming a Student* (2005); Elizabeth A. Armstrong and Laura Hamilton, *Paying for the Party: How College Maintains Inequality* (2013). For a more optimistic, though somewhat dated, account, see Michael Moffatt, *Coming of Age in New Jersey: College and American Culture* (1989).

6. K. Baier et al., *College Students' Textbook Reading, or Not! American Reading Forum Annual Yearbook* (2011); C. Burchfield and J. Sappington, "Compliance with Required Reading Assignments," 27 *Teaching of Psychology* (2000), p. 58.

7. See Sara Goldrick-Rab, *Paying the Price: College Costs, Financial Aid, and the Betrayal of the American Dream* (2016).

8. *The Chronicle of Higher Education, Almanac 2015–16* (2015), p. 32.

9. US Department of Education, *The Nation's Report Card: Trends in Academic Progress 2012* (2012), p. 27; Noel-Levitz, Inc., *National Freshman Attitudes Report* (2007).

10. Mark Bauerlein, *The Dumbest Generation: How the Digital Age Stupefies Young Americans and Jeopardizes Our Future* (2007), pp. 53–54.

11. Rebekah Nathan, note 5.

12. Nancy Jennings, Suzanne Lovett, Lee Cuba, Joe Swingle, and Heather Lindkvist, "What Would Make a Successful Year for You? How Students Define Success in College," 99 *Liberal Education* (Spring 2013); Ani Yazedjian, Michelle L. Toews, Sevin Tesarra, and Katherine E. Purswell, "It's a Whole New World," 49 *Journal of College Student Development* (2008), p. 141.

13. National Survey of Student Engagement (NSSE), *Experiences That Matter: Enhancing Student Learning and Success* (2007), p. 46.

14. See, e.g., Roger L. Geiger, *Knowledge and Money: Research Universities and the Paradox of the Marketplace* (2005), pp. 244–49; James E. Coté and Anton Allaher, *Lowering Higher Education: The Rise of Corporate Universities and the Fall of Liberal Education* (2011).

15. For an extensive treatment of the self-esteem movement and its effects on college student behavior, see Jean M. Twenge, *Generation Me: Why Today's Young Americans Are More Confident, Assertive, Entitled—and More Miserable Than Ever* (2008).

16. See, e.g., Valen E. Johnson, *Grade Inflation: A Crisis in College Education* (2002); Stuart Rojstaczer and Christopher Healy, "Where A Is Ordinary: The Evolution of American College and University Grading, 1940–2009," 114 *Teachers College Record* (2012), p. 1. For a diversity of views about the existence and extent of grade inflation, see Lester H. Hunt (ed.), *Grade Inflation: Academic Standards in Higher Education* (2008).

17. National Survey of Student Engagement (NSSE), note 13.

18. See Peter Sacks, note 5, pp. 31–38, 48–51, 78–80.

19. Philip Babcock, "Real Costs of Nominal Grade Inflation? New Evidence from Student Course Evaluations," 48 *Economic Inquiry* (2010), p. 983.

20. Ibid.

21. Ibid.

22. Ashley Finley (Association of American Colleges & Universities), *Making Progress? What We Know about the Achievement of Liberal Education Outcomes* (2012), p. 14.

23. See p. 73.

24. See p. 76.

25. Kenneth C. Green, *The 2011–12 Inside Higher Ed Survey of College and University Chief Academic Officers* (2012), p. 2.

26. Roger L. Geiger, note 14, p. 129.

CHAPTER FIVE   EMPLOYERS

1. Hart Research Associates, *It Takes More than a Major: Employer Priorities for College Learning and Student Success*, survey carried out for Association of American Colleges & Universities (2013).

2. Jeff Selingo, "Skills Gap? Employers and Colleges Point Fingers at Each Other," *Chronicle of Higher Education* (September 12, 2012).

3. Pearson, *Breakthrough to Greater Student Achievement* (2013), p. 30.

4. Ibid., p. 29.

5. Ibid., p. 5.

6. Ibid., p. 15.

7.

Relative Importance of Competencies

Competency	Students	Employers
Communicate orally	78	85
Work with others in teams	77	83
Communicate in writing	75	82
Ethical judgment	74	81
Critical thinking	79	81
Apply analytical skill in real-world settings	79	80
Solve complex problems	73	74
Locate, organize, solve complex problems	73	68
Innovate, be creative	69	65

Hart Research Associates, *Falling Short? College Learning and Career Success*, survey carried out for Association of American Colleges & Universities (January 20, 2015), p. 8.

8.

	Doing Good Job	Minor Improvement Needed	Moderate Improvement Needed	Major Improvement Needed
For first job	74%	6%	16%	2%
For advancement	64%	10%	20%	6%

Pew Research Center Survey (May 19, 2014).

9. Bentley University, *The Prepared U. Project: An In-Depth Look at Millennial Preparedness for Today's Workforce* (2014).

10. Cited in Public Agenda, *Profiting Higher Education: What Students, Alumni, and Employers Think about For-Profit Colleges* (February 2014).

11. See John Bridgeland, Jessica Milano, and Elyse Rosenblum, *Across the Great Divide: Perspectives of CEOs and College Presidents on America's Higher Education and Skills Gap* (March 2011), pp. 4, 10.

12. Economist Intelligence Unit, *Closing the Skills Gap: Companies and Colleges Collaborating for Change* (2014), p. 7.

13. *Chronicle of Higher Education* and American Public Media's *Marketplace, The Role of Higher Education in Career Development: Employer Perceptions* (December 2012).

14. Public Agenda, note 10, p. 25.

15. John Bridgeland, Jessica Milano, and Elyse Rosenblum, note 11, p. 4.

16. Ibid., p. 15.

17. Peter Capelli, *Why Good People Can't Get Good Jobs: The Skills Gap and What People Can Do* (2012), p. 70.

18. Ibid., p. 88.

19. David Smith and Katherine LaVelle (Accenture Outlook), *The New Skills Imperative: Reconnecting Work with the Workforce* (May 2013), p. 2.

20. Hart Research Associates, note 7, p. 10.

21. Bentley University, note 9, p. 9.

22. William G. Bowen and Derek Bok, *The Shape of the River: Long-Term Consequences of Considering Race in College and University Admissions* (1998), pp. 208–9.

23. P. 34; Philip S. Babcock and Mindy Marks, "The Falling Time Cost of College: Evidence from Half a Century of Time Use Data," 91 *Review of Economics and Statistics* (2011), p. 468.

24. Stuart Rojstaczer and Christopher Healy, "Where A Is Ordinary: The Evolution of American College and University Grading, 1940–2009," 114 *Teachers College Record* (July 2012), p. 1.

25. See Roger L. Geiger, *Knowledge and Money: Research Universities and the Paradox of the Marketplace* (2004), pp. 98–100. As Geiger describes what has occurred: "Universities became increasingly averse to the traditional negative sanctions of college—not just bad grades and the threat of failure, but everyday matters like mandatory attendance, pop quizzes, and comprehensive final examinations. Grade inflation, whatever else its cause, is consistent with this reluctance to coerce, as opposed to cajole, effort from students" (p. 247).

26. Bentley University, note 9, p. 9.

27. See, e.g., John H. Pryor, Sylvia Hurtado, Victor B. Saenz, Jennifer Lindholm, William S. Korn, and Katharine M. Mahoney, *The American Freshman—National Norms for Fall 2005*, Higher Education Research Institute, University of California, Los Angeles (2006).

28. See, e.g., Paul Faia, "New Assessments from Testing Firms Have Job-Market Potential," *Inside Higher Ed* (August 2, 2013).

29. See Don Peck, "They're Watching You at Work," 312 *Atlantic* (December 2013), p. 1, https://www.theatlantic.com/magazine/archive/2013/12/theyre-watching-you-at -work/354681/.

30. Paul LeBlanc, "Making Sense of Disruptive Technologies and Higher Education: A Theory of Change, the Growth of Online Programs, and the Next Generation of Delivery Models" (paper prepared for the American Enterprise Institute Conference "Stretching the Higher Education Dollar," August 2, 2012), p. 20.

CHAPTER SIX   COMPETITION, OLD AND NEW

1. See, e.g., Paul E. Peterson, "Forum: Post-Regulatory School Reform," 119 *Harvard Magazine* (September–October 2016), p. 37.

2. According to one survey from the *Chronicle of Higher Education*, competition for students is the second most cited worry of college presidents. *The View from the Top: What Presidents Think about Financial Sustainability, Student Outcomes, and the Future of Higher Education* (2015), p. 7.

3. Peter Drucker is quoted in an interview by Robert Lenzner and Stephen S. Johnson, "Seeing Things as They Really Are," *Forbes* (March 10, 1997), p. 127; see also Clayton Christensen, Michael Horn, Louis Calderon, and Louis Soares, *Disrupting College: How Disruptive Innovation Can Deliver Quality and Affordability to Postsecondary Education* (2011); Nathan Hardin, "The End of the University As We Know It," *American Interest* (January–February 2013), p. 35.

4. See, e.g., David W. Breneman, Brian Pusser, and Sarah E. Turner (eds.), *Earnings from Learning: The Rise of For-Profit Universities* (2006); Guilbert C. Hentschke, Vincent M. Lechuga, and William G. Tierney (eds.), *For Profit Universities: Their Markets, Regulation, Performance, and Place in Higher Education* (2010).

5. General Accounting Office, Statement of Gregory D. Katz, *For Profit Colleges: Undercover Testing Finds Colleges Encouraged Fraud and Engaged in Deceptive and Questionable Marketing Practices* (August 4, 2010).

6. See, e.g., Patrick Denice, "Does It Pay to Attend a For-Profit College? Vertical and Horizontal Stratification in Higher Education," 52 *Social Science Research* (2015), p. 161.

7. Public Agenda, *Profiting Higher Education: What Students, Alumni, and Employers Think about For-Profit Colleges* (February 2014).

8. Clayton Christensen et al., note 3.

9. Mamie Lynch, Jennifer Engle, and José L. Cruz, "Subprime Opportunity: The Unfulfilled Promise of For-Profit Colleges and Universities," *Education Trust* (November 2010).

10. See, e.g., Kevin Carey, *The End of College: Creating the Future of Learning and the University of Everywhere* (2015); Ryan Craig, *College Disrupted: The Great Unbundling of Higher Education* (2015).

11. Candace Thille, "Building Open Learning as a Community-Based Research Activity," in Toru Iiyoshi and M. S. Vijay Kumar (eds.), *Opening Up Education: The Collective Advancement of Education through Open Technology, Open Content and Open Knowledge* (2008), p. 165; William G. Bowen, Matthew M. Chingos, Kelly Lack, and Thomas I. Nygren, *Interactive Learning Online at Public Universities: Evidence from Randomized Trials* (May 2012). These ventures, however, have as yet not penetrated deeply into our higher education system. As Laura Perna and Ramon Ruiz have recently concluded, "online teaching has had relatively little impact on instructional approaches at

most colleges and universities.... technology has largely been used to enhance traditional approaches to delivering higher education without fundamentally changing the nature of teaching and learning." "Technology," in Michael Bastedo, Philip G. Altbach, and Patricia J. Gumport (eds.), *American Higher Education in the Twenty-First Century* (4th ed., 2016), pp. 432, 440.

12. Derek Bok, *Higher Education in America* (2013), p. 36.

13. Di Xu and Shanna S. Jaggars, "The Impact of Online Learning on Students' Course Outcomes: Evidence from a Large Community and Technical College System," 37 *Economics of Education Review* (2013), p. 96.

14. Steve Kolowich, "The New Intelligence," *Inside Higher Ed* (January 25, 2013).

15. Kim Reid, *Wake-Up Call, Eduventures' Student Success Ratings Are Here* (June 7, 2016), http://www.eduventures.com/2016/06/eduventures-student-success-ratings -are-here/.

16. Ellen Wagner and David Longanecker, "Scaling Student Success with Predictive Analytics: Reflections after Four Years in the Data Trenches," *Change* (March 7, 2016), pp. 52–59.

17. Carol A. Twigg, "New Models for Online Learning: Improving Learning and Reducing Costs: Outcomes from Changing the Equation," *Change* (July–August 2013), p. 6.

18. E.g., Richard R. Hake, "Interactive Engagement versus Traditional Methods: A Six-Thousand-Student Survey of Mechanics Test Data for Introductory Physics Courses," 66 *American Journal of Physics* (1998), p. 64. Louis Deslauriers, Ellen Schelew, and Carl Wieman, "Improved Learning in a Large Enrollment Physics Class," 332 *Science* (2011), p. 862.

CHAPTER SEVEN   THE MAJOR FOUNDATIONS

1. Quoted in Roger L. Geiger, *The History of American Higher Education: Learning and Culture from the Founding to World War II* (2015), p. 479.

2. See, e.g., Ernest V. Hollis, *Philanthropic Foundations and Higher Education* (1938).

3. Steven C. Wheatley, *The Politics of Philanthropy: Abraham Flexner and Medical Education* (1988).

4. Abraham Flexner, *Medical Education in the United States and Canada: A Report to the Carnegie Foundation for the Advancement of Teaching*, Bulletin No. 4 (2010).

5. Ernest V. Hollis, note 2, p. 289.

6. Quoted in Merle Curti and Roderick Nash, *Philanthropy in the Shaping of Higher Education* (1965), p. 221.

7. Quoted in Steven C. Wheatley, note 3, p. 147.

8. Cassie Hall and Scott L. Thomas, "Advocacy Philanthropy and the Public Policy Agenda" (paper prepared for the annual meeting of the American Educational Research Association, April 2012).

9. Quoted in ibid., p. 24.

10. Ibid., p. 20. More generally, see *Current Trends in National Foundation Funding for Higher Education: With a Focus on National Foundations, Corporate and Foundation Research*, Michigan State University (October 17, 2013).

11. E.g., Katherine Mangan, "How Gates Shapes Higher Education Policy," *Chronicle of Higher Education* (July 14, 2013), www.chronicle.com/article/How-Gates-Shapes-States/140303/; Cassie Hall and Scott L. Thomas, note 8, p. 32.

12. E.g., Stanley N. Katz, "Beware Big Donors," *Chronicle of Higher Education* (March 25, 2012), http://chronicle.com/article/Big-Philanthropys-Role-in/131275/.43.

13. Ibid.

14. Joel Fleishman, *The Foundation: A Great American Secret* (2007), p. 196.

15. Alexander K. Mayer et al., *Moving Ahead with Institutional Change: Lessons from the First Round of Achieving the Dream Community Colleges*, Executive Summary (April 2014).

CHAPTER EIGHT   THE ROLE OF GOVERNMENT IN RAISING LEVELS OF EDUCATIONAL ATTAINMENT

1. John Bound and Sarah Turner, "Going to War and Going to College: Did World War II and the GI Bill Increase Educational Attainment for Returning Veterans?" 20 *Journal of Labor Economics* (2002), p. 784; Marcus Stanley, "College Education and the Midcentury GI Bills," 118 *Quarterly Journal of Economics* (2003), p. 671.

2. John Bound and Sarah Turner, note 1, pp. 807.

3. College Board, *Trends in Student Aid, 2013* (2013), p. 12.

4. Suzanne Mettler, *Degrees of Inequality: How the Politics of Higher Education Sabotaged the American Dream* (2014), p. 24; William G. Bowen and Michael S. McPherson, *Lesson Plan: An Agenda for Change in American Higher Education* (2016), p. 30.

5. David S. Mundel, "What Do We Know about the Impact of Grants to College Students?" in Sandy Baum, Michael McPherson, and Patricia Steele (eds.), *The Effectiveness of Student Aid Policies: What the Research Tells Us* (2008), pp. 9, 21.

6. Jacqueline King, *Missed Opportunities: Students Who Do Not Apply for Financial Aid*, American Council on Education, Education Issue Brief (2004).

7. Eric P. Bettinger, Bridget Terry Long, Philip Oreopoulos, and Lisa Sambonetsu, *The Role of Simplification and Information in College Decisions*, National Bureau of Economic Research, Working Paper No. 15361 (September 2009).

8. Kelly Field, "Obama Takes Steps to Ease Applications for Federal Student Aid," *Chronicle of Higher Education* (September 25, 2015), p. A6.

9. E.g., Susan Dynarski and Judith Scott-Clayton, "Financial Aid Policy: Lessons from Research," 23 *The Future of Children* (2013), pp. 67, 79.

10. E.g., Lyle McKinney and Andrea B. Burridge, "Helping or Hindering: The Effect of Loans on Community College Students' Persistence," 56 *Research in Higher Education* (2015), p. 299. One state that promised free tuition and fees for up to four years to students with minimum course loads and grade point averages found that five-year graduation rates rose by only 4 percent. Susan Dynarski and Judith Scott-Clayton, note 9, pp. 67, 82.

11. See, e.g., Joshua Angrist, Daniel Lang, and Philip Oreopoulos, "Incentives and Services for College Achievement: Evidence from a Randomized Trial," 1 *American Economic Journal: Applied Economics* (2009), p. 1; Charles T. Clotfelter, Steven W. Hemelt, and Helen F. Ladd, *Multifaceted Aid for Low-Income Students and College Outcomes: Evidence from North Carolina*, National Bureau of Economic Research, Working Paper No. 22217 (May 2016).

12. John Bound and Sarah Turner, "Cohort Crowding: How Resources Affect Collegiate Attainment," 91 *Journal of Public Economics* (2007), p. 877. See also John Bound, Michael Lovenheim and Sarah Turner, *Why Have College Completion Rates Declined?* National Bureau of Economic Research, Working Paper No. 15566 (December 2009). Lyle McKinney and Andrea B. Burridge, note 10, p. 299.

13. Eric Bettinger, "Financial Aid: A Blunt Instrument for Increasing Degree Attainment," in Andrew P. Kelly and Mark Schneider (eds.), *Getting to Graduation: The Completion Agenda in Higher Education* (2012), pp. 157, 172.

14. For an extensive treatment of these problems, see Sara Goldrick-Rab, *Paying the Price: College Costs, Financial Aid, and the Betrayal of the American Dream* (2016).

15. Ralph Stinebrickner and Todd Stinebrickner, "Academic Performance and College Dropout: Using Longitudinal Expectations Data to Estimate a Learning Model," 32 *Journal of Labor Economics* (2014), p. 601.

16. Lori Patton Davis, Carla M. Morelon, Dawn M. Whitehead, and Don Hossler, "Campus-Based Retention Initiatives: Does the Emperor Have Clothes?" *New Directions for Institutional Research*, No. 130 (Summer 2006), p. 9.

17. Jay P. Greene and Greg Forster, *Public High School Graduation and College Readiness Rates in the United States*, Education Working Paper, Manhattan Institute (2003).

18. See, e.g., Thomas Bailey, "Challenges and Opportunity: Rethinking the Role and Function of Developmental Education in Community College," *New Directions for Community Colleges*, No. 145 (2009).

19. Sara Goldrick-Rab, Douglas W. Harris, and Philip A. Trostes, "Why Financial Aid Matters (or Does Not) for College Success: Toward a New Interdisciplinary Perspective," in J. C. Smart (ed.), *Higher Education: Handbook of Theory and Research* (2009), pp. 1, 18.

20. US Department of Education, *Trends in Academic Progress 2012: The Nation's Report Card* (2012).

21. Andrew P. Kelly and Mark Schneider (eds.), *Getting to Graduation: The Completion Agenda in Higher Education* (2012), p. 298.

22. *Building a Foundation of 'Actionable Knowledge': Research That Can Improve the Performance of Federal Student Aid Policies*, American Enterprise Institute (June 24, 2013), p. 8.

23. Sara Goldrick-Rab, Douglas W. Harris, and Philip A. Trostes, note 19.

24. Susan Dynarski and Judith Scott-Clayton, note 9, pp. 67, 86.

25. Bridget Terry Long, "Remediation," in Andrew P. Kelly and Mark Schneider, note 21, pp. 175, 189.

26. National Center for Education Statistics, *Educational Attainment of Young Adults* (May 2016), p. 2, figure 3.

27. William Doyle and William Zumeta, "State-Level Responses to the Access and Completion Challenge in the New Era of Austerity," 655 *Annals of the American Academy of Political and Social Science* (September 14, 2014), p. 81.

28. See, e.g., Tom Sugar, "Boosting College Completion at Community Colleges: Time, Choice, Structure, and the Significant Role of States" (2010) (unpublished document).

29. See, e.g., Thomas R. Bailey, Shana S. Jaggars, and Davis Jenkins, *Redesigning America's Community Colleges: A Clearer Path to Student Success*, Community College Research Center (2015); James E. Rosenbaum, Regina Deil-Amen, and Ann E. Person, *After Admission: From College Access to College Success* (2006).

30. Laura W. Perna and Joni E. Finney, *The Attainment Agenda: State Policy Leadership in Higher Education* (2014), p. 291.

31. E.g., Joseph C. Burke and Associates, *Funding Public Colleges and Universities for Performance: Popularity, Prospects, and Performance* (2002); Donald E. Heller (ed.), *The States and Higher Education Policy: Affordability, Access, and Accountability* (2nd ed., 2012), p. 191.

32. E.g., David Tandberg and Nicholas W. Hillman, *State Performance Funding for Higher Education: Silver Bullet or Red Herring*, Policy Brief, Wisconsin Center for the Advancement of Postsecondary Education (2013), p. 4; Donald E. Heller (ed.), note 31, p. 191.

33. E.g., Kevin Dougherty and Rebecca S. Natow, *The Politics of Performance Funding for Higher Education: Origins, Discontinuations, and Transformations* (2015); Amanda Rutherford and Thomas Rabovsky, "Evaluating Impacts of Performance Funding on Outcomes in Higher Education," 655 *Annals of the American Academy of Political and Social Science* (September 2014), p. 185.

34. E.g., Fredericks Volkwein and David A. Tandberg, "Measuring Up: Examining Connections among State Structural Characteristics, Regulatory Practices, and Performance," 49 *Research on Higher Education* (2008), p. 180; Amanda Rutherford and Thomas Rabovsky, note 33, p. 205; Kevin J. Dougherty and Vikash Reddy, *The Impacts of State Performance Funding Systems on Higher Education Institutions*, Community College Research Center, CCRC Working Paper No. 37 (2011), p. 26.

35. Justin Kaplan (ed.), *Bartlett's Familiar Quotations* (16th ed., 1992), p. 316.

CHAPTER NINE   GOVERNMENT EFFORTS TO IMPROVE THE QUALITY OF EDUCATION

1. *Sweezy v. New Hampshire*, 354 U.S. 234, 263 (1957).

2. Ibid.

3. See Robert Zemsky, *Checklist for Change: Making American Higher Education a Suitable Enterprise* (2013), p. 56.

4. Elaine Seymour and Nancy M. Hewitt, *Talking about Leaving: Why Undergraduates Leave the Sciences* (1997), p. 33.

5. E.g., Robert L. DeHaan, "The Impending Revolution in Undergraduate Science Education," 14 *Journal of Science Education and Technology* (2005), p. 253; James Fairweather, *Linking Evidence and Promising Practices in Science, Technology, Engineering, and Mathematics (STEM) Undergraduate Education* (n.d.).

6. Richard Hake, "Interactive Engagement versus Traditional Methods: A Six-Thousand-Student Survey of Mechanics Test Data for Introductory Physics Courses," 66 *American Journal of Physics* (1998), p. 64.

7. Louis Deslauriers, Ellen Schelew, and Carl Wieman, "Improved Learning in a Large-Enrollment Physics Class," 332 *Science* (2011), p. 862.

8. Paul Basken, "Crusader for Better Science Teaching Finds Colleges Slow to Change," *Chronicle of Higher Education* (June17, 2013), http://chronicle.com/article/Crusader-for-Better-Science/139849.

9. See pp. 47–51.

10. See, e.g., Carol L. Colbeck, "State Policies to Improve Undergraduate Teaching: Administrator and Faculty Responses," 73 *Journal of Higher Education* (2002), p. 3.

11. See, e.g., Joseph C. Burke and Associates, *Funding Public Colleges and Universities for Performance: Popularity, Prospects, and Performance* (2002), p. 80.

12. Community College Research Center, *Performance Funding: Impacts, Obstacles, and Unintended Outcomes* (February 2014), p. 2.

13. Quoted by Grover J. Whitehurst in his testimony before the House Subcommittee on Early Childhood, Elementary, and Secondary Education, *The Federal Role in Education Research* (November 16, 2011).

14. Anthony Bryk, Louis Gomez, Alicia Grunder, and Paul LeMahieu, *Learning to Improve: How America's Schools Can Get Better* (2015), p. 240n10.

CHAPTER TEN   ACCREDITATION

1. See, e.g., Peter T. Ewell, *Transforming Institutional Accreditation in U.S. Higher Education*, National Center for Higher Education Management Systems (NCHEMS) (March 2015).

2. Frans A. Van Vught and Don F. Westerheijden, "Toward a General Model of Quality Assessment in Higher Education," 28 *Higher Education* (1994), p. 355.

3. See Andrew P. Kelly and Chad Aldeman, *False Fronts? Behind Higher Education's Voluntary Accountability Systems*, American Enterprise Institute (March 2010).

4. The development of the federal role in accreditation has been described by Barbara Brittingham, "Accreditation in the United States: How Did We Get to Where We Are?" 145 *New Directions for Higher Education* (2009), p. 7.

5. General Accounting Office, *Higher Education: Education Should Strengthen Oversight of Schools and Accreditors*, Report No. 15-59 (December 2014).

6. See, e.g., Ben Miller, *Improving Gainful Employment: Suggestions for Better Accountability*, New America Foundation (November 2013).

7. See, e.g., Senate Committee on Health, Education, Labor, and Pensions, *Higher Education Accreditation: Concepts and Proposals* (2015), pp. 13–14.

8. S.3380, a Bill to amend the Higher Education Act of 1965 to provide for accreditation reform, and for other purposes, submitted by Senators Warren, Durbin, and Schatz (September 22, 2016).

9. E.g., Andrew Gillen, Daniel L. Bennett, and Richard Vedder, *The Inmates Running the Asylum: An Analysis of Higher Education Accreditation* (October 2010), pp. 20–23.

10. Sylvia Manning, *Launching New Institutions: Solving the Chicken-and-Egg Problem in American Higher Education*, American Enterprise Institute (October 2014).

11. See pp. 16–17.

12. Eric Kelderman, "How Many French-Literature Degrees Is Kentucky Really Paying For?" *Chronicle of Higher Education* (February 19, 2016), p. A11.

13. According to a survey by George D. Kuh, Natasha Jankowski, Stanley O. Ikenberry, and Jillian Kinzie, with a response rate of 83 percent, 84 percent of institutions in

2013 had developed learning goals for all their students. *Knowing What Students Know and Can Do: The Current State of Student Learning Outcomes Assessment in U.S. Colleges and Universities* (2014). The figure today is probably somewhat higher.

14. See, e.g., Vicky Schray, *Assuring Quality in Higher Education: Recommendations for Improving Accreditation*, Issue Paper prepared for Secretary of Education's Commission on the Future of Higher Education (n.d.); Robert C. Dickeson, *The Need for Accreditation Reform*, Issue Paper Prepared for Secretary of Education's Commission on the Future of Higher Education (n.d.). The Department of Education appears to have endorsed this recommendation, US Department of Education, *Department of Education Advances Transparency Agenda for Accreditation* (November 6, 2015), p. 4.

15. See, e.g., Peter T. Ewell, note 1.

16. E.g., Andrew Gillen, Daniel L. Bennett, and Richard Vedder, note 9, p. 45.

17. Ibid., pp. 37–38; David D. Dill, "Ensuring Academic Standards in Higher Education," *Change* (May/June 2014), pp. 53, 56.

18. E.g., Fredericks Volkwein, Lisa R. Lattuca, Betty J. Harper, and Robert J. Domingo, "Measuring the Impact of Professional Accreditation on Student Experiences and Learning Outcomes," 48 *Research in Higher Education* (2007), p. 25.

19. David D. Dill, note 17, pp. 53, 56.

20. Vicky Schray, note 14, p. 5.

21. Such difficulties seem to have arisen in some countries that use professional inspectors. John Brennon and Tarla Shah, "Quality Assessment and Institutional Change: Experiences from 14 Countries," 40 *Higher Education* (2000), pp. 331, 347.

22. See George D. Kuh et al., note 13.

23. Ibid., p. 5.

24. Ibid., "Nearly three-quarters of provosts reported either 'very much' or 'quite a bit' of support for assessment on their campus," p. 11.

25. Peter Ewell, Karen Paulson, and Jillian Kinzie, *Down and In: Assessment Practices at the Program Level* (2011).

26. George D. Kuh et al., note 13, p. 15.

CHAPTER ELEVEN   INCREASING EDUCATIONAL ATTAINMENT

1. Joseph C. Burke and Associates, *Funding Public Colleges and Universities for Performance: Popularity, Prospects, and Performance* (2002); David Tandberg and Nicholas W. Hillman, *Funding for Higher Education: Silver Bullet or Red Herring?* Policy Brief, Wisconsin Center for the Advancement of Postsecondary Education (2013).

2. Jeffrey L Selingo, *What Presidents Think: A 2013 Survey of Four-Year College Presidents* (2013), p. 23.

3. Kenneth C. Green, *The 2011–12 Inside Higher Ed Survey of College and University Chief Academic Officers* (2012), p. 8.

4. On overall attainment growth, see National Center for Education Statistics, *Digest of Education Statistics: 2014 Tables and Figures*, table 104.20. On racial disparities, see National Center for Educational Statistics, *Educational Attainment of Young Adults* (May 2016), p. 2, figure 3.

5. See William G. Bowen and Michael S. McPherson, *Lesson Plan: An Agenda for Change in American Higher Education* (2016), pp. 11–14.

6. US Department of Education, *The Nation's Report Card, Trends in Academic Progress 2012* (2013), pp. 15, 16.

7. James E. Rosenbaum, *Beyond College for All* (2001), p. 208. For estimates of how many students complete remediation successfully and how many of these eventually earn a degree, see Community College Research Institute, *What We Know about Developmental Education Outcomes* (2014).

8. Erin Velez, *America's College Drop-Out Epidemic: Understanding the College Drop-Out Population*, National Center for Analysis of Longitudinal Data in Education Research, Working Paper No. 109 (January, 2014).

9. Tom Loveless, *How Well Are American Students Learning?* The 2012 Brown Center Report on American Education (2012), p. 14. See also Brian Jacob, Susan Dynarski, Kenneth Frank, and Barbara Schneider, *Are Expectations Alone Enough?* National Bureau of Economic Research, Working Paper No. 22013 (February 2016).

10. Robert Putnam, *Our Kids* (2015), p. 231.

11. Katherine Mangan, "Obama Proposes Free Community College for Millions of Students," *Chronicle of Higher Education* (January 8, 2015).

12. Emily Deruy, "The Debate over Free Community College," *Atlantic* (July 27, 2015).

13. See Sara Goldrick-Rab, *Paying the Price: College Costs, Financial Aid, and the Betrayal of the American Dream* (2016).

14. Ralph Stinebrickner and Todd Stinebrickner, "Academic Performance and College Dropout: Using Longitudinal Expectations Data to Estimate a Learning Model," 32 *Journal of Labor Economics* (2014), p. 601.

15. Susan Dynarski and Judith Scott-Clayton, "Financial Aid Policy: Lessons from Research," 23 *The Future of Children* (2013), pp. 67, 82.

16. See Steve Kolowich, "The New Intelligence," *Inside Higher Ed* (January 25, 2013).

17. See Lindsay C. Page and Judith Scott-Clayton, *Improving College Access in the United States: Barriers and Policy Responses*, National Bureau of Economic Research, Working Paper No. 2178 (December 2015), p. 31.

18. See p. 119.

19. The relevant studies are discussed and reinforced in a recent study of the Carolina Covenant Program for Low-Income Students at the University of North Carolina, Chapel Hill. Charles T. Clotfelter, Steve W. Hemelt, and Helen F. Ladd, *Multifaceted Aid for Low-Income Students and College Outcomes: Evidence from North Carolina*, National Bureau of Economic Research, Working Paper No. 22217 (May 2016).

20. For an extended analysis of this type of reform, see Thomas R. Bailey, Shana S. Jaggars, and David Jenkins, *Redesigning America's Community Colleges: A Clearer Path to Success*, Community College Research Center (2015).

21. See, e.g., CAEL Forum and News, *Competency-Based Education* (2013); see also Amy Laitinen, "Cracking the Credit Hour," *New America Foundation and Education Sector* (September 2012).

22. See, e.g., Lumina Foundation, *Connecting Credentials: Making the Case for Reforming the U.S. Credentialing System* (2015).

23. *Corporation for a Skilled Workforce: Making a Market for Competency-Based Credentials* (n.d.), p. 1.

CHAPTER TWELVE   IMPROVING THE QUALITY OF EDUCATION

1. Eric A. Hanushek and Ludger Woessmann, *How Much Do Educational Outcomes Matter in OECD Countries?* National Bureau of Economic Research, Working Paper No. 16515 (2010).

2. Philip S. Babcock and Mindy Marks, "The Falling Time Cost of College: Evidence from Half a Century of Time Use Data," 93 *Review of Economics and Statistics* (2011). See generally, chapter 2.

3. See chapter 5.

4. See, e.g., M. Kevin Eagan and Audrey J. Jaeger, "Closing the Gate: Part-Time Faculty and Instruction in Gateway Courses and First-Year Persistence," in John M. Braxton (ed.), *The Role of the Classroom in College Student Performance* (2008), p. 39.

5. John Bound and Sarah Turner, "Cohort Crowding: How Resources Affect Collegiate Attainment," 91 *Journal of Public Economics* (2007), p. 877.

6. See pp. 73–74.

7. See p. 53.

8. See p. 54.

9. See, e.g., Derek Bok, *Higher Education in America*, pp. 183–200 (2013).

10. Rebekah Nathan, *My Freshman Year: What a Professor Learned by Becoming a Student* (2005); Mary Grigsby, *College Life through the Eyes of Students* (2009).

11. John M. Braxton, "Selectivity and Rigor in Research Universities," 64 *Journal of Higher Education* (1993), p. 657; "Selective Liberal Arts Colleges: Higher Quality as Well as Higher Prestige?" 56 *Journal of Higher Education* (1985), p. 538.

12. See pp. 71–72.

13. Justin Miller, "When Adjunct Profs Go Union," *American Prospect* (Summer 2015), p. 46.

14. See, e.g., Paul D. Umbach, "How Effective Are They? Exploring the Impact of Contingent Faculty on Undergraduate Education," 30 *Review of Higher Education* (Winter 2007), p. 91.

15. Stephen R. White and Mark K. McBeth, *A History of the Doctor of Arts Tradition in American Higher Education* (2003).

16. A survey of faculty revealed that more than two-thirds of tenured faculty would favor giving adjunct instructors a share in governance on matters affecting their responsibilities. Adrianna Kezar, David Maxey, and Elizabeth Holcombe, *The Professoriate Reconsidered: A Study of New Faculty Models* (2015).

CHAPTER THIRTEEN   ENCOURAGING REFORM

1. See the Council of Independent Colleges and Universities, *A Study of Presidents of Independent Colleges and Universities* (2011), p. 11.

2. Coalition for Evidence-Based Policy, *Randomized Trials Commissioned by the Institute of Education Sciences since 2002: How Many Found Positive versus Weak Effects* (July 2013).

3. Eric Mazur, "Peer Instruction: Ten Years of Experience and Results," 69 *American Journal of Physics* (2001), p. 970; Uri Treisman, "Studying Students Studying Calculus," *College Mathematics Journal* (1992), p. 362.

4. Dan Berrett, "The Next Great Hope for Measuring Learning," *Chronicle of Higher Education* (October 21, 2016), p. A30; Association of American Colleges & Universities, *The LEAP Challenge: Education for a World of Unscripted Problems* (2015); Association of American Colleges & Universities, *College Learning for a New Century: A Report from the National Leadership Council for Liberal Education and America's Promise* (2016).

5. Justin Kaplan (ed.), *Bartlett's Familiar Quotations* (16th ed., 1992), p. 322.

6. Charles Henderson and Melissa H. Dancy, "Barriers to the Use of Research-Based Instructional Strategies: The Influence of Both Individual and Situational Characteristics," 3 *Physics Education Research* (2007).

7. E.g., Carnegie Foundation for the Advancement of Teaching, *International Survey of the Academic Profession* (1992).

8. James S. Fairweather, "Beyond the Rhetoric: Trends in the Relative Value of Teaching and Research in Faculty Salaries," 76 *Journal of Higher Education* (2005), p. 401.

9. See pp. 54–55, 74.

10. See Elaine D. Baker, "The Challenge of Scaling Successful Policy Innovations: A Case Study of Three Colorado Community College System Grants," in Andrew P. Kelly and Mark Schneider (eds.), *Getting to Graduation: The Completion Agenda in Higher Education* (2012), p. 225.

11. Malcolm Getz, John J. Siegfried, and Kathryn H. Anderson, "Adoption of Innovation in Higher Education," 37 *Quarterly Journal of Economics* (1997), p. 605.

12. See pp. 70–71 and 66.

13. Lion F. Gardiner, *Redesigning Higher Education: Producing Dramatic Gains in Student Learning* (1994), p. 57.

14. For further analyses about the process of reform in colleges and universities, see Jessica L. Jonson, Robert J. Thompson, Jr., Timothy Guetterman, and Nancy Mitchell, "The Effect of Informational Characteristics and Faculty Knowledge and Beliefs on the Use of Assessment," *Innovation in Higher Education* (March 9, 2016), doi:10.1007/s10755-016-9366-7; Adriana Kezar, "Institutionalizing Student Outcomes Assessment: The Need for Better Research to Inform Practice," 38 *Innovative Higher Education* (2013), p. 189; M. W. Peterson and C. H. Augustine, "Organizational Practices Enhancing the Use of Student Assessment Information in Academic Decisions," 41 *Research In Higher Education* (2000), p. 21.

INDEX

Accenture, 75
accountability, educational, 7–8, 125–26
accreditation, 136–54; American system of,
    138–39; educational improvement as goal
    of, 144–52; effectiveness of, 153; financial
    aid linked to, 139, 141–44; government role
    in, 137, 139–42, 148, 150; grading system
    for, 147–48; graduation rates as focus of,
    151; importance of, 152–54; innovation as
    affected by, 142–44, 143n; learning as focus
    of, 151–53, 198; methods of, 145; minimum
    standards in, 139–44; professionalization of,
    149; program characteristics, 137–38; pub-
    lishing results of, 146–47; reform role of,
    197–98; role and purposes of, 136, 146;
    scope of, 148–50; scrutiny of process of, 136;
    of strong vs. weak colleges, 145n; suggested
    reforms to system of, 146–54; teaching as
    focus of, 151–53, 198
adjunct faculty: educational quality threatened
    by poor employment conditions of, 49n, 51,
    64–65, 170, 175–78; effectiveness of, 176,
    176n; graduation rates affected by, 46, 176;
    percentage of workforce represented by,
    49n, 170, 175; voice of, in educational
    decisions, 179
advising. *See* student support and advising
Alverno College, 57
American Civil Rights Initiative, 100
American Dream, 12, 19, 188
Anderson, Kathryn, 194
area studies, 100
Arizona State University, 57, 94, 164, 199
Arum, Richard, 29–31
Association of American Colleges &
    Universities, 103, 144n, 191
Association of Concerned Trustees and
    Alumni, 100
athletics, 44, 46

Babcock, Philip, 34–35, 36, 65
Bayer Corporation, 9
benefits of education: economic, 7–15, 38;
    noneconomic, 14–17, 38, 180
Berea College, 113, 163

Bettinger, Eric, 112
Blackboard, 91
boards of trustees. *See* trustees
Bound, John, 117n
Boylan, Myles, 48
Brigham Young University–Idaho, 45, 46
Bureau of Labor Statistics, 9, 10
Bush, George W., 125
Business Roundtable, 9
Butler, Murray, 99

Campus Reform, 101n
Capelli, Peter, 10–11, 75
Carnegie Foundation, 98–100, 104, 108
Carnegie Mellon University, 90
Carnevale, Anthony, 9
Center on Education and the Workforce,
    Georgetown University, 9
Christensen, Clayton, 88–90, 93
Chronicle of Higher Education (newspaper), 191
City University of New York (CUNY), 165n,
    199
civic education and citizenship, 14–15, 24
civil rights, 129n
CLA. *See* Collegiate Learning Assessment
Clark, Kim, 45
class. *See* income groups
Clinton, Bill, 16
Clinton, Hillary, 162–63
coeducation, 59–60
college presidents and other leaders: chief
    activities of, 52; in community colleges,
    54–55; on employment preparation as
    educational mandate, 70–71; faculty
    relations with, 52–53; and grade inflation,
    65–66; reform role of, 51–54, 197; self-
    perception of, 53, 70–71, 170, 195; trustees'
    relations with, 56–57
Collegiate Learning Assessment (CLA), 29–31,
    125–26, 130
Columbia University, 99
Common Core curriculum, 160–61
community colleges: curricula of, 22, 24;
    drawbacks of, 86; dropout rates at, 47, 159;
    employment preparation by, 87; financing

Perna, Laura, 213n11
philanthropy. *See* foundations
politics: and educational accountability, 7–8,
125–26, 139; polarization of, 132, 164, 185;
and purpose of education, 16–17, 68, 73,
143–44, 204n35, 205n38. *See also* government role
presidents. *See* college presidents and other
leaders
President's Council of Advisors on Science and
Technology, 128
prestige, 83–84
professors. *See* faculty
publication, as measure of faculty achievement, 50, 84, 193
Putnam, Robert, 161

quality. *See* educational quality
quality assurance programs, 137–38

race: and admission to selective colleges, 19;
and civil rights progress, 129n; educational
attainment by, 13
rankings, 83–84
Read, Sister Joel, 57
reform, 183–202; challenges for, 47–58,
184–88, 193–94; college leaders' role in,
51–54; faculty as obstacle to, 45–46, 48–51,
128–29, 192–93; history of, 2–3; instructional, 48–51; of open-admission institutions, 43–47; opportunities for, 2, 183;
process of, 188–94; responsibility for,
194–95; in STEM subjects, 128–29; tortoise
and hare fable applied to, 200–201; trustees'
role in, 54–57
religiously affiliated colleges, 98–99
remedial education, 46–47, 113, 115, 159, 164,
180
research. *See* education research
research programs, university, 84, 99–100
research universities, 49n, 116, 134–35
Rockefeller Foundation, 98–99, 104, 108
Roksa, Josipa, 29–31
Rosenbaum, James E., 159
Rudolph, Frederick, 25
Ruiz, Ramon, 213n11

Sanders, Bernie, 162–63
Schneider, Mark, 114
scholarly journals, 190

Scott, Rick, 16
Scott-Clayton, Judith, 115, 164
selective colleges: accreditation of, 145n;
educational opportunities at, 19–20; grades
in, 64; reluctance of, to evaluate their teaching and learning, 53
self-paced learning, 166
Siegfried, John, 194
skills: contemporary workforce, 166; debates
over, 10–11; declines in, 11n; of immigrants,
12–13; intellectual, 28–31; measurements of,
79–80; predictions concerning, 11; shortage
of, 1, 9–10, 65; soft, 11n; valued by employers, 68; workplace training deficits and, 75
Smith, Adam, 81
society, benefits of education for, 14–17,
82–83, 205n38
socioeconomic conditions, 114, 161
soft skills, 11n
Southern New Hampshire University, 57, 79
Spellings, Margaret, 125
Spencer Foundation, 100
state government role, 115–21, 129–31,
134–35, 160, 170
STEM (science, technology, engineering, and
mathematics), 9–10, 12, 127–29
StraighterLine, 90
student loan defaults, 87, 90, 140, 187, 200
students: as consumers, 59, 63, 82; curricular
preferences of, 21, 25–26, 59; dropout
decisions of, 60–61; effect of, on educational
quality, 59–67; effort exerted by, 35–36,
61–65; evaluations of professors by, 50,
64–65; grades as concern of, 62–65; high-
risk, 91, 94, 187, 200; measurement of
learning by, 27–37, 79–80; motivations of,
for educational attainment, 17, 61, 68, 78,
205n39; motivations of, on assessments,
31; preparation of, for college-level work,
113–14, 119, 159–61, 169–70, 187; quality of
effort exerted by, 35–36; relevance of courses
to, 171; self-perception of employment
qualifications by, 71–72, 76, 211n7, 211n8;
self-perception of learning by, 65, 172–73;
self-reported significant learning experiences of, 34–35, 62; time spent on class and
studying by, 34–35, 61, 63–64, 169, 172;
voices of, on campus concerns, 59–60;
workforce readiness of, 70–74. *See also*
income groups; race

student support and advising, 44, 89, 91, 113, 118, 164–65, 181
sunshine laws, 56

task forces, 196
teaching faculty, 175–78, 197
teaching methods: computer-based, 90, 164, 213n11; effectiveness of, 27, 36–37, 49n; government role in, 127; graduate school instruction in, 173–75, 197, 199; new, 36–37; persistence of traditional, 48–51, 128–29, 192–93, 196–97; in STEM subjects, 127–29. *See also* pedagogy
technology: and educational quality, 93–94; in higher education, 92–96, 191–92; unintended consequences of, 95–96
tenure-track faculty. *See* faculty
Terenzini, Patrick, 28–30, 32–33
test scores: on critical thinking, 29–31; declines in, 1, 158–59; student motivation as factor in, 31
tortoise and hare fable, 200–201
Treisman, Uri, 190–91, 195
Trostes, Philip, 115
Truman, Harry, 205n38
Trump, Donald, 122, 140, 161
trustees: appointment of, 56; backgrounds and expertise of, 56; chief activities of, 55; college leaders' relations with, 56–57; hiring

decisions of, 54–55; reform role of, 54–57, 197
Turner, Sarah, 117n
Twigg, Carol, 103

Udacity, 90
University of Phoenix, 87–90
US Congress. *See* government role
US Department of Education, 87, 90, 125–26, 133, 140–42, 144, 199
U.S. News and World Report (newspaper), 83–84

Veterans' Readjustment Act, 139
Vietnam War, 35
vocational education, 86, 143–44, 166–68, 167n

Walker, Scott, 16
Western Governor's University (WGU), 45, 91–92, 208n4
WGU. *See* Western Governor's University
Wieman, Carl, 128, 192, 193
Woessmann, Ludger, 26–27, 38
women, equal opportunities for, 129n
working population, higher education options for, 85, 86, 91, 166–68
writing, 24–25

year-round education, 45, 46